GRIMSBY
BOOK
OF
DAYS

LUCY WOOD

The History Press

LUCY WOOD qualified as a journalist in 1999 and is now working in public relations following a long career in regional newspapers. She is a contributor to the British Comedy Guide (www.comedy. co.uk) and attends the Edinburgh Fringe Festival every year. She lives in Lincolnshire and has a keen interest in local history.

First published 2014

The History Press
The Mill, Brimscombe Port
Stroud, Gloucestershire, GL5 2QG
www.thehistorypress.co.uk

British Library Cataloguing in Publication Data.
A catalogue record for this book is available from the British Library.

ISBN 978 0 7524 9947 5

Typesetting and origination by The History Press
Printed in India

— January 1st —

1945: On this day, the Mayor of Grimsby, C.W. Hewson, issued his New Year message. It read:

> We hope that the coming year may be a year of success and safe landings to our fishermen in their dangerous occupation; and may the time quickly come when we shall hear the crashing peal of the church bells telling us not of peace on earth and goodwill to men at Christmastime only, but peace on earth for all time and to all men.

(*Grimsby Evening Telegraph*, 1945)

2006: On this day, the man behind one of Grimsby's most prominent pieces of public art passed away peacefully, aged 84. Peter Todd created the five bronze figures, known as the Guardians of Knowledge, attached to the south elevation of Grimsby Central Library.

The artwork, measuring 11ft high, is among the last examples of its kind in public library buildings in the UK. Todd designed and built the figures in 1968 at his studio in Walesby. Generations of artists were taught by Todd, who was the head of Grimsby School of Art for thirty years. Among his many students was the actor John Hurt. (*Grimsby Evening Telegraph*, 2006)

— JANUARY 2ND —

1970: On this day, pop star Freddie Garrity, of Freddie and The Dreamers, underwent an emergency operation after a car crash in which a 19-year-old Grimsby girl was also injured. The girl was a passenger in his Lotus Elan sports car when it hit an unlit roundabout junction at South Mimms in Hertfordshire.

The 19 year old was described as 'quite comfortable' in hospital despite suffering a head injury and some abrasions. Her mother said the pair had been friends for some time.

Recently, Freddie and his group had performed at The Beachcomber and The Flamingo, in Cleethorpes, and the girl had renewed her friendship with the singer at this time. On the night of the crash she had been to see him performing in *Cinderella* at the Odeon, Golders Green, London. Freddie's role of Buttons was taken over by Peter Birrwell, the group's guitarist. (*Grimsby Evening Telegraph*, 1970)

− January 3rd −

1949: On this day, the Service Food Company was counting the cost of the biggest blaze Grimsby had seen since the Second World War. Four nights before, the sky had been lit up by flames, when fire engulfed the firm's imposing premises in Victoria Street. The building was gutted, despite a huge fire-fighting operation which saw sailors and soldiers voluntarily join in. It was reminiscent, said the local newspaper, of the great air raids of 1943. The building, which adjoined Spillers' Mill, was completely destroyed and at one stage, sparks were blown across the Alexandra Dock, threatening to set fire to wood yards in the area. Timber in JG Cutting's began to smolder as sparks ignited sawdust in the shaft of a lift. The company estimated the blaze had cost £14,000 – £4,000 for the building itself and the rest for the machinery and cattle food inside. (*Grimsby Telegraph Bygones*, 1996)

1976: On this day, flood warnings came too late to save towns along the Lincolnshire coast – from Cleethorpes to Skegness – from their worst night in years. Huge waves sent water and mud pouring through hundreds of properties. Within an hour, houses were engulfed in miniature tidal waves, the Grimsby–Cleethorpes railway line washed away and offices at Grimsby's Royal Dock badly damaged. Cleethorpes Bathing Pool was also wrecked. (*Grimsby Evening Telegraph*, 1976)

~ JANUARY 4TH ~

2002: On this day, the stricken 3,000-ton oil tanker MV *Willy* was stranded on rocks near Cawsand, East Cornwall. The Cypriot-registered vessel had been chartered by Conoco in Grimsby and left Immingham on December 28th 2001, heading for Plymouth. The tanker ran aground on New Year's Day and remained stranded.

Although the 21-year-old vessel had offloaded the petrol she was carrying for Conoco, because vapour was still in her tanks, officials were worried about the risk of explosion and 150 villagers from Kingsand and Cawsand were evacuated from their homes.

The vessel's tanks still contained more than 80 tonnes of fuel, which could have been spilled if the vessel moved too violently on the rocks. Salvage workers removed as much of the fuel as they could, and absorbent booms were placed all around the vessel to ensure that any leakage was contained.

It wasn't until January 11th that the operation to refloat her, employing specialist teams, began. (*Grimsby Telegraph*, 2002)

— January 5th —

1980: On this day, thousands of Grimsby Town Football Club fans packed into cars, coaches, vans and trains for the mass exodus to Merseyside for the FA Cup clash with League leaders Liverpool.

Every street corner in Grimsby and Cleethorpes became a meeting place for eager supporters waiting for transport to ferry them on the three-and-a-half hour journey. As things began to move, the main roads out of Grimsby became a one-way system full of cars and coaches with black-and-white scarves streaming from their windows. It was estimated that between 7,000 and 8,000 Mariners fans made the trip.

Among them were Mr and Mrs John Baker, who had been going to watch Grimsby Town since 1947. 'We go to all the home matches and, whenever we can, we go to the away games as well,' said Mr Baker. 'We certainly were not going to miss this one.'

He predicted that Grimsby could humble the mighty League champions if Town played in their usual style, predicting a score of 2-1.

Unfortunately for the black-and-white army, Liverpool won 5-0. (*Grimsby Evening Telegraph*, 1980)

~ January 6th ~

1949: On this day, a record low landing of fish paralysed Grimsby's fish market and contributed to a fish famine throughout the country.

Bad weather at sea and a hold-up of trawlers over Christmas resulted in three North Sea trawlers landing only 393 kits. There were no deep-sea landings. Though an allocation of frozen fish alleviated the shortage to some extent, a large percentage of merchants were unable to fulfill their orders and Grimsby Fish Market was idle by 9 a.m.

Grimsby was not the only port where supplies were abnormally short. The eight major fishing ports in England totalled only 10,895 kits. Landings at Hull, for example, were 7,100 kits compared with over 19,000 the previous day.

Prospects for the following day were very bad; no deep-sea ships were expected to land. Landings had been lower in the past, but only when abnormal conditions, such as strikes, existed. (*Grimsby Evening Telegraph*, 1949)

~ January 7th ~

1850: On this day, the freemen divided land in Grimsby's East Marsh pasture into paddocks. In 1849, the Pastures Act stated that the 'borough hath of late years increased in trade and resort, and such pastures have become very valuable for building purposes'. That year, members of the freemen's Pastures Committee were appointed, and they deliberated on the best scheme for making their pastures productive.

Although turning the East Marsh pasture into a building plot would generate large amounts of revenue, it was decided that laying out roads and installing drainage would be expensive and unprofitable – that is, until the demand for building was great enough to take up a large plot of the pasture. The land was cut off by railway lines and the East Marsh Drain, so building was unlikely there at that time. So, in the meantime, the freemen divided most of their pastures into paddocks and allotment gardens. This yielded higher rents than pasture, and it also meant individual plots could be reclaimed for building when required.

On this day, 151 acres in the East Marsh, Haycroft and Little Field of Grimsby were let as paddocks and gardens, producing an annual rental altogether of £408. This continued throughout the 1850s. (Alan Dowling, *Grimsby: Making The Town 1800–1914*, 2007)

1814: On this day, Susannah Knight was baptised in Grimsby. Her life was to end many miles away from home, the wife of a transported convict.

William Borrowdale was charged in 1835 with stealing a bay mare from a field in Halifax. He was convicted at the York Assizes on July 18th that year and promptly transported, aged in his early 20s, to Van Diemen's Land in 1836 on the ship the Elphinstone.

His convict records describe him as 5ft 4in tall, with light brown hair, a long head and dark hazel eyes. His profession was given as a groom.

He arrived in Tasmania on May 24th 1936, and was sent to Port Arthur, a convict prison settlement. On June 26th 1845, he was recommended for pardon, which was granted on June 12th 1846. He moved to Stanley, in the North West, where he ran an inn called the Black Horse.

In 1843, his wife, Susannah, travelled for weeks across the sea with their son James, leaving her family and friends in Grimsby behind to be with her husband. Sadly, James died shortly after the trip, aged about 10, of illness.

William later ran the Commercial Hotel and a butchery, and he was devastated when, after about sixteen years in Tasmania, Susannah died.

After a few years, he met Jane Carr. They married, had at least three children, and farmed land on the Stanley peninsular. William died, aged 69, much loved and respected, and is buried with his wives in Stanley. (*Grimsby Telegraph Bygones*, 1999; www.ancestry.com)

～ January 9th ～

1986: On this day, fishing magnate John Carl Ross died at his home in Humberston, aged 84.

He began his career modestly as a barrow boy on the docks, but went on to head a multi-million-pound frozen food empire. Today the Ross name is still synonymous with the fishing industry.

Mr Ross started working for his fish merchant father, packing and selling fish, at the tender age of 17. He planned on becoming a stockbroker or accountant and worked hard for the next ten years, studying accountancy in the evenings.

When Mr Ross Senior had a heart attack in 1929, John took full control of the business – at that time consisting of thirty-four workers – and set about expanding it. He began by building his own trawler with fish merchant Jack Vincent, who became a joint managing director of the empire after the two amalgamated their businesses.

In 1942, his good friend Sir Alec Black died, and Mr Ross purchased nine of Sir Alec's vessels. He also bought two businesses, which led to the firm becoming a public company, and then more, including Young's.

As the decades passed, the workforce grew to 15,000 and at its peak the firm was turning over £100 million a year. (*Grimsby Evening Telegraph*, 1986)

~ January 10th ~

1936: On this day, the *Grimsby News* carried the following report:

> While the bells were being pealed before evening service on Sunday, the congregation gathered in the parish church were startled to hear the regular changes stopped by a terrific crash, followed by violent discord. The prolonged frost preceding Christmas had affected the rope of the largest bell, which weighs one ton, it parted and the bell careered violently in its cradle, then fell to the floor of the bell chamber with a crash which resounded through the church. The peal was brought to an abrupt finish and as the bell is the one on which the hours are struck, the clock was affected until the Tuesday, when the St James bell ringers managed to get the bell into position again. It was not damaged by the mishap.

1980: On this day, a Grimsby pub pool team managed to avoid defeat in a crunch game – thanks to a helping hand from one of their regulars! The Wheatsheaf Hotel team were losing 6–5 with one game to go against their rivals from the Royal Oak. Beverly Murgatroyd, of Grimsby, stepped up and got her hand firmly stuck as she attempted to release the balls for the last game, after the mechanism inside the table failed to release them. After the drama, landlord Tom Parkinson said, 'Beverly plays on the table a lot, but that was the first time she was in it!' Sadly we don't know exactly how they managed to extract Beverley's hand from the table but it obviously took some time! (George H. Black, *Tales of Grimsby Long Ago*, undated booklet)

— January 11th —

1912: On this day, Strand Street School – which famously had a rooftop playground – officially opened for business. Construction had begun two years previously, by H.C. Scaping of Grimsby, for the Grimsby Education Authority, although it actually began life as St Andrew's School in 1860. Commemorating its opening under the name of Strand by Lady Doughty, a plaque was fixed inside the west entrance.

The playground, towering high above neighbouring buildings and giving panoramic views of the town, was a talking point for many years. Even the Second World War did not prevent hundreds of children enjoying the fresh air and fun activities to be had there. A former pupil recalled:

> I distinctly remember playing up there with some mates with our tennis ball. In fact, we were doing just that on the day a German plane bombed Burgon's Store. That's when the bullet marks appeared in the wall of the playground – and that's when I broke the land speed record! I can recall playing up there right until I was evacuated to Gainsborough.

(Grimsby Central Library)

– January 12th –

1898: On this day, Grimsby learned of the death of Albert Goodwin. He had died the day before in Ireland – horrifically murdered for £2 of savings. Many people knew him as the nephew of a one-time magistrate and councillor.

Against advice, he had taken the Queen's Shilling and joined the 8th Royal Irish Hussars, but chose a grim friend in Wilfred Kenny. A few days before he was to return home to Grimsby on leave, Albert revealed he had saved £2 for the trip. It was for this sum that Kenny, using his carbine and sword, cut Albert's throat.

Albert's body was found near the officers' mess at the camp at Cahir, his head terribly battered. At first it was thought a civilian had committed the crime and dragged the corpse back to camp but the blood-soaked carbine and a shovel was found in the cavalry stables.

Kenny – who had various aliases but was really Willie Kreutze from Germany – said nothing throughout his trial, never confessed and was hanged at Clonmel Prison.

Albert was buried with full military honours in Ireland. The entire regiment was on parade. (*Grimsby Telegraph Bygones*, 2001)

⁓ JANUARY 13TH ⁓

1968: On this day, Don McEvoy resigned as Grimsby Town Football Club's manager – less than six months after taking over at Blundell Park. McEvoy took on the role, without a contract, after the club dispensed with the services of Jimmy McGuigan, who moved on to manage Chesterfield at the top of the fourth division.

McEvoy had been a centre half with Huddersfield Town, Lincoln City, Sheffield Wednesday and Barrow. After a period as coach with Halifax Town, he returned to Barrow as manager and after three seasons, took the club to promotion to the third division.

Before McEvoy took over, the Grimsby club – at the foot of the table – had gone ten league games without a win, apart from the shock dismissal from the FA Cup by Bradford, the bottom club in division four. The Mariners' last win had been against Bury on October 28th the year before.

No reason was given for McEvoy's departure. (*Grimsby Evening Telegraph*, 1968)

– January 14th –

1987: On this day, Grimsby was virtually isolated as driving snow cut off major routes, leaving a siege-like situation which lasted for several days.

Ambulance workers slept in their stations and had to be dug out to attend casualties. The cold weather brought on a spate of heart attacks, as well as a myriad of broken bones from people slipping. Tragically, one woman died and another man, aged in his early 40s, collapsed and died outside Scartho Road Swimming Baths. A 62-year-old died at the wheel of his car while attempting to start it.

Ploughs were sent out in a desperate bid to make headway but even they were defeated by the drifts, caused by strong winds. One motorist had to dig himself out three times in the space of 80 yards and eventually gave up; another, George Smith, was stranded for thirteen hours after setting off for work.

Milk supplies and morning paper deliveries were disrupted, bread was rationed at many shops and wholesale meat suppliers were selling three times their normal amount. (*Grimsby Evening Telegraph*, 1987)

– JANUARY 15TH –

1937: On this day, Grimsby was shrouded in the worst fog it had seen for twenty years. Fifty ships were unable to leave dock, ambulance crews were hampered in getting to emergencies and a driver had a narrow escape in a crash between a lorry and a tram.

The Grimsby trawler *Abronia* had to be beached off Immingham after it was damaged in a collision with an unknown vessel in the fog. Thankfully, nobody on board was injured. (*Grimsby Evening Telegraph*, 1937)

1959: On this day, a tragic discovery was made. A youth found the body of a newborn child on the level crossing at Suggitt's Lane. The child was wrapped in old newspapers, and it was reported that police were studying the sheets to see if they could provide any clues to the infant's identity. Chief Inspector J. Cottingham told the local newspaper: 'The body was wrapped up in newspapers to make it look like a parcel, but the youth was able to see what was in it.' (*Grimsby Evening Telegraph*, 1959)

– JANUARY 16TH –

1992: On this day, Grimsby welcomed a royal visitor, Princess Anne, to the town. She officially opened Ross Young's pizza factory, hailed as a world beater in terms of production. It not only produced pizzas as near as possible to authentic Italian recipes, but it was also technically state-of-the-art.

The factory was built to produce pizzas for Marks & Spencer and for United Biscuits' brand label, San Marco. The company's food technologists had spent long periods in Italy to see how the home of pizza did things. Most of the ingredients were sourced in Italy, while Tuscany was used as a location for the TV adverts.

In 2000, Heinz bought the business for £190 million when United Biscuits pulled out of the chilled and frozen market. At the time the factory was one of Grimsby's biggest employers, with a workforce of over 900. But Heinz didn't reckon with the fierce competition and in March 2003, Heinz announced it was closing the factory, with a loss of 405 jobs. (*Grimsby Evening Telegraph*, 1992 and 2003)

⟶ January 17th ⟵

1909: On this day, Freddie Frinton was born, the son of a Grimsby fisherman. He was born Frederick Bittiner Coo and is still a cult hero to millions of Germans, even though he died in 1968, four months after suffering from a heart attack.

He grew up to become a comedian, beginning his career on Cleethorpes beach with Jimmy Slater's Follies. He appears on television in Germany every New Year's Eve in a classic comedy routine, *Dinner For One*. The film has been shown consecutively for years, and many Germans believe that New Year is incomplete without it.

Freddie plays the long-suffering butler to Miss Sophie, a deluded dowager celebrating her 90th birthday. Places are set for her friends – the only trouble being that they are all dead! To keep the charade alive, Freddie circles the table as he drinks a toast to Miss Sophie's health at the end of each course.

Freddie was famous for playing a drunk, and his catchphrase was 'good evening ossifer'. He scratched a living on variety circuits for many years before finding fame in the TV sitcom *Meet the Wife*, with Thora Hird. The series came to an abrupt end in 1968, when he died. (*Grimsby Telegraph Bygones*)

– January 18th –

1962: On this day, a doctor was rushed to sea by the Spurn Lifeboat after a member of the crew of the 8.047-ton British cargo ship *Ben Cruachan* was reported to have fallen down a hold aboard the vessel off the Humber.

Spurn Lifeboat met the ship and Dr Ralph Jones sadly confirmed that the man had died. The *Ben Cruachan* proceeded on her voyage to Grangemouth, where the body was landed.

Also on this day, magistrates heard evidence in a court case involving a stabbing incident on board the British collier *Sir Alexander Kennedy* 'on the high seas off the coast of Lincolnshire'. One shipmate was accused of causing grievous bodily harm to another by stabbing him in the face. Although he was receiving treatment in hospital in Grimsby, the victim appeared before court and said, 'I want to tell you about the trouble I have had with another fellow'. The defendant was remanded in custody. (*Grimsby Evening Telegraph*, 1962)

⁓ January 19th ⁓

1948: On this day, Grimsby suffered the biggest demand for electricity ever experienced up to this point in time. The power surge that morning coincided with the sharpest frost of the year so far and resulted in forty minutes' load shedding.

This prompted a warning from the Borough Electricity Department that only drastic voluntary economy would avert power cuts if the forecasted cold spell materialised. If cuts were necessary, it said, they would be made on a district rotation basis.

Temperatures in the town had fallen during the night to 28 degrees Fahrenheit, with 2 degrees of ground frost. It was 2 degrees colder than on any night so far that year, and ended a spell of exceptionally mild weather for January.

On the same day, it was reported that Grimsby was to play its part in relieving the potato famine being experienced in London and the south. Enough Lincolnshire-grown potatoes to supply nearly 12,000,000 people with their 3lbs ration for a week were shipped from Grimsby throughout the following fortnight. On the instructions of the Ministry of Food's Potato Division, 16,000 tons was to go to London, the South Coast and South Wales. The first two ships, small coasters which carried about 600 to 800 tons each, were expected to arrive at Grimsby within two days. (*Grimsby Evening Telegraph*, 1948)

~ January 20th ~

1854: On this day, the *Grimsby Gazette* published a report on the burial ground at St James. It was the only burial ground for people in Grimsby at the time (about 12,000 bodies had been interred in an area of about 1 acre), and concerns over space had been raised as early as 1846.

In the following year, a letter to the Bishop of Lincoln asking for help read:

> It is with the greatest difficulty that the sexton can find a clear spot. In too many instances he is compelled to disturb the decomposing remains of the respective tenants to make room for new occupants. So full is the churchyard that he is obliged to dig and probe to find unoccupied space.

In 1848, a complaint was made to the General Board of Health:

> On leaving clothes out on a line to dry, people living in a house nearby to the graveyard complained that the nausea which had been absorbed was so bad as to render it needful to rewash them. A coffin had been disturbed one day and a human head taken out with the hair fresh on it, and the decomposing matter shovelled out.

At this time coffins were being buried 2ft below the surface, and graves were being reopened after a few days to receive further occupants.

St James was officially closed in June 1854. (*Grimsby Gazette*, 1854)

~ JANUARY 21ST ~

1905: On this day, a letter appeared in the *Liverpool Echo* from a schoolteacher living in Binbrook, a village outside Grimsby, claiming terrifying paranormal activity was taking place at Binbrook Farm.

The Society for Psychical Research said the first instance of paranormal activity was reported by Mrs White in December 1904, when a milk pan was overturned by unseen hands. Throughout January 1905, objects were repeatedly thrown around and fires ignited.

A servant was sweeping the kitchen when the back of her dress caught fire. She was admitted to Louth Hospital in a critical condition with extensive burns.

During this time, something began killing the chickens on the farm. Farmer White claimed that out of 250 fowl he had in January 1905, only twenty-four survived. He explained:

> They have been killed in the same weird way. The skin around the neck has been pulled off and the windpipe drawn from its place and snapped. The fowl house has been watched night and day and, whenever examined, four or five birds would be found dead.

In early February, the activity stopped. (Jason Day, *Haunted Grimsby*, 2011)

– January 22nd –

1970: On this day, there was a growing indignation in the towns and villages of the Lincolnshire countryside – and it was going to take more than well-intended words to waft it away. As the *Grimsby Evening Telegraph* reported:

Look no farther than the end of your nose for the cause – the evil smells that for too long have been accepted as a part of progress in industry and agriculture. When country folk, long used to farmyard odours, start complaining it is time for action.

The Association of Public Health Inspectors in London was told that smells from intensive farming and vast quantities of highly septic manure were causing an outcry. Battles are being fought between big businesses and health officials, who are right to urge stronger laws to cope with the problem.

Nearer home, there is a whiff of reassurance. Brigg's medical officer says that the nuisances which cause most public concern are often least harmful to health. This does not make them any easier to stomach. But research and preventative measures have not, at the moment, the stimulus of absolute compulsion. It is time the law lent more weight to those efforts being made to clear the air. It might start by recognising such offensive odours for what they are - an assault on the person.

(*Grimsby Evening Telegraph*, 1970)

— JANUARY 23RD —

1980: On this day, the Grimsby seiner *Fiona Jane* – which had been out of radio contact for two days – was reported safe in the North Sea, minutes after an aircraft had taken off to search for her.

Concern for the 58ft vessel began to mount after she failed to report in. Her last reported position had been 140 miles east/north-east of the Humber, and strong gales had been lashing that area. As dawn broke on this day, an RAF Nimrod took off from Kinross to comb the area were the vessel had last been reported.

Only minutes afterwards, shortly before 8.30, Skipper Enjar Sorensen put out a 'safe and well' call, reporting that he and his two-man crew were safe. The Nimrod was returned to base. Sorensen – who had been fishing for forty-five years – told the Post Office station that he only knew there were worries about his vessel's safety when he heard a news broadcast at 6 a.m. that morning. A spokesperson for Humber Radio said, 'He [the skipper] seems to have lost a day. He thought he had reported in.' (*Grimsby Evening Telegraph*, 1980)

— January 24th —

1987: On this day, faulty phone lines were causing chaos at a frustrated Grimsby fish merchant's ... and a John Cleese farce had nothing to do with it!

Pandemonium broke out at T. Chapman and Sons, in Kemp Street, when the telephone system packed up – smack in the middle of the nationwide BT strike. Three out of six lines went completely dead. On the others, the only person to answer was the speaking clock and, to make matters worse, every time an incoming call was made, the Telex machine went berserk.

'It's absolute chaos,' said company secretary Loretta Skade. 'We have about 30 miles of meaningless Telex messages.'

When they eventually succeeded in getting past the speaking clock, there were further surprises in store – more often than not, it was a wrong number. Seeing the funny side though, employees of the firm posed for amusing photographs for the local newspaper.

Disruption caused by the strike lasted about a fortnight, until BT agreed to a two-year pay rise worth 12.66 per cent. (*Grimsby Evening Telegraph*, 1987)

~ January 25th ~

1969: On this day, a 12-year-old missing Grimsby boy was safe – after being found at Heathrow Airport, in London, late the night before.

The Havelock School pupil had been reported missing to the police by his mother the day before. Officers in Grimsby began a search but it was called off when they received a message that the youngster had seen by an airline official looking at the planes. He was handed over to the police, who looked after him for the evening.

On this day, his father took a day off work to return him from the airport to his home in Grimsby. His mother told the *Grimsby Evening Telegraph* how she and her son had had a 'tiff' and she had sent him to bed earlier than usual. The following morning, he was quite cheerful when he left home for school at the usual time, saying he would see her in the evening.

The youngster wanted to pursue a career in the navy, said his mother, and she would have understood his actions if he had gone to a seaport, not an airport. (*Grimsby Evening Telegraph*, 1969)

— January 26th —

1953: On this day, a homeless fisherman bravely dived into the cold and murky waters of Grimsby Dock to rescue a screaming woman. Charles Frederick Lodge – better known as Tabby Lodge – was congratulated by magistrates and the police for his gallantry.

The woman had thrown herself into the water at the Corporation Road lifting bridge following a row with her boyfriend. When Mr Lodge arrived at the scene, the woman was screaming in the water, in the deepest part of the dock.

Three men had already climbed down underneath the bridge and were trying to reach her.

After taking off his overcoat and shoes, Mr Lodge dived in and swam to shore with the woman, where the other men pulled them both out.

The woman, who could not swim, was seen by medics at hospital.

Accommodation was found for Mr Lodge that night at the Salvation Army Hostel, and the particulars of his actions were sent to the Royal Humane Society. (*Grimsby Evening Telegraph*, 1953)

~ January 27th ~

1947: On this day, severe snowfall brought Grimsby to a halt. In fact, mention 1947 to anyone who was there at the time and their thoughts turn immediately to snow drifts, frozen pipes, biting winds and huddling round a flickering fire, trying to keep warm.

Trains were stranded on blocked lines, people were marooned for days on end, there was a coal shortage and rationing was still in force. Bread ended up being delivered on the rope railway, used in normal times to move ironstone to isolated communities.

On this day, 2ins of snow fell; three days later, there were reports of drifts 5ft high. One man walking on the Wolds stubbed his toe on something, dug down and discovered an abandoned bus. Even Grimsby Town's players were stranded in a train on their way back from a match.

When it looked like the cold spell was ending, it came back with a vengeance. In early February, the first of the great blizzards struck – people awoke to a buried world and Grimsby was completely cut off. But even when it thawed in March, flooding forced 7,000 people to evacuate. Melting snow left 3ins of water in some Grimsby streets. (*Grimsby Telegraph Bygones*, 1940s special edition, 1985)

JANUARY 28TH

1938: On this day, the Grimsby vessel *Leicestershire* was lost, with fifteen men on board, in one of the town's worst fishing disasters. The vessel had arrived in the port two years previously, when she was one of the big new additions to the Shire Trawlers fleet, built by Smith's Dock, in Middlesbrough.

The *Leicestershire* was homeward bound from Iceland on this day when it's believed she was overwhelmed by a violent storm off the Orkneys. Her last message was picked up by another Grimsby trawler, the *Northern Chief*, when she was some 30 miles from the Skerries.

The following day, islanders on Hoy found bodies and wreckage washed ashore on the rocky coastline. Part of a trawler's boat was found bearing the name 'Grimsby' and later parts of a radio set identified as coming from the *Leicestershire* were discovered.

Grimsby's Port Missioner had the grim task of visiting fifteen homes, informing twelve women they were widows and twenty-three children that they were fatherless.

The tragedy could have claimed a sixteenth life, were it not for good fortune. While the vessel was fishing off Iceland, her galley boy complained of feeling unwell. The skipper was so concerned he put the boy ashore at Isafjord, where he was found to have appendicitis. (*Grimsby Telegraph Bygones*, Great Trawlers edition, 1996)

— January 29th —

1982: On this day, furious residents slammed the builders of the new Grimsby Town football stand after sheets of corrugated iron fell 'like giant daggers' from its roof during high winds.

Three sheets of the roof, measuring 12ft by 3ft, fell 50ft from the top of the stand being constructed at Blundell Park, in Cleethorpes.

Famously, the ground is one of only a handful in the UK that is situated in a different town to which the club belongs. (*Grimsby Evening Telegraph*, 1982)

1987: On this day, Blundell Park was once again in the news, as neo-Nazi thugs had begun infiltrating the terraces of Grimsby Town Football Club. They had produced crude 'calling cards' designed to be stuck on their victims, prominently featuring the Grimsby Town club motif. The managing director of the club at the time, Tom Lindley, pledged to take action. (*Grimsby Evening Telegraph*, 1987)

– January 30th –

1959: On this day, it was announced that about £8,000 was to be spent on re-modelling Grimsby's Old Market Place, making it open to one-way traffic only. The scheme was due to be submitted by Grimsby Town Council to the Ministry of Transport and Civil Aviation in April, as soon as possible after the beginning of the new financial year.

From Eason's corner towards Victoria Street, the road was to be widened to 21ft, and traffic would flow towards Victoria Street. At the junction of Bull Ring Lane, there was to be a small, semi-circular projection from the footpath for a small garden. The remainder of the historic Corn Exchange and the recently closed conveniences were to be demolished. The object of the plan was to lead traffic from Eason's corner and the church into a single line of traffic before it met that entering from Bull Ring Lane.

The Old Market Place and Corn Exchange were much loved areas of Grimsby in days gone by. Modernisation plans – which sprung up in many places after the hardships of the Second World War – were later, and still are, criticised by Grimbarians. (*Grimsby Evening Telegraph*, 1959)

— January 31st —

1953: On this day, the Lincolnshire coast flooded; the biggest peacetime tragedy the country had even seen. Some 307 lives were lost and 24,000 homes damaged or destroyed, and days later, more than 1,000 people remained untraced along the battered, flooded coastline.

Lashed by winds of hurricane force, the North Sea ripped gaps in the sea defences. From Grimsby and Cleethorpes in the north to Canvey Island in the south, roads turned into rivers and the sea smashed through people's homes and businesses along the entire east coast.

Peter Blanchard was a projectionist at the Ritz Cinema, in Grimsby Road, and was working when the waves hit. He recalled going up on the roof with a friend, the wind so strong that they had to cling on to each other:

> We could see water coming along Grimsby Road towards the cinema. The chief projectionist, Sid Melhuish, had gone home because his house backed onto the railway. When the sea broke the embankment, it smashed through the walls of his house. We could see straight through to what was left of the embankment with the railway tracks hanging across the gap and nothing inside the house.

(*Grimsby Telegraph*; Met Office)

1950: On this day, with all their flares gone and their tiny vessel in danger of being wrecked on the rock-strewn Durham coast in a gale, the crew of the Grimsby motor fishing boat *Sunray* stripped off some of their clothes and burnt them on the deck as distress signals.

For nearly four hours the *Sunray*, pounded by heavy seas, drifted helplessly in the darkness after her engines had broken down.

Coastguards saw her SOS, and Hartlepool's lifeboat, after searching for her for three hours, took the *Sunray* in tow and brought her and her crew safely to port. (*Grimsby Evening Telegraph*, 1950)

1976: On this day, women won their campaign to become dockers at the twin Humber ports of Grimsby and Immingham. A meeting of the Grimsby and Immingham Dock Labour Board decided that women's applications for dockers' jobs would be treated the same as men. (*Grimsby Evening Telegraph*, 1976)

— February 2nd —

1934: On this day, a monster rising from the depths of the Humber sparked a mystery in Grimsby. Cleethorpes' inshore boatmen, who earned a precarious living line fishing in the river, realised their lines were being stripped of fish. At first poachers were blamed, so early on February 2nd, two fishermen – Kirman and Reeder – decided to keep a vigil.

Kirman, who had been standing up in the boat watching and waiting, gave a yell and fell back on to Reeder. Speechless, he could only point at the water. The men saw a terrific swirl, rapidly moving away from the boat, travelling in the direction of Tetney Haven. At a distance of 100 yards, a huge black shape broke the surface of the waves and, in a few seconds, disappeared as though diving.

Two days later, William Croft, who had spent fifty-one of his sixty years fishing, also saw the Humber Monster – though this was not for the first time. He'd seen it ten years before.

'You can take it from me, it's no porpoise,' he said. 'It had a big head, like a Great Dane, ears and a mane on its neck. There was about two feet of head and neck out of the water.'

It was decided to kill the creature. The first attempt was initially thought successful when a 'huge dark shape' was seen on a sandbank – but it was a tree trunk and was instead sawn up for logs. Two days later, another armed squad set out but nothing was found … and mention of it was never publicly made again. (*Grimsby Telegraph Bygones*, 1996)

– February 3rd –

1905: On this day, the *Scarborough Post* published a report about Grimsby's very own 'musical' trawler, the *Syrian*. It read:

> A novel courtesy of the sea was paid Filey by the Grimsby trawler Syrian, which put into the bay for shelter from the strong westerly gale. She had no sooner anchored under the lee of the Brigg and swung round with her head to the wind than, by means of an organ pipe arrangement on her siren, she gave full blast to Auld Lang Syne. The tune was most admirably played and brought scores of people running to the foreshore and cliff tops to investigate the strange occurrence. After a pause, the siren broke into Life on an Ocean Wave. The Bay of Biscay was next rendered, the melody later giving place to The Death of Nelson. Later in the afternoon, the steamer obliged with Rule Britannia and God Save the King.

The *Syrian* had a short seagoing life. She was launched in 1904 for Sir Thomas Robinson, but was sunk by a U-boat on July 11th 1915, off Hornsea. (*Scarborough Post*, 1905)

— February 4th —

1967: On this day, two people who attended a jumble sale at a local school must have been convinced they had bagged a bargain. In the half-hour rush between 2.30 p.m. and 3 p.m. at the sale at Bursar Street School, two coats belonging to helpers were inadvertently sold for a song!

One of the helpers was Mrs Hettie Heaton, who lived in Bentley Street, and when she went to collect her coat at the end of the sale, she found it had been sold, together with another coat belonging to her daughter.

She was told that her daughter's had fetched the handsome price of 3s. Her own – a three-quarter-length brown foam-backed coat with metal figured buttons – had gone for a similar sum. It had been a Christmas present from her husband, and had cost £8.

A plea was made for the bargain-hunters who unwittingly claimed the articles to return them to their owners … but it was never reported if they came forward! (*Grimsby Evening Telegraph*, 1967)

~ February 5th ~

1940: On this day, authorities in London were reporting that attacks by German planes on shipping in the North Sea had been a failure. Nine ships – among them the Grimsby trawler *Rose of England* – had been attacked by German bombers the previous weekend and authorities said four, possibly five, German planes were lost, with seven of their airmen dead and six taken prisoner. The Grimsby trawler *Harlech Castle* brought to port three German airmen who had been shot down, and the body of a fourth who had died of head wounds on board the trawler. Two of the men had leg wounds, a fifth man drowned before the trawler could reach the scene and others remained missing.

Captain T.T. Rendall, skipper of the *Harlech Castle*, said that during a scrap between German and British machines one of the Germans dived into the sea. 'I swung the ship round and saw five men standing on the fuselage of the plane,' he told the Press. 'Then the plane sank and only four were on the surface when we arrived. We picked them up and dressed their wounds. Two could speak a little English and they thanked us and said more planes were coming over in the afternoon.'

Although one neutral ship was sunk and one British steamer set on fire, the other seven of the nine attacked vessels escaped with minor damage. (*The Recorder*, South Australia, 1940)

⟶ FEBRUARY 6TH ⟵

1923: On this day, a high-society affair which shocked Grimsby was revealed. Australian journalist Eugenia Bertuance Stone swept widowed Sir George Doughty, Grimsby's MP, off his feet. The 6ft 2in tall beauty was 28 and he 53, and they married. Sir George owned the *Grimsby Evening Telegraph*, and she wrote a column in it, under her own name, in a high and moral tone, on many subjects.

Following Sir George's death in 1914, she left Grimsby for London, and was a frequent visitor to the Riviera. But Sir George's great friend T.G. Tickler − a famous name in Grimsby − had become infatuated with her, despite being married with four children. By 1920, he was living half with his wife and half with Lady Doughty, and had told his wife that if she didn't like it, she could leave.

In 1923, Mrs Tickler discovered erotic letters to her husband and decided to divorce. The court was told Tickler had broken into his wife's bedroom, brandishing a loaded pistol, and threatened to kill them both. The divorce was granted.

Tickler never married Lady Doughty nor returned to Grimsby − he married eventually in 1955, to a Mrs Brown, whom he had known for thirty-three years. (*Grimsby Telegraph Bygones*, 2007)

FEBRUARY 7TH

1954: On this day, the Grimsby trawler *Laforey* hit a reef called Sendingane off the coast of Norway. Skippered by the much-respected William Mogg, the *Laforey*, just 5 years old, was returning to Grimsby, carrying a catch of 1,500 kits.

The first sign that the 609-ton vessel was in trouble was when the wireless operator sent the first of two mayday messages. A Norwegian salvage vessel, the *Conrad Langaard*, located the position of the stricken trawler and its crew. A wire from Norway reported the capsized ship had been spotted lying bottom up on a reef near Floroe. Several vessels rushed to the scene to help, but it was too late. All twenty crew men died, and the sinking was officially recorded on February 8th, the following day.

Back in Grimsby, flags were dropped to half-mast when the rescue operation was abandoned, and a memorial service, attended by almost 1,000 people, was held at the Central Hall. Nearly 300 of those present were relatives of the dead crew. The body of Johanness Besselling was the only man recovered. He was found about 70 miles north of where the vessel sank several days later, in an unmarked lifejacket.

The wreck lay undiscovered until Norwegian divers found the vessel in September 2010. (www.grimsbytelegraph.co.uk; David Boswell, *Loss Lists of Grimsby Vessels 1800–1960*, 1969; verbal account by Ronald Limb)

~ February 8th ~

2006: On this day, a film which went on to achieve international success had its first screening. And a boy from Grimsby, who had no acting experience whatsoever, was in the lead role.

Thomas Turgoose landed the part of Shaun in *This is England* when legendary director Shane Meadows sent scouts to Grimsby to find undiscovered talent. The auditions, held at a community centre, unearthed Thomas who, at just 13, displayed an indifference Shane knew he wanted for his character.

On this day, Shane aired the first cut of the gritty film to the powers-that-be, and it was later premiered in Grimsby. Filmed partly in the town, Thomas starred alongside Stephen Graham and Joe Gilgun. Shane said, 'To come from the streets of Grimsby having never acted and deliver the performance Tommy has is breathtaking.'

The young Thomas – known as Tommo to his friends – was once excluded from school for throwing chairs at teachers, swearing and smashing up classrooms. He dedicated his performance to his late mum, Sharon. (*Grimsby Telegraph*, 2006)

~ February 9th ~

1844: On this day, the first pile was driven at the New Docks. Within six years, in 1850, 1,000 men had been employed in the construction of the docks; the work would be completed in 1852. The space enclosed measured 83 acres which, when finished, would 'be a safe refuge for vessels in stormy weather'. (David Kaye, *The Book of Grimsby*, 1981)

1931: On this day, a story of gallantry was told with the arrival of the trawler *Resmilo* into port, which had lost her mate and third hand at sea. The incident happened at night, 50 miles off Spurn Point, in the Humber. The gear was being shot when the mate became entangled in it and as the trawl went over the side, he was dragged overboard with it.

The third hand saw him go and, without waiting to throw off his heavy sea clothing, dived into the rough water in the darkness – an act of extreme courage. The mate went under the water and was never seen again. The third hand clung to the gear and was brought back on to the trawler unconscious. Resuscitation failed and his body was landed in Grimsby on this day. (*Grimsby Telegraph Bygones*, 1999)

~ February 10th ~

1956: On this day, British and Icelandic trawler owners agreed on principles under which Icelandic fish could be landed in Britain after a four-year ban imposed during the Cod War (disputes between the two countries over fishing territories lasted from 1952–76). The president of the British Trawlers Federation, Mr J. Croft Baker, of Grimsby, said it was impossible to forecast a date when Icelandic fish would again be unloaded in Britain, but 'the principle in resuming these landings was clearly agreed on'. The breakthrough ended two days of negotiations in Paris. (*Grimsby Evening Telegraph*, 1956)

1967: On this day, The Who played the Gaiety Ballroom in Grimsby. Only three members of the legendary band appeared on stage though: Roger Daltrey was apparently ill. The show climaxed in Pete Townshend smashing his Stratocaster on the stage and throwing the remains into the eager crowd. Keith Moon's drum kit was totally wrecked, and he threw handfuls of drumsticks into the audience. They were fought over with vigour, and no doubt remain prized possessions in some local households. (www.grimsbytelegraph.co.uk)

~ February 11th ~

2013: On this day, archaeologists were awaiting the results of scientific tests on a prehistoric forest engulfed in the cold North Sea, and which has been preserved for thousands of years.

Radiocarbon dating of the wood was expected to determine the exact date when the trees grew, and palaeo-environmental analysis of the peat layers had also been conducted.

Starting at the toe of the Wonderland groyne on Cleethorpes promenade, the stumps of a sunken forest stretch the length of the coastal plain. The stumps are believed to date back to 2,000 BC, suggesting the area was once home to green oak, birch and alder.

In 1949, wood salvaged from the ancient forest was used to create caskets and other carved objects for the mayor's parlour. Tools relating to the New Stone and Bronze Age, including flint hand axes, were also discovered there.

Little is known about the forest, only that when the trees grew, they were probably 20ft above sea level, preserved through being bedded in peat. (*Grimsby Telegraph*, 2013)

~ FEBRUARY 12TH ~

1940: On this day, the rescue of the Grimsby trawler *Gurth* was staged in complete darkness, not to mention a snow blizzard, and it went down in history as one of the most daring.

The incident was a triumph of endurance and dedication for Coxswain Robert Cross, who is probably one of the most famous lifeboat men from the Grimsby area. He twice won the RNLI gold medal for gallantry, as well as three silver and two bronze medals. Cross, who was also awarded the George Medal, held the post of coxswain for thirty-one years, retiring in 1943 aged 67. He lived to the age of 88, having taken part in the rescue of 453 lives.

Cross won both the RNLI gold medal and the George Medal for the rescue of the *Gurth*, and his five-man crew each won the silver medal – deserved honours for extraordinary perseverance. Two of the crew were ill, so it was manned by only six and Cross couldn't spare anyone to operate the search light. So, in total darkness and fighting a blizzard, they worked the lifeboat alongside the trawler. The rescuers were repeatedly knocked down by the sea and were only saved from being washed overboard by hanging on to the handrails.

Three-and-half hours after the rescue began, the entire crew of the *Gurth* were safe on shore, albeit bruised and battered, and eternally thankful to Cross and his shattered men. (Ivan E. Broadhead, *Portrait of Humberside*, 1983)

– February 13th –

1934: On this day, Grimsby magistrates made a deputation to the Home Office … the subject – drinking. Clubs were the focus of the Grimsby Brewster Sessions, held on this day at the town hall.

The Chief Constable of the town, Mr C. Tarttelin, said there were forty-six fully licensed houses in the borough, twenty-eight beer houses and others, making 141 in all. According to the last census, that meant there was one licensed house for every 855 inhabitants.

During the year before, there had been fifty-one incidents of drunkenness reported, including the arrest of eleven females. The sitting heard that the custom of drinking was 'dying' and that only very few young people indulged; it was the old people who were keeping it up. (*Grimsby Evening Telegraph*, 1934)

***

1968: On this day, angry scenes erupted at the Central Hall when Lilian Bilocca appealed to 150 Grimsby fishermen's wives to support her campaign for greater safety on board trawlers.

Several people, including wives who had lost relatives at sea, and Herbert Joys, radio operator on the Notts County, protested to Mrs Bilocca and Vera Tidswell-Howard, leader of the Grimsby wives' protest. The women were told to leave the fight for safety to the men. But the two campaigners finally won the day and were cheered as they outlined their plans for better conditions at sea. (*Grimsby Evening Telegraph*, 1968)

~ February 14th ~

1862: On this day, an enraged mob sparked a riot in the centre of Grimsby. A fierce political battle was being fought between election candidates John Chapman and George Heneage. It was in the days before the Reform Act, so every single vote counted, and a rumour was circulating that Heneage was expecting two voters from Liverpool to boost his count.

On Valentine's Day, the day of the election, the out-voters were met at the railway station and taken to the nearby Yarborough Hotel. This was spotted by a local who told Chapman's supporters – by now fuelled with alcohol.

Chapman's men gathered outside the hotel entrance, demanding that the two show themselves. To calm the situation, landlord Mr Stephens allowed some into the hotel to meet the out-voters upstairs. Chapman's supporters returned to their friends and all seemed quiet – until the hotel came under attack. It was pelted with stones and the incensed mob burst through the doors. The rioters attacked patrons, broke windows and threw furniture into the street.

At the time, Grimsby's police force only had eight officers, and they were soon overpowered. Fortunately, there had been suspicions that Election Day would spell trouble, so officers from Hull were in town.

The mob was removed and sixteen rioters were arrested and tried at the Lincolnshire Summer Assizes. Four were convicted of wounding, assaulting, beating and ill-treating their opponents and the police, and sentenced to three months' hard labour in Lincoln Prison.

The election itself was close-run, with Chapman polling 458 votes and Heneage 446. (www.grimsbytelegraph.co.uk)

~ February 15th ~

1937: On this day, inspired by the approaching Coronation, a Grimsby Girl Guide wrote some verses addressed to the king and queen, and forwarded them, without the knowledge of her family, to Buckingham Palace. The young girl, Sybil Ward, was thrilled to receive a thank-you from Her Majesty's Lady-in-Waiting, praising her 'charming verses'.

The 15 year old wrote:

> I will always try to serve
> You; King and Queen, as you deserve;
> And I know that I will be
> Unswerving in my loyalty.
> May God always be with you –
> Bless each little act you do:
> Grant you and our Empire peace,
> Happiness that will not cease.

Also on this day, two 15-year-old boys appeared before the Grimsby Juvenile Court, charged with carrying out a raid on a railway van in the East Marsh Sidings the night before. They were accused of stealing chocolates valued at £2 1s, belonging to the LNER Railway.

A sack containing seven cartons of chocolates had been found hidden against the wheel of a railway van. A policeman was called, who changed into plain clothes and visited the home of one of the suspected youths, who admitted they had stored the chocolates with the intention of going back for them later.

Both boys were remanded for eight days. (*Grimsby Evening Telegraph*, 1937)

— February 16th —

1962: On this day, the Spurn lifeboat made a dramatic sixty-minute dash to save the two-man crew of a small yacht which was in danger of being smashed to pieces in the Humber in gale-lashed seas.

The alarm was given at about 9.30 a.m., when a diver, engaged on repair work of British Titan Products' discharge pipeline from the Humber Bank, went down to see if the weather would allow work to continue. He saw a yacht was in difficulties, then saw two red flares and immediately telephoned the Grimsby Dockmaster, Captain R.L. Freeman, who called the lifeboat.

The diver, Jack Parker, said, 'I could see he was in trouble, and he must have seen me because he fired two flares. I let the tug owners know and the dockmaster.'

As the lifeboat tossed towards the little vessel, a yellow Air Sea Rescue Service helicopter from Leconfield hovered above, marking the yacht's position and standing by in case of emergency.

The lifeboat made three attempts to get alongside the vessel, and the two crewmen were able to jump on board. They had been heading for Grimsby from Ferriby when the engine 'conked out', and they lost their bearings, mistaking Titan's chimney for the Dock Tower. (*Grimsby Evening Telegraph*, 1962)

~ February 17th ~

1950: On this day, the Grimsby trawler *Pollard* became stranded at Trannoy, West Fjord, Norway. Owned by the Crampin Steam Fishing Company, she had sailed earlier that week for the White Sea fishing grounds and, in the ordinary course, would have been returning to Grimsby in another seventeen or eighteen days. But high seas and a stiff south-west breeze caused her to become stranded and she began taking on water.

Dramatic radio distress calls were picked up by the Norwegian vessel *Ornes*, and the twenty-two-strong crew, all from Grimsby or Cleethorpes, were safely rescued.

Water was in the engine room when the crew left the *Pollard* and the skipper, mate and wireless operator returned to the vessel aboard the salvage steamer *Jason* the following day. The ship, although wrecked, was not going to sink. Her skipper, George Albert Peacock, had served continuously on the vessel for three years, first as a deck hand then third hand, mate and since August 1949, as skipper. He had been fishing since he was a boy and during the war served as a skipper in the Royal Naval Reserve, minesweeping. (*Grimsby Telegraph Bygones*, 2009)

⌐ February 18th ⌐

1953: On this day, hope for the safety of the Grimsby trawler *Sheldon* and her crew, silent since January 30th, was officially abandoned by the owners, Sir Thomas Robinson and Son (Grimsby) Ltd.

'In view of the evidence, only a miracle could bring her home now,' a spokesman for the firm told the *Grimsby Evening Telegraph*.

Studying all the reports of other vessels, and knowing the approximate position of the *Sheldon*, the owners came to the conclusion that a gale hit her in the early hours of January 31st and that she probably took an exceptional sea broadside and was sunk.

Other trawlers reported the suddenness with which the gale hit them. Skipper Shepherd, of the Cunningham, was reported as saying: 'The storm hit us at about 5 a.m. It came on literally within ten minutes. I have never seen anything like it.'

The *Sheldon*, with her crew of fourteen – including the skipper and his son – had sailed from Grimsby on January 26th for the Faroes fishing grounds, but put into Kirkwall to land two of the crew, the cook and a deckhand, who were ill. She then sailed from Kirkwell on her ill-fated voyage at noon on January 30th. Because of her silence since that date, intensive air, sea and radio searches were made, but no trace of her was discovered. (*Grimsby Evening Telegraph*, 1953)

— February 19th —

1977: On this day, popular Grimsby MP Anthony Crosland died, aged 58. He had been in a week-long coma after suffering a massive stroke.

Mr Crosland – or Tony, as he was known – played a big role in the town, and went on to have an internationally important career. Born in 1918 in St Leonards-on-Sea, the Labour man studied at Trinity College, Oxford. He entered politics in 1949, and was regarded as a 'moderniser' of his day. During his political life he was the Secretary of State for Foreign and Commonwealth Affairs, Secretary of State for the Environment, President of the Board of Trade, Secretary of State for Local Government and Regional Planning and Secretary of State for Education and Science. He served Grimsby from October 8th 1959, taking over from Kenneth Younger, and left office on February 19th 1977, when Austin Mitchell took over. He also was an author. Mr Crosland was a keen football fan and an avid viewer of *Match of the Day*. He would regularly attend Grimsby Town matches at Blundell Park.

His ashes were scattered at sea near Grimsby the following month. (*Grimsby Evening Telegraph*, 1977)

— February 20th —

2002: On this day, Australian soapstar-turned-musician Jason Donovan was playing a poorly attended gig at Chicago Rock Cafe nightspot in Grimsby. More than 150 miles down the road in London, his ex-girlfriend Kylie Minogue was picking up two Brit awards.

They used to be good *Neighbours*, but by then they weren't even good friends … the gulf between the teen idols' careers had never been wider.

While Kylie sang chart-topper 'Can't Get You Out Of My Head', bearded Jason, in an overcoat and sweatshirt, netted about £2,000 and free booze in Grimsby, a sad reflection of a career which began in *Neighbours*, took him to the music charts and the West End … and then mercilessly dumped him.

But it was the *Grimsby Telegraph*'s front page about Jason's fall from popularity that prompted national newspaper *The Sun* to launch the Let's Get Donovan On Again campaign – and he later credited it with reinvigorating his career. It was backed by music mogul Pete Waterman, who brought Jason and Kylie together for their 1988 number one hit, 'Especially for You'. He told the *Sun*: 'It'd be nice to see him back.'

Since that fateful day in Grimsby, Jason has made more music, presented TV shows and toured in theatre productions. Could it be largely down to Grimsby's local newspaper? (*Grimsby Telegraph*, 2002; *The Sun*, 2002)

1887: On this day, Richard Insole was hanged by James Berry at Lincoln Prison. He had been convicted of the murder of his estranged wife, 22-year-old Sarah Ann, shooting her four times at point-blank range.

The couple had separated following domestic arguments, and Sarah moved out to live with her parents. In January that year, Insole, a 24-year-old apprentice fisherman, bought a revolver and followed Sarah to her parents' home. Reports say Insole shot at his wife, but she threw up his hand and the shot missed. He fired again and she fell into a chair. When he fired a third time, she fell on to the floor. Pushing her mother aside, Insole placed the revolver close to Sarah's heart and fired twice more.

He did not try to flee the scene. When the police arrived, Insole was found sitting in a chair. He pulled out a knife and tried to slash his own stomach, but an officer knocked him out.

At Sarah's inquest, Insole said he had caught his wife committing adultery with his friend, James Shepherd. The jury in the court case recommended mercy on the grounds of provocation and a public petition, signed by 4,000 Grimsby residents was raised – including signatures from magistrates, council members and the Bishop of Lincoln – but he was sentenced to death. (Stephen Wade, *Foul Deeds and Suspicious Deaths in Grimsby and Cleethorpes*, 2007)

~ February 22nd ~

1947: On this day, Grimsby Corporation bus drivers, answering an SOS call from the LNER, fought their way through a blinding blizzard of snow and sleet in the early hours of the morning to evacuate nearly 200 passengers from trains stranded at Waltham. They had become stuck because a goods wagon had derailed, and engines were embedded in deep drifts near Peak's Tunnel, in Grimsby. (*Grimsby Evening Telegraph*, 1947)

1963: On this day, Grimsby was officially twinned with Bremerhaven, in Germany – making it one of the oldest twinning arrangements in the UK.

Bremerhaven is the largest town on the North Sea coast of Germany and, like Grimsby, is a commercial port with fishing links. The fish docks there are now developed to house processing facilities, restaurants, offices and training centres. There are also car ferry terminals and an international distribution centre.

Much of the town was destroyed in the Second World War, but it has maintained its old charm and architecture, including a maritime museum, a lighthouse, art centres and a promenade.

As well as Grimsby, Bremerhaven's partners also include Cherbourg, Fredrickshaven, Pori, Scezin and Kalininegrad. (*Grimsby Evening Telegraph Bygones*, 1993)

~ February 23rd ~

1937: On this day, the timely return of his mother saved the life of a 2-year-old Grimsby boy. The youngster, playing in the back kitchen of his home in Kent Street, had detached the tube from a gas boiler and placed the end in his mouth.

His mother was washing clothes in the yard at the time. When she returned into the house, she saw her son lying on his back on the floor, black in the face and unconscious, with the rubber tube of the gas boiler in his mouth.

A policeman called to the house administered first aid and accompanied the child to hospital, where he was given oxygen. The boy was allowed to return home later the same day. (*Grimsby Evening Telegraph Bygones*, 1994)

1940: On this day, three Grimsby men were feared lost on the trawler *Fifeshire*, which the Admiralty reported as lost through enemy aircraft action.

The families of Second Hand Robert Wilson Loades, Stoker James Lawson, and Seaman Robert Armstrong Platt all received the sorrowful news, and Grimsby grieved with them. The shock of Mr Lawson's parents was recounted on the front page of the *Grimsby Evening Telegraph*.

His mother had heard from him just a few days before to say he was expected home on sick leave. She had no idea that he'd gone to sea again. Mr Lawson had been in the navy for only two months. (*Grimsby Evening Telegraph*, 1940)

— February 24th —

1958: On this day, the crew of the *Wolverhampton Wanderers* was honoured for their part in one of the most dramatic sea rescues ever launched by a Grimsby trawler.

On December 22nd the previous year, the merchant vessel *Bosworth*, with a fourteen-man crew, was on its way from Granton, Scotland, to Sweden with a cargo of coal. The weather deteriorated so the captain put out a call for other shipping to stand by as she had developed a list. Vessels, including the *Wolverhampton Wanderers*, headed to the location, as the wind blew at force 11.

Skipper Bob Drew recalled:

> It took us five hours to do just 30 miles. The Bosworth had a 20 degree list and was taking water. We kept a searchlight trained on her all night. In the early hours we got a message from her crew saying she was sinking. We got life rafts ready but we could not get the lines aboard the Bosworth.

Then, the waves lifted the *Bosworth* high in the water and crashed her down on top of the trawler's starboard bulwarks, causing extensive damage. The Grimsby crew took to their boats, picking up the *Bosworth*'s men in the process.

On this day, at a special ceremony, Skipper Drew and his officers received waterproof watches from the collier's owners, while the rest of the crew got cigarette lighters. (*Grimsby Evening Telegraph*, 1958)

FEBRUARY 25TH

1936: On this day, seventeen houses which Grimsby Town Council had scheduled as slums were the subject of an inquiry at the town hall. They were situated in Red Hill and Burgess Street, and in certain instances, the owners objected to their demolition because the loss of revenue from them would cause hardship. In every instance, the owners of the properties made applications for compensation.

The hearing was conducted by Mr B. Fitch-Jones, an inspector from the Ministry of Health.

One homeowner contended that the house was not unfit for human habitation, nor 'injurious to the health of the inhabitants', and that any defects which existed could easily be remedied.

Work began to clear the slums but halted in 1939 at the outbreak of the Second World War. It wasn't until the 1950s that housing conditions began to improve. (*Grimsby Evening Telegraph*, 1936)

1957: On this day, a Grimsby family was awarded £6,000 in damages at the Lincolnshire Assizes. Rene Roberts, who had five daughters, was the widow of Cuthbert William Roberts, the son of a former mayor, who had died two years previous, after a fall at the West Marsh paper mills of Peter Dixon and Son Ltd. He fell from the girders of a crane track which ran across the machine house at the mill.

The family claimed damages from the firm, and the conclusion made the front page headline of the *Grimsby Evening Telegraph*. It was ruled that the factory method used by Mr Roberts and other workers as standard was not 'reasonably safe'. (*Grimsby Evening Telegraph*, 1957)

~ February 26th ~

1977: On this day, a band of men had been recruited to take part in what was later branded as a 'day of shame' for the town and British shipping. A group of forty men were brought together in Grimsby and, a week later, under the cover of darkness, boarded the *Globtik Venus*, an oil tanker stranded in the French port of Le Havre, and overpowered its thirty-strong crew.

According to eyewitnesses, the group boarded the vessel screaming, waving sticks and iron bars. The Filipinos stood with their hands in the air. Camera crews captured the storming on film, and journalists were there to witness it.

The dramatic storming happened because the Filipino crew was striking over pay, and the vessel's owner, shipping tycoon Ravi Tikkoo, brought in the Grimsby seamen. As far as he was concerned, the Filipinos had mutinied, taking over his ship and demanding a £150,000 ransom. The Grimsby men, he told the press, had recovered his property and were standing over it as security guards.

In Grimsby, unions warned that the men would be 'severely disciplined' when they came home, and that their names had been put on a black-list.

Little was known about the group, apart from that they were believed to be out-of-work fishermen. (*Grimsby Evening Telegraph*, 1977)

- February 27th -

2008: On this day, at about 1 a.m., Grimsby residents had a rude awakening – they were shaken from their sleep by the worst earthquake to hit the UK in twenty-four years. While most homes escaped relatively unscathed, some buildings had to undergo twelve months of structural repairs.

Its epicentre was several miles away in the Lincolnshire village of Market Rasen, and the quake measured 5.2 on the Richter scale. One field away was where chicken farmer Peter Sargent kept his poultry. He said, 'I went into the shed as normal and there, in one corner, were 72 dead birds without a mark on them. I am convinced they flocked to one corner when the ground shook and died of suffocation and fright.'

For the majority of residents, the aftermath was relatively short-lived – though many awoke to find firefighters tackling collapsed chimney stacks and removing rubble from their streets and gardens. One resident said, 'I can still remember the mess in the garden when we got up. We lost our chimney stack, the roof was damaged and the kitchen window was smashed.'

The effects were not limited to Lincolnshire – the quake was felt widely across England and Wales. (*Grimsby Telegraph*, 2008)

FEBRUARY 28TH

1969: On this day, the wreckage of what was thought to be that of a Second World War aircraft was found on the beach. Police carried out an examination of the hulk – thought to be a Spitfire – after it was spotted by a Humber Bank worker on the sands at South Killingholme.

Only a small portion of the wreckage – a section of the wheel covering – was visible when it was noticed by an eagle-eyed Fison worker, James Moore, who lived in Grimsby. He had been walking on the beach between the Regent Oil and BP jetties at the time. Pieces of twisted wreckage were strewn around it for an area of about 50 yards, and a number of small bullets were recovered from the scene.

The RAF was called to investigate the discovery, but it was thought to be impossible to recover the plane as it was too deeply buried.

One suggestion was that it could have been the wreckage of one of two fighter aircraft believed to have crashed in that area about twenty years before. (*Grimsby Telegraph Bygones*, 1999)

~ February 29th ~

1604: On this day, Archbishop John Whitgift died and was buried at St Nicholas' church in Croydon. He was born in Grimsby in about 1530, the oldest son of a wealthy merchant. His uncle, Robert Whitgift, was the abbot of the nearby Wellow Augustinian monastery. He took a keen interest in his nephew's education and, on his advice, John was sent to St Anthony's School in London for tutorage.

He attended Queen's College, Cambridge, but swapped to Pembroke Hall, where he graduated with a Bachelor of Arts degree in 1553. In May 1555, he was elected to a fellowship and took Holy Orders in 1560.

A staunch Protestant, his first sermon was preached at the University Church of Great St Mary's, and in that year he became chaplain to the Bishop of Ely. This title was the first of many in his long and illustrious career, and he was in royal favour; the queen was frequently his guest at his London home, Lambeth Palace. (John Ketteringham, *Lincolnshire People*, 1995)

~ MARCH 1ST ~

1848: On this day, the East Lincolnshire railway line, taking in Grimsby, Louth and Boston south of the county, was opened, as was Grimsby's connection with New Holland. The town's mayor, William Heaford Daubney, gave notice that all shops and offices had to be closed that day. And there were scenes of great celebration as the first train into Grimsby passed under Deansgate bridge. (Edward Dobson, *A Guide and Directory to Cleethorpes*, 1850)

1938: On this day, at a County Court hearing, a pilot whose aeroplane had crash at the Grimsby Municipal Aerodrome, in Waltham, was sued by the owner of the machine for damage.

The proceedings heard that the pilot, an amateur, made an error of judgement and crashed in a Taylor Cub when attempting to land in the aerodrome, and afterwards declared he was 'glad to be alive'. The pilot had been giving demonstrations to Lincolnshire Aero Club members. It was alleged his piloting was erratic, even making the plane stall on one occasion, and that it had frightened people on the ground below.

The owner was a London-based agent and distributor for the American Taylor Cub aeroplane. (*Grimsby Evening Telegraph*, 1938)

~ March 2nd ~

1967: On this day, Grimsby's town clerk, Mr F.W. Ward, sent a protest telegram to the Home Secretary, Roy Jenkins, over the appointment of the new Deputy Chief Constable for Lincolnshire. It followed a walk-out by the town's six representatives on the Lincolnshire Police Committee from a meeting in Lincoln when it failed to appoint the borough's Chief Constable, James Angus – described as being 'unquestionably the right man for the job'. Instead, on the casting vote of the chairman of the committee, Sir Weston Cracroft-Amcotts, the appointment went to the then Assistant Chief Constable of Lincolnshire, Mr A. Johnson, who, under the existing system, was subordinate to Mr Angus.

Grimsby's council, in protest, also declared that the mayor would take up the issue with the town's MP, Anthony Crosland.

'It is not a question of crying over spilt milk or creating a furore because our man was not appointed,' said Councillor A. Peters. 'We felt so strongly that justice was not done that we walked out in protest.' (*Grimsby Evening Telegraph*, 1967)

~ March 3rd ~

1937: On this day, the eighteen-strong crew of the Grimsby trawler *Lord Ernle* was rescued at 3 a.m., after the vessel ran on to the rocks between Flamborough and Bridlington.

A cheery wireless operator kept up the spirits of the rescuers. An early message said: 'I think the job is OK and going well, but I cannot see. They have got a line on board. Cheerio.'

His final message before leaving the stranded trawler was: 'I have got a call to come. I'll be seeing you sometime.'

Only one of the crew had been rescued when the breeches buoy line snapped, and the rest of them had to jump into the lifeboat below. (*Grimsby Evening Telegraph*, 1937)

1938: On this day, a proposal by the Grimsby Corporation to widen Cleethorpe Road, from Hilda Street to Park Street, was held up to scrutiny at a public inquiry. Conducted on behalf of the Minister of Transport, it investigated an application for an order made in 1937 for the compulsory purchase of the necessary land to enable the widening to be carried out. The owners of the freehold and a number of private owners lodged their objections. (*Grimsby Evening Telegraph*, 1938)

– MARCH 4TH –

1971: On this day, Grimsby Fish Docks became the centre of a bitter dispute when fishermen decided to strike in support of a pay claim. In February, a ballot had showed overwhelming support for a stoppage. The port's deep-sea fishermen wanted an extra £3.75 a week. The owners responded with a new pay structure, offering an increase of £7 on the basic rate, but with substantial cuts in the poundage.

The two sides got together to resolve the situation but crews, meeting at the Mariner's Rest pub, rejected the owners' offer. On this day, hopes of avoiding a showdown disappeared when the trawler owners decided not to make a new offer.

The rush to meet the midnight deadline began. At least seven trawlers sailed that day, and the North Wall was almost empty of vessels. The next morning, March 5, pickets were patrolling dock entrances trying to persuade crews to join their cause.

The 280-ton *Ross Kestrel*, with eight men, became the first trawler to break the strike as she sailed. However, she was on a completely different pay structure to the distant water crews.

Despite the vigilance of the pickets, four distant water trawlers broke out of Grimsby undercover on March 8th; the first big attempt to break the strike. By March 16th, some 350 men had defied the strike and it collapsed. (*Grimsby Telegraph Bygones*, trawlers edition, 2008)

~ MARCH 5TH ~

1192: On this day, Old Clee Church – the oldest building in Grimsby – was dedicated. For many centuries, Holy Trinity and St Mary served as the parish church for Clee, a farming village, and the separate fishing hamlet of Clee Thorpes.

It was the long-standing settlement of Saxon fishermen and their families, but their peace was frequently disrupted by Viking raiders pillaging the area after landing on the east coast.

The Vikings soon colonised the area, as far as Scunthorpe, and within twenty years it became their hub, and soon after, a small principality ruled by Prince Havelock of Denmark.

St Hugh, the first Bishop of Lincoln, dedicated Old Clee Church on this day, during the reign of Richard the Lionheart.

The Saxon tower of the church dates back to around 1050. The nave was rebuilt and the transepts added in Norman times.

In 1992, celebrations to mark the 800th anniversary of this dedication were held. A tablet, worded in Latin, was installed in one of the Norman pillars. The inscription translates as: 'This church dedicated on the third of nones of March in 1192 in honour of the Holy Trinity and Blessed Virgin Mary by Hugh, Bishop of Lincoln in the time of Richard.' (Grimsby Central Library)

— MARCH 6TH —

1965: On this day, a police inquiry into a £9,000 safe raid was widened to a national one. Two days before, a gang using gelignite blew a safe in an office on Grimsby Fish Docks and got away with the cash – all in front of a terrified security guard.

The daring raid took place at Associated Fisheries, in Wickham Road, and the stolen cash was destined as wages to trawler crews. The gang of three men, one of them masked, broke in, planted the explosive and muffled the noise with a carpet. A watchman was seized by the men but thankfully unharmed. When they left, he phoned the police and road blocks were set up, but they escaped.

On this day, the watchman told the local newspaper how he was still suffering from shock:

> It seems like a nightmare now. I was on my rounds and as I passed the entrance to the offices, a man grabbed hold of me by the right shoulder and with his hand, caught me under the chin. They said, 'Don't shout, and you'll be all right. If you start talking, that is just too bad.'

(*Grimsby Evening Telegraph*, 1965)

~ March 7th ~

1991: On this day, lions were on the loose in Grimsby. Four ferocious beasts brought the town to a standstill after they broke free during a performance at Chipperfield's Circus. It was the stuff of a Hollywood film script, but it became reality at 7.40 p.m.

The animals escaped after their cage was sabotaged, and roamed the streets for more than an hour before being captured. Michael Strandt needed twenty-four stitches after a lion pounced on him and sunk its teeth into his neck. He owed his life to policeman Ron Harrison, who rammed the animal with his patrol car.

A clown – complete with red nose, big feet and costume – trapped one of the lions in an alley at Victoria Street bus station. He had earlier rushed into the nearby Grimsby Police Station to raise the alarm. Along with Sgt Stewart Bellamy, the clown used the stick and chair to keep the animal at bay until help arrived.

Another of the lions was captured after being trapped in the Grimsby Cleethorpes Transport bus depot.

Despite the escape – and protests by activists – the show went on the next night as normal. (*Grimsby Evening Telegraph*, 1991)

- March 8th -

1976: On this day, twelve men were rescued when a gas rig supply helicopter crashed into the North Sea, 35 miles off the Humber. The helicopter came down soon after leaving a British Petroleum gas rig in the West Sole Field, heading for BP's Easington terminal.

A massive air-sea rescue operation was immediately launched, with rescue helicopters from Leconfield and Coltishall being scrambled. The twelve men, who had managed to get into a life-raft, were picked up shortly afterwards by the standby vessel *Margaret Christina*.

Meanwhile, as the drama at sea unfolded, train services ground to a halt as a drivers' lightning strike threw the timetable into chaos.

The dispute centred around new working schedules introduced by British Rail and was brought to head when one driver refused to take his train over an amended route.

As a result, ten trains to and from Cleethorpes were cancelled that morning, followed by four more later on. (*Grimsby Evening Telegraph*, 1976)

~ MARCH 9TH ~

1967: On this day, it was announced that top-level talks on the possibility of a Humber hovercraft service, to be run by British Railways, were due to take place in London. The news was made public just hours after it was disclosed that British Railways had begun an intensive passenger research survey to determine the future of the Hull to New Holland paddle-boat ferry service, famously served by the PS *Lincoln Castle*.

One object of the survey was to determine whether the present ageing vessels should be kept in service as long as possible, or replaced by new ships or hovercraft. Geoffrey Fiennes, of British Railways (speaking on the topic of hovercrafts), said, 'This solution attracts me, but whether it is technically possible, I don't know.'

Mr Fiennes was due to meet with Tony Brindle, the manager of British Rail Hovercraft Ltd, a wholly owned subsidiary of the Railways Board and the man responsible for operating the hovercraft service between the Isle of Wight and Southampton and Portsmouth.

It was to be some years before the Humber Bridge was constructed, changing the landscape of the River Humber to how we know it today. (*Grimsby Evening Telegraph*, 1967)

~ MARCH 10TH ~

1903: On this day, Devonian mariner Samuel Henry Smith was hanged for murder. He and mother-of-four Lucy Lingard were close. Soon after he had befriended Lucy, she left her husband and, along with her children, moved into Smith's house in Hope Street.

On November 18th 1902, the pair went on a drinking binge, rowed all afternoon and returned home with a quart of ale. Smith was simmering with rage and Lucy's oldest daughter witnessed him giving Lucy a black eye.

Two neighbours went to talk to Lucy and told Smith off for his behaviour. He apologised and the neighbours left at about 11 p.m. Shortly afterwards they heard a scream and another resident, Mrs Ward, ran to the scene to see Smith standing over Lucy's body. She had been stabbed eleven times, in the head, chest and arms. She died four days later.

Smith said Lucy was not to blame and had not provoked him. He had killed her in a rage and thrown the knife into the fireplace.

He was found guilty at Lincoln Assizes and his life was taken from him by hangman William Billington at Lincoln Prison. (Stephen Wade, *Foul Deeds and Suspicious Deaths in Grimsby and Cleethorpes*, 2007)

~ MARCH 11TH ~

1889: On this day, William Connelly, skipper of the *Doncaster*, died on board. His nephew, Walter Tennant Gempton, was charged with his murder – but he was never brought before the courts.

An initial hearing was told that Gempton, 18, murdered his uncle at sea on the sailing smack, which belonged to the Grimsby Ice Company. The judge said:

> The prisoner was the cook and had been subject to fits. He never had any quarrel with the skipper, but one day he sprang upon the deceased and inflicted a blow at the back of the neck. The man fell on deck and cried out, 'I am stabbed!'

Within ten minutes, he was dead.

Gempton made no attempt to escape, but claimed the skipper had intended to make away with the vessel, endangering the lives of those on board – an accusation wholly without foundation.

The judge told the jury to consider the prisoner's state of mind. 'Gempton is, at present, in a lunatic asylum and perhaps would not be in a position to take his trial,' he said.

The hearing was a formality and soon ended. Throughout it, the dock remained empty – and Gempton was never heard of again. Presumably, he spent the rest of his life in an asylum. (*Grimsby Telegraph Bygones*, 1997)

‒ March 12th ‒

1934: On this day, four Grimsby people were recovering after the car they were travelling in crashed into a drain, nearly drowning them. The party was driving towards Thoresby Bridge when the car skidded on the wet road and overturned into the Fleet Drain, which ran alongside the Tetney-Grainthorpe road. The drain was full of flood water, in consequence of recent heavy rain.

Fortunately for the occupants, the car fell over on its side and, though it was practically submerged, they were able to escape through the windows. One of the party, a young man, sustained a fractured right leg. He actually climbed out of the car and helped two of his companions out before realising he was injured.

A farmer who lived close by plunged into the chest-high water to help with the rescue operation. A gate was laid from the bank to the car, and across this the four people were able to get back on to the road.

All were wet through but were given every attention at the farmer's home. A doctor from North Thoresby was sent for, and attended to the young man's fracture. Another man had also hurt his leg, and the others – a man and a woman – were unhurt. (*Grimsby Evening Telegraph*, 1934)

— MARCH 13TH —

1607: On this day, the politician, lawyer and antiquarian Gervase Holles was baptised in Grimsby. He had been born in the town five days previously, a son to Frecheville Holles.

Holles went on to become Mayor of Grimsby in 1636 and 1638. He was called to the bar in 1639 and sat in the House of Commons from 1640 to 1642. In April 1640, he was elected MP for Grimsby in the Short Parliament and was re-elected for the Long Parliament in November that year.

He fought in the English Civil War, and Oliver Cromwell came to Grimsby to ransack the home of the Royalist supporter.

After the Restoration, Holles was re-elected MP for Grimsby in 1661, serving on the Cavalier Parliament until he died in 1675, aged 67. He was also Mayor of Grimsby once again in 1663, as well as secretary of petitions to Charles II and one of the Masters of Requests.

Twice married, his only son, Freschville, was also an MP for Grimsby.

Among the interesting stories relating to his life is this: Gervase was convinced a curse rested upon the desecration of Grimsby's St Mary's church and the stone it was made from. His great-uncle, Densel Holles, who lived at Irby, had plans to build a new house in the village and, disregarding his nephew's fears, bought a stone from the old church. But before a single stone could be laid, he died, suddenly. (Francis Frith, *Grimsby: An Illustrated Miscellany*, 2004)

~ March 14th ~

1919: On this day, Joseph Woodhall, a kindly former sergeant in the Manchester Regiment, murdered a well-known charity worker, Sarah Robinson, by hitting her on the head with an Indian club.

The two had been friends: Woodhall working for respectable Mrs Robinson at the Brighton Street Home for soldiers, in Cleethorpes. That evening, they took supper with another friend, Elisabeth Ann Evans, and a small argument ensued. Mrs Robinson teased Woodhall about his plans for the weekend, and this exchange led to tragedy of the worst kind.

Mrs Evans was stirring a saucepan on the fire when, out of the corner of her eye, she saw movement. Mrs Robinson said, 'Oh sergeant, you mustn't hurt Annie.' That was the last Mrs Evans heard, for Woodhall knocked her unconscious.

When she woke, Mrs Robinson was on the floor in a pool of blood. Woodhall had vanished.

He became a fugitive, eventually surrendering to the police in Waltham. Wrapped in a rug and exhausted, the 50-year-old had to be lifted out of the police cart into the station – and was found to be suffering from malaria.

He was subsequently charged with Mrs Robinson's murder, declared insane and detained at His Majesty's pleasure. The last the world saw of Woodhall was his hunched figure, sandwiched between two policemen, led, stumbling from the dock. (Stephen Wade, *Foul Deeds and Suspicious Deaths in Grimsby and Cleethorpes*, 2007)

⁓ MARCH 15TH ⁓

1848: On this day, Margaret Shafto Robinson was born in Grimsby. She was reportedly the youngest of twenty-two children to Margharetta Elisabetta Robertson, a Denmark native, and her English husband, William Robinson.

Margharetta was an actress and her daughter went on to become Dame Madge Kendal GBE, a famous actress of the Victorian and Edwardian era. With her husband, W.H. Kendal, Dame Madge became an important theatre manager.

Madge was taught at home by a governess and her father, who read Shakespeare to her from an early age.

Although she sang, she contracted diphtheria as a child and her tonsils were removed, so her voice suffered. But she went on to have a long and varied career – and five children. She was even a featured character in the 1979 play and later film *The Elephant Man*. In the film, she was played by Anne Bancroft. (*Grimsby Telegraph Bygones*, 1997)

1967: On this day, there was a gloomy outlook for northern Lincolnshire in the new railways network announced by the government. The Cleethorpes to New Holland and the coastal Grimsby to Peterborough passenger lines were not included in a new basic network of 11,000 miles agreed between the government and British Rail. (*Grimsby Evening Telegraph*, 1967)

~ MARCH 16TH ~

1915: On this day, a conversation between two men revealed a spy operating in Grimsby. Ernest Olsson was working with a fellow Swede, called Erander, when they were heard saying that in the coming war, the Germans were sure to win. Olsson mentioned that some German friends in Rotterdam were trying to extract details of the naval and military situation in Grimsby, and asked Erander for that type of information.

Unfortunately for Olsson, he was being tailed and the conversation was recorded. A week later, he asked Erander if he had made a decision about passing on information, and again, the exchange was recorded by officials. Erander replied, 'Life is sweeter than money to me; I have been in Grimsby fifteen years and I have been treated like a man, and it would be the last thing I should do.'

Olsson said some of his friends were Germans with big liners laid up at Rotterdam. He was later overheard speaking of a fleet of 130 or 170 zeppelins that were ready to fly over the sea to drop bombs on England when the weather was good.

Olsson was convicted of trying to gather information that would constitute an offence under the Official Secrets Act at Lincoln Assizes and sentenced to four years' penal servitude. (Stephen Wade, *Foul Deeds and Suspicious Deaths in Grimsby and Cleethorpes*, 2007)

~ MARCH 17TH ~

1920: On this day, Lord Heneage auctioned off 206 acres of his land at Highfield Farm. It was at a time when the running costs of estates were on the rise. Agricultural rents were low, and there was the prospect of 'interference' from local and central government. These conditions sparked a deluge of land sales throughout the country, starting in 1919.

The corporation purchased 104 acres of what Lord Hengeage had put on the market. Now, the land is the location of Scartho Road, Barrett's Recreation Ground, the school in Weelsby Avenue and Grimsby Crematorium.

On September 29th that year, 217 acres of the Grant Thorold estate went under the hammer. This is now home to private and council houses, Hardy's Recreation Ground and the King George V playing field.

Lord Yarborough held two sales during 1919 and 1920. He sold approximately 100 acres – which included the 71-acre Grange Farm, as well as building plots in Bargate and Laceby Road – to Sir Alec Black, the famous shipping magnate.

The lord's second sale was of six business premises in Haven Street, South Dock Street and West Dock Street, raising a total of £6,420. He also sold 128 acres to the corporation for the Nunsthorpe Estate for £19,200. (Alan Dowling, *Grimsby: Making The Town 1800–1914*, 2007)

— MARCH 18TH —

1966: On this day, the new Tor Line Terminal at Immingham was officially opened. Lady Kirby, the wife of Sir Arthur Kirby, the chairman of the British Transport Docks Board, did the honours.

A touch of the vintage arrived with the modern when the car ferry *Tor Anglia* completed her maiden voyage to the new roll-on, roll-off terminal just after dawn. As the flags of Britain, Sweden and Holland fluttered over the terminal forecourt, the *Tor Anglia*'s stern door lowered to reveal ... a 1904 Cadillac. The first car ashore was driven by Ragnar Kallstrom, one of the four owners of the Tor Line. Also on board was a trial shipment of thirty Saabs.

The gleaming blue and white ferry, which had sailed from Gothenburg, in Sweden, a little over twenty-four hours before, tied up alongside the terminal opposite the Henderson Quay. After Mr Kallstrom drove ashore, dockworkers moved into action with new equipment for unloading and loading cargo. (True North Books, *More Memories of Grimsby*, 2001)

— March 19th —

1703: On this day, Grimsby woman Elizabeth Spar, desperate to find some work for her son, wrote a heartfelt letter to Arthur Moore, the MP for Grimsby at the time, requesting his help. We are fortunate that the document was kept, as it opens a window on living conditions and life in Grimsby at this time. She said:

> I having one only child who is ready to be disposed of in some employ in the world either as an Apprentife to some trade or any other wayes to which he may be capable of this to desire your afsistance and advice in what may be thought fitt for him, he is now past 13 years of age and I thought to put him to one Mr Samuell Harneis a barber in Marks Lane who is our countryman and a very honest man, but my purfe will not stretch so far, without afsistance … he being a fatherlefs child, and his father-in-law not very kind to him …

(Grimsby Central Library)

~ March 20th ~

1969: On this day, the Belmont television mast was declared completely safe again – after fears that it might snap. The mast towers across the landscape on the outskirts of Grimsby, glowing gently at night.

The cold weather of 1969 had resulted in tons of ice encasing a number of the guy ropes. This, combined with freezing fog and a cold 12 knot wind, had made the mast bend. It developed a tilt which amounted to about 5ft from the perpendicular, later reducing to about 2 or 3ft.

Bright sunshine brought the threat of a rapid thaw, prompting fears that the mast would snap. Staff working at the transmitting station on BBC2 services were evacuated and the police closed nearby roads. Experts took regular readings to check the condition of the top 150ft of the structure – at that time the highest of its type in Europe.

Large chunks of ice began falling off the mast and engineers were drafted in. The drama continued overnight until this day, when the Independent Television Authority announced that all the ice had fallen off and the mast had resumed its normal vertical position. It remained a restricted area for some time afterwards. (*Grimsby Evening Telegraph*, 1969)

~ March 21st ~

1954: On this day, the weather was once again the topic on everyone's lips. Temperatures soared to over 60°F and Cleethorpes benefited from enormous crowds of trippers. It was a stark contrast to March 2nd that year, when there was 12 degrees of frost, and ice formed 4ins thick on Cleethorpes beach. On March 3rd, violent storms lashed Grimsby and Cleethorpes; the tide breached the railway line at Suggitt's Lane and the fear of a repeat of the floods of 1953 grew. Petitions were drawn up and sandbags were at the ready. But the weather turned – rather dramatically – and the fears subsided. The summer of 1954, however, was dreadful, with torrential rain and storms, lightning and howling gales. (*Grimsby Evening Telegraph*, 1954)

1969: On this day, dockyard workers were surprised to see what they took to be a penguin cavorting in the water. They were even more surprised when the 'penguin' flew away … it was later revealed to be a guillemot.

Also on this day, pigswill, rubbish, two dustbins, a desk, a chair and a ladder were among refuse discovered in the £3,450 newly opened swimming pool at North Cleethorpes Secondary School, putting the pool out of action. It is unclear how the refuse got there. (*Grimsby Telegraph Bygones*, 2002)

1935: On this day, it was reported that councillors had adopted a 'scrap the trams' policy. The minutes of a meeting of the Grimsby Tramways Committee were expected to be published, showing that, after examining the figures and giving attention to expert opinion, they regarded the tramway system as obsolete.

Cleethorpes was also faced with the great problem of the trams and transport of passengers in the resort.

While the council there wished to buy out the Tramway Company and create a trolleybus service on the Grimsby Road route, the Tramway Company was anxious to improve its service by substituting trolley buses for trams. Councillor E. Harrison, the chairman of the tramways committee, said:

> We have minutely considered the whole position and there is not the slightest doubt that the scrapping of the trams is the only decision any businessman could take. The existing track from the Clee Park Hotel to the Old Market Place is to all intents and purposes worn out, and if the trams are to be retained, the entire length must be re-laid sooner or later – and sooner than later. This would cost £24,000.

(*Grimsby Evening Telegraph*, 1935)

— MARCH 23RD —

1968: On this day, a strange incident on board a trawler was reported in the local press. Skipper Vic Sampson nosed his 40-ton trawler out of Grimsby, all set to begin a four-day fishing trip.

As the 45-year-old veteran trawlerman headed for the open sea, he called to one of his crew – but there was no reply. When he went below, he found that he was the only man on board. He had left his four-man crew standing on the quayside back at Grimsby. Somewhat red-faced, Skipper Sampson and his vessel, the *Birkdale*, returned to port without a single fish to show for the 'trip'.

'I thought they were all on board when I started the engines,' he explained. 'I even thought I could see one of them down below. It is all very embarrassing but I can see the funny side of it.'

Skipper Sampson, a former Ross Group skipper who lived at Tetney, added, 'I discovered my mistake when I wanted a job doing and called for some help. It has never happened to me before in all my thirty years as a fisherman.'

The mate, Ferdinand de Castelle, explained, 'We had gone to pick up some bobbins and were walking back to the ship when we saw her heading out into the river.' He went to the Prince of Wales pub, in Freeman Street, to telephone the vessel but without success. (*Grimsby Evening Telegraph*, 1968)

~ MARCH 24TH ~

1937: On this day, remarkable scenes at Grimsby Docks were reported on as 2,020 tons of fish were landed in only one day. The jetties were packed with fish from end to end, and boxes were stacked eight high in some places. In the first four days of that week, landings reached 6,266 tons.

Exactly fifty years on, in 1987, the local newspaper reported a dismal affair, with only 1,650 kits of fish on display. (*Grimsby Evening Telegraph*, 1937)

1965: On this day, Grimsby and northern Lincolnshire was bracing itself for a population boom. Such were the possibilities of economic growth in the area, that the population was expected to increase to 3,750,000 by 1981 – a rise of 100,000 in the twenty years from 1961.

It was one of the many possibilities outlined in a survey conducted as part of the first statutory review of the county's development plan.

The development plan needed to go before the county planning committee and county council before it had any legal effect – and they had the power to reverse it. But because so many big development projects had been mooted in the past year, the authority authorised immediate publication of the report.

It broke down the population like this: Immingham was presently home to 7,350 and could rise to 15,000; and in Cleethorpes, Waltham and Humberston currently had a population of 49,650, which was estimated to rise to 56,850. (*Grimsby Evening Telegraph*, 1965)

~ March 25th ~

1976: On this day, local farmers warned that the new Government-guaranteed price for potatoes was putting home-grown supplies 'in serious jeopardy'. The executive of the Lincolnshire National Farmers' Union had suggested that unless a guaranteed price above £40 per ton from that year's annual review was forthcoming, many farmers would choose to plant other crops. As the association's secretary, Newton Loynes, explained:

> Lincolnshire is the main producer of the end of season reserves, and if the farmer is not going to get back the £58 per ton cost of production, he is not going to plant them. And if you don't grow them in Lincolnshire, where are you going to go? The Government must be made aware that farmers will be forced to seek other crops to replace their potato acreages in order to obtain a fair return for their land.

(*Grimsby Evening Telegraph*, 1976)

1939: On this day in 1939, the highest recorded attendance at Manchester United's ground was all thanks to Grimsby. A grand total of 76,962 was recorded on the gate at Old Trafford for the FA Cup semi-final between the Wolves and the Mariners. Unfortunately, Grimsby Town lost. (*Grimsby Telegraph Bygones*, 1995)

1927: On this day, a re-modelled Freeman Street was officially opened amid much pomp and circumstance. Once Grimsby's most famous shopping street, it was first built in the early 1860s and the pubs there were popular among fishermen coming off the docks.

In 1926, the council spent £41,000 constructing a new road, and disruption was caused there for several months while old tram lines were removed and new trolley buses introduced. To mark the transformation, a committee created the Red Star shopping week, featuring special events and discounts or free gifts in the shops. The then Mayor of Grimsby, Councillor L.K. Osmond, officially re-opened Freeman Street at 2.30 p.m. on this day.

The ceremony took place on a platform erected in the grounds of the Cyclists' Club at Hainton Square. A parade formed in Freeman Street, headed by the British Legion Band and a detachment of St John Ambulance, and set off in procession to Riby Square. By the time the parade reached Duncombe Street, the crowds were so large that the trolley buses were at a standstill.

It so happened that some Grimsby Town Football Club supporters were heading to Blundell Park at the time. One of them decided to let loose a large goose. Excited at this sudden freedom, the goose strutted for a few yards in front of the dignitaries. (*Grimsby Evening Telegraph*, 1927)

— MARCH 27TH —

1852: On this day, Grimsby Dock Tower was completed. One of the best-known land-based sea marks of the Humber, the tower is 309ft – taller than Lincoln Cathedral – and contains about a million bricks.

It is twin to the tower of Sienna's town hall and elder brother of Birmingham University. It was designed by J.W. Wild, who travelled widely in in Egypt, Syria and southern Europe, gathering sketches of ideas, some of which he used in Grimsby.

Although it looks ornamental, it was initially built as part of the hydraulic system to open the lock gates and operate cranes. About 247ft up is housed a 30,000-gallon capacity water tank. It was later used for the washing down of the fish markets and for firefighting.

On the North West face is a plaque commemorating the men of the minesweepers who lost their lives in the Second World War. Unveiled in 1948, it is the only tribute of its kind to the minesweeping service, of which Grimsby was one of the largest bases. (Ivan E. Broadhead, *Portrait of Humberside*, 1983)

~ March 28th ~

1941: On this day, George Daniel Revell was declared insane ... and then of sound mind the following day. Revell, a fisherman who always carried a Bible, took to drink after one of his children died and suffered mental health problems, attempting to take his own life several times. Eight more years were to pass until his problems came to a tragic head.

Until August 1949, Edna Curtis and Revell had never heard of each other. Edna was a music hall singer and came to Cleethorpes when her marriage failed in 1935. She created a successful double act with comedian Roy Curtis, who she eventually married in Grimsby.

On August 19th, Edna met with a friend and visited the pubs around Freeman Street. That day Revell was on a day-long drinking session and his path crossed with Edna's. Brazen with drink, he approached her and the pair went off to drink some more.

At 8.45 p.m., both very drunk, they boarded a bus for Humberston. What happened after they disembarked is unclear, but at 10.45 p.m., Revell waited at a bus stop with blood on his clothes.

He told the conductress: 'Take me to a police station. I have killed a woman. God told me to do it.'

The following morning, Edna was found dumped in a field. She had been strangled. Revell was found guilty of murder while insane, and detained at His Majesty's pleasure. (Grimsby Central Library)

─ MARCH 29TH ─

1966: On this day, a Grimsby man was at the heart of an idea to launch Britain into the space race. A revolutionary new concept in space travel had been produced by a study group in Lancashire, headed by Grimsby-born researcher Tom Smith. Code-named Mustard, the group was based at the British Aircraft Corporation Centre in Warton, the home of the Lightning, Canberra and TSR-2. Mr Smith, 39, leading the team, was also the chief of the Aerospace Department at the BAC's Preston division. He was born in Old Clee, Grimsby, and was a former pupil of Wintringham Grammar School.

The study 'swept away' the present system of launching rockets with various boosters dropping off as the vehicle gained altitude. Instead they devised a three unit 'nest' of manned spacecraft, two as boosters and the third as the actual craft. The boosters would carry and feed fuel to the spacecraft up to about 50 miles, and then return to base. After the craft had completed its mission in space, it would return to earth by the normal aircraft landing method.

With advances in technology, it was reckoned this method was twenty times cheaper than the American Gemini or Apollo programme, which hoped to put a man on the moon by 1970. (*Grimsby Evening Telegraph*, 1966)

— March 30th —

2010: On this day, Gerry Burks celebrated his 75th birthday – and became the focus of national media attention when the *Sun* newspaper named him as the oldest father of a newborn child in Britain. His wife, Dawn, then aged 41, had given birth to their second son, Ryan, earlier in the month. He weighed 5lb and 7oz.

Gerry, from the market town of Louth, a few miles from Grimsby, worked as a lorry driver until he was 71 to support his family, and attributed his virility to bananas. 'People might say things about my years, but I look after myself,' he said.

Soon after Gerry hit the headlines, a great-grandfather who had recently recovered from brain surgery became Britain's oldest-known new father at the age of 76. Dennis Ealam, proud dad to daughter Jessie, jokingly said Gerry was a mere 'whipper-snapper'. By coincidence, Dennis, also a retired lorry driver, lived just 25 miles away in Lincoln. He credited his virility to clean living. (*Grimsby Telegraph*, 2010)

— MARCH 31ST —

1964: On this day, the last pints were pulled at the Honest Lawyer, a popular watering hole in Kent Street, Grimsby. Sunday nights in the pub had a touch of the 'legal' about them, complete with judges and defendants. These theme nights were the pub's way of raising money for outings for children and the elderly, with fines being imposed for those who broke the simplest of 'rules'.

The pub served the East Marsh for more than 100 years and was demolished in 1964, the last pints being supped on this day. The Honest Lawyer was well-known for the sign above its door showing a lawyer with his head underneath his arm. It vanished after being taken down for repairs, but a similar sign was created when a new Honest Lawyer was built in Ladysmith Road. (*Grimsby Evening Telegraph*, 1964)

———

2013: On this day, Wonderland closed. Wonderland was an amusement park with a big dipper, dodgems and carousel that could entertain up to 20,000 people. Inside there was a ghost train and skill tests such as darts, firing ranges and hoopla. During the 1920s, one of the many attractions to be found at Wonderland was the Mancho Tables.

The big dipper was demolished in 1974, but the historic site remained open, in later years becoming an indoor market for locals and tourists alike. It closed its doors in 2013, when the current owners sold the land. (*Grimsby Telegraph*, 2013)

~ April 1st ~

1976: On this day, a streaker who ran on to the pitch at Blundell Park told Grimsby magistrates he did it because he wanted a house. The 21-year-old civil engineer, who was fined £20 by the court, ran on to the pitch during half-time at the match between Grimsby Town and Southend.

Long-distance runner Brian Jones was just about to do a lap of honour after running 100 miles when the defendant ran on to the pitch wearing only a hat, a scarf round his waist and a pair of red football socks. He managed to evade two police officers, but was finally caught.

He told the court, 'I did it to get publicity.'

He was getting married soon and his girlfriend was expecting a child, but they could not find anywhere to live. (*Grimsby Evening Telegraph*, 1976)

1981: On this day, it was announced that Grimsby was to get grants totalling more than £209,000 from the European Economic Community (EEC) to pay for the modernisation of nine fishing vessels in the port. The grants were part of about £2.4 million being provided from community funds to aid fifty-three projects around Britain involving the modernisation of vessels under 80ft. (*Grimsby Evening Telegraph*, 1981)

~ APRIL 2ND ~

1945: On this day, the untimely death of a Grimsby boxer was announced. Well-known in local boxing circles as Dido Dixon, middleweight champion of Lincolnshire, Lance Corporal John William Dixon died from pneumonia while training as an instructor in Scotland. He was just 34.

Lance Corporal Dixon joined the Queen's Own Cameron Highlanders, an infantry regiment of the British Army, in October 1944. Before that, he had been a police war reserve constable in Grimsby for five years. He was married and an old scholar of St John's. (*Grimsby Evening Telegraph*, 1945)

1958: On this day, the Bishop of Grimsby, Dr A.I. Greaves, announced his resignation – because of his age. The 85-year-old was consecrated to the role in 1937, before which he was Bishop of Grantham for two years. As a bishop, he instituted more than half the beneficiaries in the Lincoln Diocese and had confirmed more than 20,000 candidates.

Dr Greaves was ordained deacon in Peterborough Cathedral in 1897 and ordained priest the following year. He had an honorary degree of Doctor of Divinity conferred on him by the Archbishop of Canterbury in 1947. His experience of a parish priest was obtained in Kettering, Northampton and Leicester. (*Grimsby Evening Telegraph*, 1958)

~ April 3rd ~

1941: On this day, Grimsby mourned the death of seaman Robert Abraham Dyke. Born in 1896, he served in the Royal Naval Reserve from December 1914 to December 1919. He survived three major naval battles during the First World War, including a skirmish in the Dardanelles.

During the Second World War, Robert was enlisted as a petty officer and engineer, serving on the *Bahram*, a seine-netter converted to Admiralty use.

He was killed when the Harbour Defence Patrol Craft struck a mine and blew up off Spurn Point. Eight of her nine-strong crew were lost. It was day 579 of the conflict, and two other vessels in the country also sank.

Robert's widow died while living in the alms houses in Doughty Road, Grimsby. (*Grimsby Evening Telegraph*, 1941)

1946: On this day, Messrs J.H. Thompson & Sons Ltd and Messrs S. Cartledge & Son both sought to complete the first post-war brick permanent house in Grimsby. It was reported that Messrs Thompson expected to complete their first pair of half-a-dozen semi-detached homes in Littlecoates Road by the end of April. Mr Cartledge said he hoped to complete a house off Carr Lane within three weeks. (*Grimsby Evening Telegraph*, 1946)

— April 4th —

1847: On this day, the Wesleyan Chapel was opened in George Street, Grimsby, seating more than 2,000.

Backtrack more than eighty years, and John Wesley, the little preacher with piercing eyes from nearby Epworth, wrote in his journal of 1764 that Grimsby was 'The Most Lively Place'. He had been greeted with an enthusiastic reception by followers who came to hear him speak, a somewhat different experience to his previous visits to the port.

On March 17th 1745, for example, he wrote that his congregation had been 'stupidly rude and noisy: encouraged thereto by their forespeaker, a drunken ale-house keeper … I singled him out, and fastened upon him, till he chose to withdraw.'

On February 22nd 1747 in the town, he was interrupted by:

a young gentleman with his companions (who) quite drowned my voice till a poor woman took up the cause, and by reciting a few passages of his life, wittily and keenly enough turned the laugh of all his companions upon him. I went on with little interruption. Since that time we have had no disturbance in Grimsby.

Describing the town in April 1766, he wrote:

It is no bigger than a middling village, containing a small number of half-starved inhabitants, without any trade, either foreign or domestic, but this they have; they love the Gospel, hardly six families excepted.

He made his final journey to the port on June 30, 1788, a respected preacher. (Edward Dobson, *A Guide and Directory to Cleethorpes*, 1850)

~ APRIL 5TH ~

1939: On this day, a Grimsby wood carter was recovering in hospital from serious injuries, caused when his horse bolted in a timber yard. The incident, in the yard off Adam Smith Street, occurred as the horse, drawing a wood cut, suddenly became frightened and bolted.

The worker, employed by timber merchants Messrs Bennett and Co. and aged in his sixties, was thrown from the cut, and the wheels passed over him. He suffered a compound fracture of the left leg and head injuries, and also suffered severely from shock.

The horse bolted out of the yard into Adam Smith Street, where the cut collided with a street lamp at the corner of Charlton Street. Such was the force of the collision that the lamp standard was broken and the wood cut was smashed.

This day also proved to be Grimsby Fish Dock's biggest day of the year so far. About 1,700 tons of fish were landed as a team of BBC journalists recorded the occasion for a radio documentary broadcast. More than seventy vessels landed the fish, occupying every single berth, and crowding the pontoons.

During the first three days of that week, 4,315 tons of fish had been landed, compared with just 3,660 tons the year before. (*Grimsby Evening Telegraph*, 1939)

‒ April 6th ‒

1863: On this day, a single railway track to Cleethorpes opened. Authorisation for a line to the resort was first given in 1846; three years on, the Manchester, Sheffield and Lincolnshire Railway met with the Freemen of Grimsby to discuss a route, but nothing came of it. Three routes were suggested but it wasn't until an application in 1861 that building work began. The line was extended to a double track in 1874. (Tim Mickleburgh, *Cleethorpes Pier and Promenade*, 2000)

‒‒

1991: On this day, a buy-out deal to secure the future of one of Grimsby's prime hotels was put forward ‒ by the woman who ran it. The general manager of the Yarborough Hotel, Myrah MacPherson, had submitted a finance deal and development plan for the town centre site. It was hoped that the deal would end years of speculation concerning the hotel, which had been up for sale for more than a year. The site is a historic landmark in central Grimsby. It served passengers travelling on the trains, and still does to this day. (*Grimsby Evening Telegraph*, 1991)

~ April 7th ~

1951: On this day, horse meat went on sale in the Sixhills Street shop owned by Mr J.W. Jeffrey. The *Grimsby Telegraph* reported: 'Very much like frozen veal in appearance, it caused considerable comment among customers. It sold at 4*s* and 4*s* 6*d* a pound, a lot cheaper than it was sold at in London last year.' Mr Jeffrey said the meat should be roasted like mutton. (*Grimsby Evening Telegraph*, 1951)

1934: On this day, the *Grimsby Telegraph* reported that Billy Wetherall broke a roller-skating challenge in the town. An underground miner as a child, Billy became a national treasure as a world champion endurance skater. He broke many records in towns around the country, continuing to do so through service in the First World War, despite being gassed and losing most of his hair and teeth. He could skate non-stop for more than five days – eating, washing and shaving in the process! (*Grimsby Evening Telegraph*, 1934)

1952: On this day, Mollie Sugden made her debut at the Empire Theatre, Cleethorpes, in repertory. The actress is best known for portraying the saleswoman Mrs Slocombe in the British sitcom *Are You Being Served?*

Meanwhile, at the Palace Theatre in Grimsby, there were some exotics treading the boards: Wee Georgie Wood, Marie Lloyd Junior, Turner Layton (of Layton and Johnston fame), Albert Whelan, Hettie King and Dickie Henderson … all of them survivors of Edwardian music halls. (*Grimsby Evening Telegraph*, 1952)

— APRIL 8TH —

1902: On this day, William Taylor Hewitt – a name synonymous with the brewing industry in Grimsby – died.

The history of Hewitt's starts in September 1806, when J. Garniss built a small brew house in Pasture Street. In March the following year, the first barrel of beer was rolled out and by 1810, Garniss sold the business to John Hobson. He ran the firm until his death in January 1871, when it was acquired by William Hewitt and Thomas Hewitt, trading as Hewitt Brothers. It became privately listed in 1888, with a share capital of about £200,000. Thomas died shortly afterwards and shrewd businessman William carried on alone. In 1891, he took over the brewing interests of Gale's Humber Brewery, located near the Bull Ring. It's reputed that William drove around in a horse and cart, persuading publicans to buy his beer rather than brew it themselves.

For eight years, he was a Conservative councillor, and was also a Justice of the Peace and a Guardian of the Poor for some years.

William was living modestly at Weelsby Old Hall when he died from illness, aged 70. His empire was inherited by his only daughter, Mary, and two sons, Henry Titus and Thomas William. The firm eventually ceased production in April 1968. (Graham Larn, *Beer, Hope and Charity: Hewitt's Grimsby Brewery Remembered*, 2008)

~ April 9th ~

1945: On this day, Grimsby trawler the *Falmouth* left port – never to be seen again. This vessel disappeared along with the *Dinorah* in the fishing grounds of the North Sea during the last spring of the Second World War. The double tragedy left fourteen widows and twenty-seven children without a father in Grimsby and Cleethorpes.

The *Falmouth* had left Grimsby on this day on a fishing trip which was supposed to last a week. When she failed to return, her owners, the Standard Steam Fishing Company, organised a search, but there was no sign of the trawler or her ten-man crew. It was supposed that she hit one of the many mines drifting in the fishing grounds.

By May 7th, a day before VE Day, it was announced that all hope had faded and her crew were missing, presumed dead. The announcement was made at the same time as one concerning the *Dinorah*, which had left port on April 27th. It was expected to return on May 4th. The owners, Thornton Trawlers, reported that, on the afternoon of April 28th, crews from the trawlers *Gurth* and *Rodistic* heard a loud explosion and saw a trawler, presumably the *Dinorah*, sinking. When they reached the spot, they found wreckage but no survivors of the eleven-man crew. (*Grimsby Evening Telegraph*, 1945)

– April 10th –

1944: On this day, Gibbons' Gulley was created. Then, Kirmington was the home of the 166 Squadron and their Lancasters were to be part of a major 1 Group attack on railway yards in Aulnoyne, France.

Four aircraft had already taken off when it came to the turn of the F-Fox, which was laden with 14 1,000lb bombs. Halfway down the runway a tyre burst and despite the efforts of the pilot, Sgt Gibbons, the aeroplane's undercarriage caught fire. The crew ran for it and it soon exploded, shattering every window in a mile radius of the airfield and leaving a crater in the main runway, measuring 50ft wide and 15ft deep.

By the following morning, more than 100 men were working flat out to move 500 tons of earth to fill the crater. By 12.30 p.m. the hole had been filled and at 8 p.m., Lancasters were again taking off from Kirmington, this time for a raid on Aachen.

A month later, the patched-up hole began to subside and Kirmington was closed for several days while repairs were carried out. When the airfield re-opened as the region's airport in 1974, there was still a noticeable dip in the runway. (*Grimsby Telegraph*, Bomber Boys supplement, 1991)

~ April 11th ~

1848: On this day, the area experienced its first fatal railway accident. Stoker Daniel Whittaker attempted to leap from the cab of a passenger locomotive on to the footplate of his ballast engine at Ulceby station. He fell under the locomotive, and his skull was crushed. Soon after, Robert Rennand, a farmer, was fined £1 and ordered to pay 15s costs for trespassing on the East Lincolnshire Railway Company line at Weelsby. The following month, railway employee David Anderson was killed in Grimsby when he jumped on to the track to warn an oncoming driver that the points were wrongly set.

The first train to pull into Grimsby did so on February 28th 1848, cheered on by scores of rejoicing residents, although the public service actually began two days later on March 1st. Deansgate Bridge, still standing near Grimsby station, was specially constructed over fifteen months in preparation.

The line's passenger carriages were built by Williams of Goswell Road. First class was described as 'handsome and convenient as any man of the nicest taste or appreciation of comfort in travelling could wish'. An express return ticket from Grimsby to London travelling in this class cost 32s 6d, whereas an ordinary return was 29s. Second-class coaches had 'good glass windows and cushions on seats', and the respective second-class fares were 25s and 22s. (*Grimsby Telegraph Bygones*, 1998)

— April 12th —

1907: On this day, the curious case of Prince Makaroo – a clever conman – made headlines. Three days previously, a young man, holding a package wrapped in a Berlin newspaper, had checked into the Royal Hotel as Prince Makaroo of Zululand.

He telephoned the mayor, who visited the prince at the hotel, where the smartly dressed African presented vouchers from the British consul in Berlin and asked for a loan of 40 or 50s. The mayor politely chatted with the prince, and then promptly phoned the police.

Within minutes, 23-year-old Makaroo was identified as having been resident in Grimsby since 1901 and was arrested on suspicion of trying to obtain money by false pretences. Police Inspector Baglee said he knew the prince as Khaki Brown, a captain attached to the British Army on holiday from South Africa.

Makaroo claimed he was on an important mission from Zululand and that he needed £200. In fact, Makaroo had established a reputation as 'a regular dandy' and a 'lady-killer', promenading around Grimsby in uniform. In court on April 17th, the magistrates were told Makaroo was, in fact, Charles Isaac Brown, also known as Isaac Uriah Brown, a native of Ceylon. He had been in trouble for impersonation before. The court decided he was a liar and sentenced him to three months' hard labour. (*Grimsby County Times*, 1907)

~ APRIL 13TH ~

1952: On this day, Easter Sunday, Grimsby fishermen were in the midst of massively successful landings – and breathing a collective sigh of relief. Easter week of 1952 saw the fish docks at full stretch. Monday landings were 18,674 kits; Tuesday, 17,886; Wednesday, 18,555; and Thursday, 68,322 – a grand total of 4,270 tons of fish landed in just four days.

The same Easter, on Good Friday, Grimsby Town Football Club played Stockport at home before a crowd of 26,390 and takings were £2,501 – a ground record for the time. The successful landings at the docks were a stark contrast to the continuing bad weather at sea experienced just a short time before in January. It brought a fish famine to the entire country. Prices at Grimsby Fish Market were sky high.

'These prices are just fantastic,' a leading merchant told the local newspaper. He was referring to Iceland bulk cod, at 10*s* to 12*s* a stone, Iceland shelf cod at 14*s* to 14*s* 6*d*, and Iceland coalfish at 8*s* to 10*s*. The prices were double those when midweek supplies had been plentiful a few weeks previously. (*Grimsby Evening Telegraph*, 1952)

~ APRIL 14TH ~

1892: On this day, a 76-ton finback whale became stranded near Spurn Point. The female – about 75ft long and with a 35ft girth – died and was towed ashore by a tug to Cleethorpes. Enterprising residents surrounded her with a screen and charged for the privilege of viewing the carcass.

She was bought at public auction for £75 by café and amusement arcade owner Matthew Dowse, banana importer Mr Hercock and butcher Mr Schulke. The blubber was sold and a shed was built near the railway station to exhibit the enormous skeleton. Dowse charged 6*d* for people to visit, and in two seasons made about £1,000 before it went on a tour of England. He then sold it for £250 to an American showman, but eventually bought it back for £15.

The jawbones were preserved and in the 1950s, became an entrance arch to a rose garden in Sidney Park. In 2010, the jawbones were donated to The Jungle Zoo, who kept them in storage. In 2011, the zoo explained how a mystery man pretending to be from the attraction removed them – and they had gone missing. The council swiftly located the bones and they have been in safe keeping at the zoo since. (*Grimsby Telegraph Bygones*, 1997)

~ April 15th ~

1932: On this day, Tom Lapidge, a mate on the *Capricornus*, vanished into thin air. The *Capricornus* was heading home, and the crew had turned in. Lapidge was alone with the compass and at 4 a.m., he called for a cup of tea. A deckhand called Remblance went to the bridge – but there was no one there. All that remained of Lapidge was his belt, sou'wester, oilfrock and pipe.

Remblance roused the skipper and the crew, and the ship was searched. They traced their path back 4 miles but nothing was found, so at 6.30 a.m., headed back to Grimsby.

An inquiry concluded Lapidge, 48, from Healing, had been washed overboard and that was the end of the matter... until August, when he turned up at his daughter-in-law's home.

Bill Weatherill, a fellow fisherman who knew Lapidge, recalled:

> He claimed that, officially, he didn't exist. He had devised a plan to defraud an insurance company by faking his death. He hid away in the ship's bunkers. When the ship docked, he sneaked ashore under the cover of darkness and made his way to Hull, where he had arranged to meet his wife. He told me his wife duly drew the insurance – but she made off with another man.

It is not known if Lapidge was punished. (*Grimsby Telegraph Bygones*, 2002)

~ April 16th ~

2001: On this day, a *Grimsby Telegraph* reporter was sitting in his car outside the newspaper office, eating a sandwich, when his car rocked unexpectedly. He thought it was a particularly strong gust of wind … until he went up to the newsroom and discovered every single phone ringing, and his boss motioning for him to get back in his car.

There had been a fire and explosion at the ConocoPhillips Oil Refinery. Some 170 tonnes of LPG gas was released from the saturate gas plant at the refinery and the gas cloud ignited. As the fire burned, it caused failures in other areas of pipework, resulting in another explosion. The flames raged for two-and-a-half hours.

Amazingly, there were no serious injuries, but considerable damage was caused to buildings there. It took the refinery some time to recover. The south bank near Grimsby is a haven of industry, and ConocoPhillips, now Phillips66, is one of many which make a large contribution to the life, not to mention the employment, of Grimsby folk. (*Grimsby Telegraph*, 2001)

~ April 17th ~

1935: On this day, the 447-ton steam trawler *Vascama* sailed into the Royal Dock at Grimsby. Dressed in bunting, the vessel – GY 164 – was the brand new addition to the fleet of Atlas Steam Fishing Company (known in Grimsby fishing circles by the family name of Lettens). And skipper Peter Christian Jensen was rightly proud: the *Vascama* was the first trawler in town to be fitted with a shower and a hot and cold water supply … luxury indeed for the fishermen on board.

She was built in Selby and at just over 158ft, she was not the biggest trawler in the port, but fitted with the latest aids, she was greatly admired. On her trials, the coal-fired boiler had supplied enough steam for the *Vascama* to achieve a speed of 12½ knots over the measured mile.

Her maiden voyage was on April 18th 1935, to the Icelandic fishing grounds. She returned to port after eighteen days, with a catch of 3,000 boxes.

In August that year, she attracted even more fame when she became the first Grimsby steam trawler to fish the Newfoundland Banks. An arduous 5,000-mile round trip, it was one of the most distant fishing grounds to Grimsby.

At the outbreak of the Second World War, she was sold to the Admiralty and was used to hunt U-boats. (Harry C. Hutson, *Grimsby's Fighting Fleet*, 1990)

~ APRIL 18TH ~

1849: On this day in 1849, His Royal Highness Prince Albert honoured Grimsby with his presence to lay the foundation stone of the New Dock. He had arrived by train the day before and stayed at Brocklesby Hall. The *Illustrated News* reported that, as the royal train made its way north, crowds of 'healthy, sturdy peasants and yeomen' had assembled at each station along the route to greet the Prince as he swept along.

The foundation stone inscription reads:

> This first stone of the Great Grimsby Docks was laid by HRH Prince Albert on the 18th day of April in the year of our Lord 1849, and in the 12th year of the reign of Her Majesty Queen Victoria. May God protect these Docks.

(*The Illustrated News*, 1849)

1990: On this day, the Humber Flats and marshes were granted international status as a haven for tens of thousands of birds. This day was a busy one for news in the Grimsby area: not only did the Secretary of State for Energy give the go-ahead for a £250 million power station at Killingholme, but Grimsby Town manager Alan Buckley received the Barclays Bank Fourth Division manager of the month award. (*Grimsby Evening Telegraph*, 1990)

~ April 19th ~

1952: On this day, prompt action by a locomotive fireman saved one of Grimsby's oldest shops from going up in flames. Mr J.B. Danby was walking near Messrs Chambers, in the Old Market Place, at 2 a.m. when he smelled burning and saw smoke coming from the shop blinds. Hundreds of pounds worth of damage was caused to shop fittings and a display refrigerator – the source of the blaze. It is thought the refrigerator suffered a short circuit. (*Grimsby Telegraph Bygones*, 1999)

1963: On this day in 1963, police officers were scratching their heads over what to do with a rather unusual item of lost property. Strange things were regularly handed into the force's lost property office, but this had to be one of the strangest. A workman walking through Railway Street in Grimsby glanced over some wasteland and saw … a skull.

He gingerly picked it up and handed it to a police officer in nearby Kent Street. No attempt was made to find the man who'd lost his head, for a doctor estimated the skull to be about 200 years old. It was thought that the relic had been buried and recently been dis-interred. It was later destroyed. (*Grimsby Evening Telegraph*, 1963)

⹀ April 20th ⹀

1976: On this day, a famous name made a date with Grimsby. Doctor Henry Kissinger decided to fly to Lincolnshire that weekend, so Grimsby MP Anthony Crosland could keep long-standing engagements in the area on his diary.

The American Secretary of State arranged a working breakfast with Mr Crosland, then the new Foreign Secretary, to discuss Rhodesia and the South African problem. The meeting with America's globe-trotting ambassador was one of Mr Crosland's first major engagements in his role as Foreign Secretary.

Doctor Kissinger was calling by en-route to a twelve-day tour of Africa. He had wanted to see Mr Crosland in London, but the MP was reluctant to let down his constituents by cancelling engagements in the town. Mr Crosland was due at a committee meeting and had also been invited to present trophies at the Humberside Leisure Conference at Cleethorpes Pier. He also had to be in Grimsby for other engagements and a morning surgery with residents. So Doctor Kissinger agreed to fly to him, on board the presidential plane US1. Mr Crosland said, 'The main topic of our meeting will be concerning problems in Africa, but I cannot really say yet what lines our discussion will take.' (*Grimsby Evening Telegraph*, 1976)

— April 21st —

1944: On this day, Laceby Women's Institute knuckled down for the war effort. Members held a Shawl Parade as part of the group's annual general meeting; just one of many different events organised to not only support the troops but bolster spirits too.

There were twenty members of the branch during 1944, and the women made and sold jam, learned how to cure rabbit skins and make them into fashionable gauntlet gloves, and bottled and canned fruit gathered from the countryside. They held whist drives and knitted small comforts for our fighting soldiers. They also raised money for hospitals throughout the British Legion's Support the Soldiers Week.

Monthly meetings, particularly the competitions, perfectly showcase the 'make do and mend' ethos during the Second World War. Members were tasked with making a collar out of newspaper, a strong bag, an apron out of scraps of material and, quaintly, successfully whistling a tune.

Edith Stanley was president during the war years. She made her members into an army of knitters, making warm, comfortable shawls for refugees forced by the conflict to roam Europe; the Shawl Parade displaying their efforts. (Laceby History Group, *The Chronicles of Laceby*, 1980)

~ APRIL 22ND ~

1842: On this day, an Act of Parliament received royal assent for inclosing the open and common land and fields of Clee, and Cleethorpes, with the hamlet of Thrunscoe. The land totalled 2,416 acres, including: 819 acres arable; 740 acres common; one rood and 53 perches; 700 acres pasture, and 15 perches. (Edward Dobson, *A Guide and Directory to Cleethorpes*, 1850)

1958: On this day, a local newspaper reported that no less than 600 women watched intently as a beauty expert gave a make-up demonstration on a model at a mannequin parade at Grimsby Town Hall.

Suddenly, excited murmuring broke out and eyes were cast upwards, with many of the women rising from their seats. For running round a ledge above the audience was a tiny mouse. And it kept on running round and round.

But the model won the day. After a hold-up lasting fifteen minutes, the demonstration continued. The mouse had got fed up and vanished, and by then, no one was bothered. 'Even a mouse cannot seriously expect to challenge beauty,' the report read. (*Grimsby Evening Telegraph*, 1958)

~ APRIL 23RD ~

1954: On this day, the Polish ship *Brygada Makowskiego* had called at Grimsby – her first visit there for three years. Her chief officer had lived in Britain during the war when he served in a Polish submarine attached to the Royal Navy.

The crew was twenty-nine-strong, and welcomed a *Grimsby Evening Telegraph* reporter on board for a polite, if guarded, interview – with no names given. The chief officer declined to comment when references were made to Poland and the Iron Curtain. Although the crew had the Iron Curtain precautions lifted to enable them to mix with Grimsby people, their 'welfare' was being carefully supervised by an on-board welfare officer.

With increasing trade developing between Poland and Britain, she had made several visits recently to other British ports. Slipping through the Iron Curtain, therefore, had become quite a routine. 'We see things a different way,' said a crewman. 'Polish sailors prefer to discuss the weather.' (*Grimsby Evening Telegraph*, 1954)

1928: On this day, a Grimsby Corporation trolley omnibus ran off the road and into a shop window at the corner of Freeman Street and Wellington Street. One passenger sustained a broken collarbone. (*Grimsby Evening Telegraph*, 1928)

~ April 24th ~

1946: On this day, the war may have been over for almost a year, but it still managed to claim the lives of ten Grimsby fishermen. They were on board the Grimsby trawler *Earl Essex*, which was fishing in the North Sea. It had been a good trip and she would have been heading home with her fish rooms almost full.

As the crew was hauling the nets over the stern, one of them spotted something among the glistening fish. There was a shout of warning but it was too late – the stern disappeared in a blinding flash.

Another Grimsby trawler, the *Vera Grace*, was fishing 5 miles away when her crew heard a 'crack like thunder'. They saw the *Earl Essex* vanish in a ball of smoke. When it cleared, just the bows were showing.

When they arrived at the scene, all they found was debris – until one of the crew spotted a man clinging to the wreckage. It was one of *Earl Essex*'s trimmers, Joe Taylor, alive and almost uninjured. He told how he had gone on deck when what everyone assumed was a mine was hauled into the nets and exploded. He was blown into the sea and when he surfaced, another crew member was nearby but he disappeared within minutes.

Earl Essex was the first of Grimsby's post-war mine casualties and several other boats were damaged in the years to come. (*Grimsby Evening Telegraph*, 1946)

~ APRIL 25TH ~

1936: On this day, Ray Edmonds, the famous snooker player, was born in Grimsby. Ray's career first took off as an amateur, taking the World Amateur title twice in the early 1970s. He then went professional, and reached the World Snooker Championship four times – in 1980, 1981, 1985 and 1986. Each time, he lost in the first round.

In 1985 though, Ray won the World Professional Billiards Championship, giving him the unique distinction of being the only player to have won that title as well as two World Amateur titles at snooker.

During this time, he established the Ray Edmonds Snooker Centre in Grimsby, opening in 1983. He also worked for ITV and the BBC as a snooker commentator before retiring in 2004. (www.rayedmondssnooker.co.uk)

~ APRIL 26TH ~

1955: On this day, Grimsby welcomed the new fishing limits around the Faroe Islands, which had been negotiated by the British, Danish and Faroe governments. The new limits were to come into force on July 1st and were regarded as a balance between the fishing interests of the two parties. The Danish Government gave an assurance that the new rules would apply to the fishing vessels of all other countries and would remain in force for at least two years.

The organisations representing the trawling industry had been kept informed of the negotiations, and Foreign Secretary Harold Macmillan was confident that a reasonable compromise had been arrived at between the interests of the Faroe inshore fishermen and those of British trawlermen.

Generally speaking, the established 3-mile limit had been adhered to, measured from the low water mark of the islands' off-lying rocks. The original proposals were for the limit to be 3 miles from base lines drawn from island to island in a rough triangle, enclosing the whole of the Faroe Islands, but the lines were modified during the negotiations.

This allowed trawlers to fish in a portion of West Bay, where many Grimsby middle-water trawlers worked, and was a concession which Grimsby skippers were anxious to obtain. (Grimsby Central Library)

~ APRIL 27TH ~

1846: On this day, Grimsby County Borough Police Force was established, made up of one officer and three constables. By 1870, the population of 1,200 was covered by ten constables and two sergeants. Records show they dealt with an average of ninety-nine crimes a year, which were mainly drunkenness. (*Grimsby Telegraph*, 2010)

1983: On this day, dock workers joined in a champagne celebration to mark a record-breaking effort – loading sugar aboard a ship bound for Iran. The gauntlet had been thrown down by their company, Lindsey Dock Services, which promised a case of bubbly to the first group of workers to load 1,000 tonnes in a single shift.

A gang of twenty-one men loaded 1,087 tonnes into the cargo ship *Aegis Harvest* during their shift on this day, which ran from 8am to 5pm. The sugar was in 50kg bags, stacked twenty-four to a pallet, which had to be lifted by crane into the hold. Each bag then had to be manhandled into place – 21,745 in all. The sugar was from the British Sugar Corporation, bound for Iran. (*Grimsby Evening Telegraph*, 1983)

← APRIL 28TH →

1981: On this day, Steve Currie, the Grimsby-born musician who achieved fame when he joined T-Rex, died in a car accident. Steve was the bassist in the original Rumble Band line-up, a well-known band in Lincolnshire. This was while he was studying at Grimsby Tech College. But he shot to worldwide fame when he became a member of glam rock band T-Rex in November 1970. They had recently been renamed from Tyrannosaurus Rex, and were still publicised as a duo.

He played bass on top hits such as 'Get It On', 'Metal Guru', and 'Telegram Sam' – Marc Bolan's most memorable singles. Steve left the band in 1976, but continued recording with Bolan until the singer died in a car crash in 1977.

Having emigrated to Portugal, he also died in a car accident in 1981. He was returning to his home near Vale de Parra, on the Algarve, at the time – less than four years after Bolan died in the car crash in Barnes, south-west London. (*Grimsby Telegraph*, 2013)

~ April 29th ~

1967: On this day, Grimsby trawler skipper Bernard 'Bunny' Newton became a legend after doing a runner when his boat was impounded. News had reached Grimsby that the trawler *Brandur* had been arrested for alleged illegal fishing off Iceland. She had been apprehended by the gunboat *Thor*, and four days later came the news that stunned Grimsby and intrigued the world.

Bunny had broken out of Reykjavik Harbour and made a run for home. What was more astonishing was the fact he had two Icelandic policemen held 'captive' on board. The escape bid lasted for eleven hours before Bunny and his crew were back in custody. The *Brandur* had managed to get some 43 miles from Iceland. To avoid detection her number, GY 111, had been painted out and H52 painted in instead.

A judge ruled that Bunny should be kept in custody for the length of the case or thirty days. As the delay went on, the 1,000 kits of fish on board the *Brandur* was starting to deteriorate. There were further problems as fire swept through the vessel as she lay in Reykjavik harbour.

Bunny – who all along denied illegal fishing – was found guilty of trying to escape with his arrested ship and obstructing the policemen with threats. He was given a three-month prison sentence, fined 300,000 crowns, and freed when the vessel's owners put up a £100,000 bond. The *Brandur* arrived home on May 9th, her catch grossing £2,500. (*Grimsby Evening Telegraph*, 1967)

~ APRIL 30TH ~

On this day every year, Walpurgis Night is celebrated. According to books published on customs, the eve of May Day is considered as a midsummer Halloween, when Pagan activities were held in high regard by many. And it was a night rumoured to be full of satanic worship.

Walpurgis was an Anglo-Saxon saint, who played a part in missions to convert the Germans in the eighth century. She died on February 25th 779, and is still remembered here.

In the book *A Lincolnshire Calendar*, a Grimsby man recalls the celebrations:

> In my younger days, we referred to the night as Wulf-er-grisle night, that's how we pronounced the name. Wolf, the animal that we spelt with a 'u', then 'er', then 'gristle', like the gristle in your leg. It was reputed to be a bad night for satanic goings-on. Certain people went out into the woods for a satanic rite and usually finished up by setting fire to the woods. It went on in the Grimsby area. Many folk hung cowslips up that night or early on May Day morning to ward off evil and protect their animals, that's why they hung cowslips up in the cowshed.

(Maureen Sutton, *A Lincolnshire Calendar*, 1997)

1991: On this day, pop music's most famous couple, Paul and Linda McCartney, were looking forward to the day when Grimsby produced a fishless fish finger. 'We are both lovers of fish – that is why we don't eat it,' Linda said.

The Wings star and wife of ex-Beatle Paul was in London to launch a new range of revolutionary vegetarian dishes developed in Grimsby for Ross Youngs. They included beefless burgers, chickenless nuggets and a ploughman's pie without steak.

Also on this day, Lincolnshire's world-beating power lifter, Roger Powell, broke the world record for the seventh time at the British Masters in Birmingham. The 55-year-old grandfather, who weighed in at 9st 6lb, lifted 195kg (30st 9lb) – a new world record by 2.5kg (5.5lb). (*Grimsby Evening Telegraph*, 1991)

~ MAY 2ND ~

1947: On this day, a boundary battle had been won – by one side, at least – when Cleethorpes came out tops in a battle of the boundaries fought out with Grimsby.

Grimsby fired the first shots by suggesting to the Boundary Commission that it took over the borough of Cleethorpes, together with the Grimsby Rural District, which included Immingham, Stallingborough, Healing, Waltham, Humberston and Laceby. It provoked a rather swift response from Cleethorpes: 'We will fight Grimsby every inch of the way,' declared the mayor, Alderman Albert Cox. 'Cleethorpes will fight to preserve its identity.'

In June 1946, Cleethorpes counter-attacked by suggesting it took over part of Grimsby – the area around Carr Lane and Clee Road.

The Commission weighed up the arguments and finally, on this day, decided there would be no changes. But changes were on the way for Cleethorpes – and they were welcomed.

Until 1946, the resort had been part of the Grimsby parliamentary constituency and had shared an MP. That year, constituencies came under scrutiny, and Cleethorpes ended up within a new Louth constituency. This came into effect in 1950 and lasted until 1983, when Cleethorpes became Brigg and Cleethorpes instead. (*Grimsby Evening Telegraph*, 1947)

~ MAY 3RD ~

1962: On this day, Grimsby trawler the *Ross Kenilworth* foundered off the coast of Iceland – another vessel which formed part of the town's rich fishing heritage. The sinking followed desperate attempts by the *Ross Rodney* and the *Thor*, an Icelandic gun boat, to save the 7-year-old vessel, which began to take on water when the main injection box fractured in the engine room.

The pumps could not cope with the inrush of water but, as the incident happened only 20 miles off the Icelandic coast, it was hoped to tow her to land. The *Ross Rodney* got a line on board and the *Thor* put a salvage pump on to the *Kenilworth*. However, it quickly became clear that she was in danger of capsizing. The seventeen-man crew was rescued and the *Kenilworth* was abandoned to the sea.

She had left Grimsby under the command of skipper Jack Simpson, and three days before the sinking landed one of her deckhands at Isafjord for medical treatment. Her crew included brothers Ronald and Charles McUrich, both of Grimsby. (*Grimsby Telegraph Bygones*, trawlers edition, 2008)

⸺ MAY 4TH ⸺

1972: On this day, an alert went out to find two large drums, which contained enough explosive to kill several people. The chemical sodium chlorate is used as a common weed killer, but when packed tight into canisters, it can become a potential bomb. The drums were part of a large consignment which had been stored in a warehouse in Grimsby since January.

Evidence of a break-in was discovered by staff, and a stocktake revealed that the drums were missing. Each one weighed about a hundredweight and stood 2ft 6ins high. Coloured leaf-green, they were marked with labels describing the contents. Police were puzzled about the motive and how the thieves got the drums out of the warehouse, for the main door was locked. The only other exit was through a loft trapdoor, at least 15ft above the ground.

The force took the unusual step of touring schools in the area to warn children of the dangers the drums posed, should they come across them. Sodium chlorate, which looks and tastes like table salt, is also a highly lethal poison. Just a few teaspoons could kill. Detective Chief Inspector Ron Smith, head of Grimsby CID, said, 'It is the sort of stuff you cannot take risks with.'

It is not known if the drums were found, as the outcome of this incident is not recorded. (*Grimsby Evening Telegraph*, 1972)

– MAY 5TH –

1907: On this day, Grimsby teacher Charlotte Collinson (*née* Urquhart) was enjoying the sights and sounds of Rome. This tour of Italy, organised during term-time especially for teachers, cost just £20, and her diary, later transcribed by her great-nephew and grandson, is a unique record. She even had an audience with the Pope during the trip, who she described as being as 'such a dear old man'. Her journal entry for this day reads:

> Rome is the most delightful and wonderful place that one could imagine. Everything is nice, to the shops, the streets, the people and the beautiful children. The little babies are carried on cushions in the most picturesque fashion. The first thing we did was visit St Peter's, where mass was held at 10 o'clock. There was nothing much to be seen except a few priests marching round, drinking wine and burning incense. Every time they pass before the altar they bow. I thought the whole thing a mockery. On the afternoon, we visited some catacombs. We each had a lighted taper and followed Dr Forbes down the dark passages in single file. The early Christians decorated their catacombs. One inscription was 'Flora … Pax'. It was the tomb of a little child and Flora was a martyr for, in the tomb, was the remains of glass containing dried-up blood which Dr Forbes told us marked the tomb of a martyr.

(*Grimsby Telegraph Bygones*, 2001)

~ MAY 6TH ~

1886: On this day, the warden of Clee parish church made a complaint to the Bishop Suffragen of Nottingham. Ernest de Lacy Read had serious concerns about the conduct of the Reverend John Peter Benson, the rector of Clee-cum-Cleethorpes, alleging he was guilty of watering down the communion wine and standing with his back to people to hide his actions. He was also 'in the habit of wearing incorrect clothes at the administration of Holy Communion', according to a report by *Hull Daily Mail*. (Grimsby Central Library)

2007: On this day, the supernatural entity which became known as the 'Grimsby Scratcher' made its presence felt in the home of the Sayles family. On Sunday, May 6th, Lynn and David Sayles were watching an episode of *Most Haunted*. Inspired, Lynn picked up a pen and tried to draw some psychic art, but instead produced the phenomena known as automatic writing. The pages of writing was narrated by the spirit of Mark Ripley, who said his partner, Mary, had been killed. Mary's spirit resided in the Sayles's home, but the pair was unable to reconnect. In the following weeks, the family experienced inexplicable happenings. A vicar blessed the house, but this made things worse: lights began turning on and off, the computer would switch on and the kettle would boil on its own – even when the mains were turned off. The couple's son said his battery-operated toys were making sounds and flashing lights when they were not turned on. Dave and Lynn suffered unexplained scratches. After the family appeared on *Living With The Dead*, things calmed down, but they eventually left the area. (Jason Day, *Haunted Grimsby*, 2011)

— MAY 7TH —

1948: On this day, an Icelandic trawler came through the lock gates at Grimsby Fish Docks with an incredible 5,709 kits of prime fish on board. The *Neptunus* had caught so much fish in Icelandic waters that she had to sell 300 kits in Iceland before it was safe to sail to the big markets in England.

The catch sold for £19,069 – a world record price for a world record landing. It included 4,293 kits of cod and 892 of haddock, and was indicative of the huge catches being then made around Iceland. (*Grimsby Evening Telegraph*, 1948)

———

1964: On this day, the town was waking up to the news that the five-man crew of a Valiant jet bomber had died when the aircraft crashed, blazing, into farm buildings near Market Rasen. The plane, on a routine flight from RAF Marham in Norfolk, was in difficulties just before the crash. An eyewitness said it looked like 'a Roman candle in the sky' and that the pilot deliberately avoided the brightly lit town nearby. If the crash had been thirty minutes later, the street lights would have been extinguished. (*Grimsby Evening Telegraph*, 1964)

~ MAY 8TH ~

1946: On this day, 80 acres of trees had been destroyed by fire – the second big woodland blaze in a week. The plantation, put down thirteen years before on the estate of Col Elwes, of Elsham Hall, was devastated. Fire crews had to fetch water in relays from a village 2 miles away to fight the flames.

The alarm had been raised by workmen felling trees. The estate's gamekeeper thought the fire had been caused due to the rekindling by the wind of a small camp fire the workmen thought had been extinguished.

Earlier in the week, more than 85 acres of the Forestry Commission's Nova Scotia wood, near Market Rasen, was also gutted by fire. (*Grimsby Telegraph Bygones*, 1999)

1956: On this day, another fire took hold in the area. By the time it was extinguished, all that was left of a picturesque thatched-roofed boys' club was a scorched and tattered Union Jack fluttering on a hedge, and a few pieces of furniture almost beyond recognition.

The scattered piles of bricks and rubble was, just a day previously, the home of the club in Ulceby, but it was consumed within such a short time that all firefighters could do was stand by helplessly and watch.

Housewives gathered buckets of water in case the high winds swept the flames towards their homes. (*Grimsby Evening Telegraph*, 1956)

~ MAY 9TH ~

1956: On this day, a teenager from Grimsby made an appearance on national television. Cadet nurse Pauline Bunn, then aged 17, had always wanted to have the bumps on her head examined by a phrenologist, and wrote to Wilfred Pickles on his show, *Ask Pickles*.

A phrenologist who had never met Pauline before was asked what career she was best suited for. He replied: 'I think she would give of her best in the nursing profession.' Pauline was training at Scartho Infirmary. (*Grimsby Evening Telegraph*, 1956)

1962: On this day, more than 200 showmen helped Grimsby Fire Brigade control what could have been a disastrous fire on the site of Grimsby's cattle market. The caravan, which was worth £200, was completely destroyed and a large £3,000 living van was badly damaged. A coal-burning stove inside the caravan was thought to have been the cause of the fire. (*Grimsby Telegraph Bygones*, 2002)

1991: On this day, a tasty £43,000 bingo win left a Grimsby dinner lady serving up bangers and cash. Lucky Sharon Stembridge celebrated her win over lunch with colleagues and youngsters at Weelsby Primary School.

Sharon was the first major prize winner in the new Coral Bingo Club, in Pasture Street, Grimsby. (*Grimsby Evening Telegraph*, 1991)

– MAY 10TH –

1937: On this day, in a ditch the wheels of a large, black, Grimsby-registered Daimler spun slowly to a halt. The car was upside down and in it was Sir James Blindell, MP for Boston, Junior Lord of the Treasury. He was dead – on Lady Blindell's 55th birthday.

She and her husband were travelling from Grimsby to open the annual Boston carnival week when two dogs ran across the road at Stickney. The chauffeur, the 19-year-old son of a Grimsby engineer, swerved but the car skidded.

Lady Blindell and the driver survived, but the life of the remarkable politician ended. In 1910, he had opened his first shoe shop, in Freeman Street. Blindells became a household name; eventually the firm had its own factories and more than 100 shops.

He made a name for himself on the town council, which he joined in 1919, and then became an MP. In 1932, he was appointed Junior Lord of the Treasury, and was knighted in 1936. (*Grimsby Evening Telegraph*, 1937)

1959: On this day, the police were hunting for an absent husband after his wife, a mother of five, was found dead at their home on the Nunsthorpe Estate. Ethel Winifred Flegg, 39, was found after two of her children knocked on a neighbour's door and asked them to 'come and waken mummy'. She had been strangled and left on the settee, where she was found by her neighbour, 29-year-old Gladys Darnell.

Mr and Mrs Flegg had lived on the estate for several years and were described as 'a quiet and pleasant' couple. Dock worker Flegg, who had served in the war, was not at the house and immediately the police circulated a description.

Ships and houses around the docks were searched; he had last been seen at about 5 a.m. on the morning Mrs Flegg had been found. Scotland Yard transmitted radio signals to trawlers on the North Sea – the widest radio search since that for the infamous Dr Crippen in 1910. The message to skippers was: 'Check your crew. If you have an Englishman called Flegg aboard, detain him.'

But it was all for nothing. Flegg's body was found in the Royal Dock. The 49 year old had drowned. (Stephen Wade, *Foul Deeds and Suspicious Deaths in Grimsby and Cleethorpes*, 2007)

~ May 12th ~

1920: On this day, the *Friesland* blew up and sank at the mouth of the River Humber. The trawler *Nairana* spotted her distress flares and took her in tow, but *Friesland* sank by the stern. The crew was rescued by Dobsons trawler *Elite*, which was returning to port.

The *Friesland*'s skipper said afterwards: 'What happened is a mystery to me.'

Although the ship had a policy, the insurance company refused to pay out. A year later, a Court of Investigation was held at Grimsby Town Hall and the suggestion of the underwriters was that Burns, the owner of the ship, had sent her to sea in the hope that she would not come back ... even suggesting that he had given orders for her to be sunk.

During the week-long hearing, Burns said he had insured the ship for £14,000, despite knowing he'd never get more than £6,000 for her, but strongly denied he'd ordered for her to be scuttled.

The court found the owner was negligent in not having the trawler examined after a period of laying up and before putting to sea, but decided the actual cause of the sinking was a mystery. Burns was told to pay £200 towards the cost of the enquiry. (*Grimsby Telegraph Bygones*, 1999)

~ MAY 13TH ~

1866: On this day, 16-year-old Lucy Sizer was assaulted by five men – and the resulting court case helped persuade Victorians to change attitudes to rape.

Lucy, a servant girl of good character, was on the way home from evening service with her younger sister when they were stopped by a man, Crawford, outside the Dock Offices. He pulled Lucy towards some railway wagons, clamping a hand over her mouth when she screamed. Crawford knocked her little sister over and, when she refused to leave, offered her money.

He dragged the older girl into a shed in the railway yard where he and four other men – all of them aged between 16 and 25 – each assaulted her. Shockingly, a dock policeman heard the noise, actually looked inside the shed and went away.

Afterwards, two of the youths helped Lucy towards home. She was ill for some time and suffered serious fits, but was able to identify an assailant, called White. He was arrested and, scared of taking the blame alone, named his accomplices.

At the trial, the defence alleged Lucy got the job in Grimsby 'to obtain money for a certain purpose from the fisher lads', but the jury found all five guilty of rape. Crawford, the ringleader, was given fifteen years' penal servitude and the others were sentenced to six years each. (Adrian Gray, *Lincolnshire Headlines*, 1993)

‑ MAY 14TH ‑

1940: On this day, a group called the Local Defence Volunteers was formed in Grimsby. Following orders from Winston Churchill, its title changed to the better-known Home Guard that July.

When Chamberlain made that dreadful announcement on September 3rd 1939, 900 men had attended Grimsby Borough Police Station offering themselves to take on worthwhile roles for the war effort. They were young and old, covering all aspects of the social scale, and within two days, they were carrying out patrols, including at Grimsby Golf Course and the railway yards on the Marsh.

A recruiting officer was appointed: Captain Frank Evison, formerly of the 4th Lincolns and the RAF.

The Home Guard made things more formal, and the initial 900 were joined by many more men. They were split into three battalions: the 5th Lindsey, responsible for Grimsby; the 6th Lindsey, patrolling Cleethorpes; and the 7th Lindsey, covering surrounding areas. (Alan Dowling, *Grimsby: Making The Town 1800–1914*, 2007; Grimsby Central Library)

− May 15th −

1912: On this day, the Great Central Railway opened the Grimsby–Immingham Electric Railway. It was described by author J. Joyce in his 1970 book, *Trams in Colour*:

> It could have made a good claim for the title of Britain's most unusual tramway. It started out as a fairly conventional type of street tramway in the town of Grimsby, then it left the roads and sped across fields to the docks at Immingham. Brush of Loughbrough built huge 54ft long single-deck tramcars for the line, although later some second-hand trams were purchased from Newcastle-upon-Tyne Corporation. In 1951, some of this earlier stock was replaced by newer trams made redundant by Gateshead & District Tramways Company. On June 30, 1956, the service lost its Corporation Bridge to Cleveland Bridge section. Many cyclists now left their machines parked at this new terminus.

The line closed for good on July 1st 1961, and was replaced by half-hourly bus routes managed by a partnership between the Grimsby-Cleethorpes Transport and the Lincolnshire Road Car Company. (J. Joyce, *Trams In Colour*, 1970)

—

1950: On this day, because of the slump in fish prices, between sixty and seventy vessels out of Grimsby's fishing fleet of 316 were laid up. It was estimated that more than 500 fishermen registered in the port were unemployed. (*Grimsby Evening Telegraph*, 1950)

— MAY 16TH —

2010: On this day, Grimsby was granted minster status at a special ceremony led by the bishops of Grimsby and Lincoln. St James' parish church, which has stood for decades in the town centre, was renamed Grimsby Minster.

Its origins begin in 1114, when the then Bishop of Lincoln, Robert Bloet, took charge of an existing religious building there. He supervised many renovations, which resulted in St James, with a nave and six bays. The central tower was created in 1365, and it became the parish church of Grimsby in 1586, when John Whitgift united the parishes of St James and St Mary's.

An entire restoration of the church began in 1856, which included extending the chancel and reconstructing the south transept.

In 1883, James College – the forerunner to St James' School – was founded by Canon Young and was the only choir school in the UK to be attached to a parish church.

The granting of minster status occurred in the first half of 2010, and a celebratory ceremony took place on this day, when the Mayor of North East Lincolnshire, the late Councillor John Colebrook, accepted the official declaration of the status on behalf of the borough. (*Grimsby Telegraph*, 2010)

⇁ MAY 17TH ⇁

1943: On this day, the Dambusters raid, with the legendary Guy Gibson at the helm, had been launched from RAF Scampton – and Grimsby girl Dora Beales was working at the airfield when that famous raid brought Germany to its knees.

Dora was just a teenager when she joined the weather department of the Women's Auxiliary Air Force (WAAF). At 18, she was posted to RAF Scampton and was on duty during one of the most famous nights in wartime history.

The late Mrs Beales recalled:

> I was giving readings for the navigators. We knew it was a crack squadron – but that was all – and worked hard through the night, measuring cloud height and atmospheric pressure. We were told not to mention anything for there could be spies around. I went home the next morning and it was all over the radio. Even the chief forecaster hadn't been told. It was shrouded in secrecy.

The overnight raid on May 16/17th under a full moon was undertaken by the newly formed 617 Squadron, formed with 24-year-old Wing Commander Gibson in command. Only at the eleventh hour did any of the crews find out what the real targets were. They were charged with flying across the English Channel, to cross the Netherlands and Germany at 0ft and to drop a bomb on the Ruhr dams. (*Grimsby Evening Telegraph*; verbal account by the late Dora Beales)

~ May 18th ~

1955: On this day, more rain had fallen in the area in the last twenty-four hours than in any single day since August 8th 1951. It was the heaviest rainfall for a May day since 1910: 1.69ins had fallen since the morning before.

The bitter, stormy night brought havoc to Lincolnshire, and Britain overall. In the county, two rivers burst their banks, a funfair was blitzed by a 60mph gale, roads became impassable and cattle drowned. In Grimsby, a falling chimney ripped through a house and the occupants spent the night sleeping on a floor. Grimsby Fire Brigade attended six call-outs to dangerous chimney stacks.

Indeed, the bad weather caused mayhem across the country. Tugs collided at sea, the *Queen Mary* liner was twelve hours late arriving at New York and some areas even experienced snowfall. (*Grimsby Evening Telegraph*, 1935 and 1955)

— MAY 19TH —

1973: On this day, the town's famous statue of Grim and Havelock was unveiled by MP Tony Crosland. Grimsby's newest statue, located on the lawns of the college at Nun's Corner, was received enthusiastically by an invited audience, with only a passing reference to the controversy it had threatened to cause. For the larger-than-life bronze statue was entirely nude. Grim the fisherman is carrying the infant Havelock ashore on his shoulder.

The statue was the work of widely respected sculptor Douglas Wain-Hobson of Manchester and was the first completely free-standing statue to be publicly set up in Grimsby since that of Prince Albert appeared more than a century before.

Welcoming the statute as a contribution to the environment in Grimsby, Mr Crosland said:

> What we must do is try to train ourselves, and other people, to walk about with eyes open. It is extraordinary how often we go about with our eyes closed. I gather some controversy has been aroused at the idea of a male nude figure. It is an odd thing about our society that this should be thought to be strange.

(*Grimsby Evening Telegraph*, 1973)

‒ May 20th ‒

1972: On this day, a mystery blaze gutted most of a 98-year-old timber mill in Grimsby. At one stage, the flames could be seen several miles away. Roads around Cooper Snowden's old mill, at the junction of Albion Street and Wellington Street, were sealed off by the police as the walls cracked with the heat and threatened to collapse.

The mill had been built by the founder of a joinery firm, Mr Cooper Snowden, in 1874 and the building had been vacated by the company two months previously when they moved to new premises in the town. They had finished clearing the old premises of timber about a fortnight before and demolition contractors had begun dismantling part of the two-storey building, which covered a 2-acre site, the week before.

Firefighters had the flames under control within an hour of receiving the alarm and were soon sifting through the charred remains in an attempt to discover the cause of the blaze. Arson had been ruled out, despite the fact crews had already been called to a small fire in the attic there the night before. (*Grimsby Evening Telegraph*, 1972)

~ May 21st ~

1940: On this day, a 14-year-old girl was remanded in custody to the Home of Help in Grimsby for seven days by the courts. Her crime was stealing £3 3s 6d. Her father told the hearing:

> I have been in prison myself and heritage counts a lot with children. Her grandfather was a well-known thief and her grandmother was a kleptomaniac. Half the time, the poor little beggar doesn't get enough to eat.

(Grimsby Central Library)

1962: On this day, a 13-year-old girl had a miraculous escape. Ann Patricia Fruen was sitting in the living room having her lunch when suddenly there was a flash of lightning and a clap of thunder, and smoke poured from the television set only 2ft away from her after the leads were blown out. The aerial was flung into the garden of a neighbour, Ann's dress was singed and decorations completed when the family had moved into the house about three months previously were damaged.

Other homes were also struck by lightning, television and radio sets were damaged, and telephone lines put out of action. (*Grimsby Evening Telegraph*, 1962)

⎯ May 22nd ⎯

1952: On this day, the crew of the *Valafell* trawler was at the centre of a mystery. Skipper Jimmy Hobson and an eighteen-man crew had been fishing 4 miles north-east of Vaida Bay, on the north Russian coast, when she was approached by two Russian naval vessels and boarded by armed sailors. Five hours later, the *Valafell* was being escorted towards the nearest port. Then came silence.

No word had been received by the *Valafell* or the Russian authorities, and the Home Office was desperately trying to find out what happened.

On this day – after eight days of silence – a brief telegram was received by owner Consolidated Fisheries that the *Valafell* was back at sea, having been released by the Russians after paying a £27 fine for fishing inside their 3-mile limit.

The crew's bumper catch would have sold for more than £8,000 but had been spoiled, so the skipper decided to put in at the Norwegian port of Honningsvaag to sell it for fishmeal. However, five men refused to return to sea, and the police were called. They were jailed for twenty-two days and the *Valafell* sailed with five Norwegians back to Grimsby – seven weeks after leaving. (*Grimsby Telegraph Bygones*, trawlers edition, 1996)

− May 23rd −

1941: On this day, a Spitfire pilot, who went on to have a very famous son, was in the midst of wartime service − flying a plane purchased by Grimsby folk.

Grimsby had launched a successful Buy A Spitfire campaign as part of the war effort and residents waited eagerly to see the aircraft for the first time. In March that year, news came that the R7231 had been released from the factory at Castle Bromwich. Just forward of the cockpit was the name 'Grimsby', emblazoned for all to see. R7231 was received by the Auxiliary Squadron 611, based at Hornchurch, and found itself in action.

Flying Officer George Duncan-Smith was soon engaged in aerial exploits, chasing enemy aircraft out to sea. This held him in good stead: eventually he led 64 Squadron in the disastrous raid on Dieppe where, in sixteen hours, more than 100 RAF Fighters were shot down.

He was later posted to North Africa and when he returned to England, took a staff job at the Ministry of Defence and was decorated for his efforts. He is, of course, the father of politican Iain Duncan-Smith.

R7231 went to 164 Squadron and then to the newly formed Norwegian Squadron 332, coming to rest at the Royal Naval Air Station, in Streeton, in May 1943.

On August 27th 1942, BL588 was on a sweep over France − and failed to return. (*Grimsby Telegraph Bygones*, 1999)

~ May 24th ~

1991: On this day, the Fishing Heritage Centre in Grimsby was opened. The nationally important museum used sights, sounds and smells to recreate the lives of trawler men – visitors could even step into the bar of the Freeman's Arms, experience a moving deck and queue for fish and chips.

In 2005, a team of ghost hunters, including *Most Haunted* investigator Phil Whyman, spent the night in the museum. Ghostly shuffling footsteps, cold spots and the strong smell of tobacco were just some of the strange experiences talked of by staff. They put it down to the spirit of a former skipper and tour guide, who had loved the place.

The investigation also focused on the *Ross Tiger*, moored nearby. As the light faded and darkness set in, the team of twelve split up. One group headed to an area set out as the bridge of a trawler and the skipper's table. The vigil was uneventful … until they heard the clang of the telegraph bell at the bottom of the staircase below them. Next was a noise on the stairs and Phil dived to the door. But it was a false alarm; the other group had come back in without telling them. (*Grimsby Evening Telegraph*, 1991; Fishing Heritage Centre)

~ MAY 25TH ~

1972: On this day, the regional group which operated Grimsby's hospital was accused of exploitation. A report prepared by young doctors claimed that overseas doctors working within the group were being 'grossly exploited' because they were too frightened to complain.

Entitled 'More in Sorrow', the report focused on fifty-three hospitals in the wider region, stating that Grimsby was one of the worst areas. It listed among the more serious problems, lack of communication between doctors and hospital administrators, poor accommodation and lack of adequate mess facilities. It read:

> Most foreign graduates have come to obtain training for higher qualifications, but most end up in service posts, often working long hours even by our standards in hospitals with very poor post-graduate teaching facilities.

The hospital group responded by admitting that communication was sometimes difficult, explaining that accommodation had recently been refurbished and declared that the 'great bulk of adverse comments came from foreign doctors which, on many occasions, were extreme'. (*Grimsby Evening Telegraph*, 1972)

~ MAY 26TH ~

1956: On this day, a gang of young boys were rescued from Haile Sand Fort, in the Humber Estuary, after being cut off by the fast incoming tide.

The police alerted the then 16-year-old Alan Sneyd, whose father owned a small rowing boat. With his two pals – 18-year-old Kenneth Broadbent and 16-year-old Arthur Bradley – Alan was rushed by police car to North Sea Lane. There, the boat was launched, and in a short while, the stranded boys were safe on land.

Soaked but cheerful, they were holding on tightly to their catch of three flatfish. The rescued boys were 14-year-old Derek Ellis, 8-year-old David Hoodless and 11-year-old Hubert Lusty.

Haile Sand Fort is one of two large fortifications in the mouth of the Humber, the other being Bull Sand Fort. Standing 59ft above the water and visible from the shore, they were used to protect the estuary and provided accommodation for 200 soldiers. They took more than four years to build and were eventually finished in December 1919. During the Second World War, they were regularly attacked by enemy aircraft. They were abandoned in 1956. (*Grimsby Evening Telegraph*, 1956)

1993: On this day, the famous politician Norman Lamont resigned as Chancellor and as a member of John Major's Cabinet – and the news was broken by him in a telephone call to his 82-year-old mother in Grimsby. Irene Lamont promptly revealed the news – in a worldwide exclusive – to the town's local newspaper, the *Grimsby Evening Telegraph*.

Mr Lamont had been at the centre of growing concern about his future as Chancellor, a position he had held for three years. His mother said she had prepared herself for an invasion of national newspaper reporters, but refused to speak to anyone else but the *Evening Telegraph*. 'For the past three years they [the national newspapers] have been at me and they have given Norman a very rough ride,' she explained.

Mr Lamont was born in the Shetland Islands and brought in in Grimsby, where his father was a surgeon. He studied at Cambridge and entered parliament in the 1970s, serving in successive governments under Margaret Thatcher and John Major for a total of fourteen years. (*Grimsby Evening Telegraph*, 1993)

— MAY 28TH —

1907: On this day, music hall escapologist Herbert Smith and his lover Lottie Roberts appeared in a Liverpool court charged with causing the death of the infant daughter of Lily Kitching, of Grimsby, and with having obtained £11 by false pretences from Lily's mother.

Pregnant and single, Lily had seen a newspaper advert from a couple wanting to adopt a baby, and requesting £15 to cover costs. She and her mother decided this could solve the problem of the unwanted child, so she wrote to Mr J. Baker in Liverpool.

The Bakers – in reality Smith and Roberts – arrived in Grimsby, telling the Kitchings they were unable to have children. They took Lily's now two-week-old baby and the money, but Lily then received a letter from them asking for another £7.

Lily's mother, suspicious, went to Liverpool but found the address was a letter call office, so informed the police. Smith – otherwise known as escapologist Leo Selwyn – and Roberts were arrested.

Lily's baby was found alive in Lincoln and the charges against the pair were reduced to that of false pretences. They had given the child to a woman to look after for a fee. When the payments stopped two weeks later, she took the baby to the workhouse.

Between January and June 1907, Smith and Roberts farmed about twenty babies, collecting £200; five of the babies brought in £66 for a total expenditure of £3. Smith was imprisoned for fifteen months and Roberts eight. (*Grimsby Telegraph Bygones*, 1999)

~ MAY 29TH ~

1856: On this day, a public holiday was declared, on order of the Mayor of Grimsby. The end of the Crimean war with Russia during 1856 held special significance for the port – it meant the re-opening of trade with the Baltic ports. The Town Council, dressed in full regalia, journeyed in procession through the town and 1,000 schoolchildren sang the National Anthem. (Edward Drury, *The Old Grimsby Story*, 1984)

1935: On this day, there was an uneasy feeling among people frequenting the Humberston Corner-Clee Crescent area of town at night, owing to attacks by a mysterious something swooping down silently on their heads.

Five residents experienced the violent attacks – always between 11.15 p.m. and 11.30 p.m., with one even hearing ghoulish chuckling. Each was left with marks and scratches on their heads, evidently made by talons, and it was suggested the culprit was a giant owl.

Ruth Mumby, of Humberston, said:

> My hat was knocked off, my head scratched and the hair nearly pulled out of my head. I swung round to see who, or what, my assailant was, but could see nothing. I did not stay to investigate. I was too frightened.

Immediately after being attacked, two male victims saw a large bird flying erratically away.

An interested party who frequented that area said he often heard shrieks, which could sound like a child crying, from owls. (*Grimsby Evening Telegraph*, 1935)

~ MAY 30TH ~

1958: On this day, production was well underway at one of Grimsby's most famous factories. The new Findus Ltd plant began operating during May, although the firm was no stranger to Grimsby: for some years, it had imported food through the port from Scandinavia.

Findus was famous for its fish fingers which, at their peak, were selling at a rate of £2.5-billion a year, and all made in Grimsby. At the height of its success, the factory employed between 3,000 and 4,000 people, recruiting mostly from the local area but also hiring large numbers of students to harvest vegetables on a part-time basis (they were later replaced by machinery).

Nestlé, its owner, re-launched Findus products under the Crosse and Blackwell label, a name usually associated with sandwich pickle. The move was seen as an effort to rival the multi-national Heinz.

Findus was a keen supporter of the town, and many a Grimsby Town fan has cheered on the team in the Findus stand at Blundell Park. (*Grimsby Evening Telegraph*, 1958)

- MAY 31ST -

1981: On this day, at 6.30 a.m., 15-year-old Tracy Johnstone tossed a message in a bottle in the sea, encouraged by her father, Alan, to let the waves take her message to a 'treasure island'.

It wasn't pirates who stumbled across the trinket, but 58-year-old Thomas Fink thirty years later in St Peter-Ording, Germany, almost 400 miles away. Mr Fink, who often holidayed there, was taking his daily walk along the beach. On a bank he found the bottle, which had been covered in sand for some time, but he could still read the message bearing Tracy's name and address.

He contacted a local newspaper to track down the owner, and Tracy was amazed at the find. She said:

> Growing up, myself and my brother Steven would send off messages in bottles, but I never expected mine to be found. One of Steven's was discovered in Finland when he was 16 and I thought 'typical, the older brother and nothing for little Tracy'. But I thought 'one day my ship will come in'.

(*Grimsby Evening Telegraph*, 1971; *Grimsby Evening Telegraph*, 2011)

— June 1st —

1968: On this day, motorists had to pay for parking in Grimsby for the first time. Today parking fees are taken for granted – a necessary part of most drivers' lives. But in 1968, they were something few had ever had to pay.

This day was the first on which motorists in Grimsby were asked to pay for parking. They did so under a 'trust the motorist' scheme agreed by the town council. The initiative should have started earlier, but was delayed for various reasons, not least being the necessity to seek loan sanction for the purchase of ticket vending machines.

Daily charges were 6*d* for two hours of parking between eight in the morning and six in the evening, with a maximum of 2*s* in any charge period. Season tickets were also available and cost 10*s* weekly, £2 monthly, £12 for six months and £24 for an entire year. (*Grimsby Evening Telegraph*, 1968)

– JUNE 2ND –

1904: On this day, the inquest was opened into the murder of Alice Prior, at the hands of Charles Smith … but what was the truth of this murder case?

Smith worked as a fitter for a box-making company on the docks. He was a sober lad who found lodgings in Daubney Street with the elderly Mrs Prior. In the same house lived her happily married daughter-in-law, Alice. Smith was friendly with her, but that was all.

At Easter 1904, Smith married Eliza Brown, taking on the house as the Priors moved to run a grocery. The new Mrs Smith liked Alice and the two became friends.

On June 1st, Alice, whose husband was at sea, called round. Smith persuaded Alice to stay for supper, so Eliza left the house at 9.15 p.m. to fetch fish and chips. When she returned only ten minutes later, Smith was on the floor, dead, shot through the left eye. Alice, shot through the temple, still alive but only survived for another five hours. A six-chambered revolver was lying on the floor.

At the inquest, Mrs Prior senior claimed Smith regretted his marriage but denied there was anything more than friendship between him and her daughter. Eliza said Smith was a good husband and she had no suspicions about him. No one knew who the gun belonged to.

With little evidence, the jury decided that Smith had murdered Alice and, being of sound mind, then killed himself. (Stephen Wade, *Foul Deeds and Suspicious Deaths in Grimsby and Cleethorpes*, 2007)

– JUNE 3RD –

1986: On this day, it was announced that Iron Age Grimsby was being brought to life as a major tourist attraction. Plans for the creation of a replica 100 BC farmstead were revealed – hailed as a dream come true for two archaeologists who unearthed the original settlement in Weelsby Road.

Councillors agreed to meet about the idea of the open-air museum at the site, between Wintringham School and the crematorium, to discuss its potential. Grimsby Borough Council granted permission but the replica site, complete with its own moat, fell foul to vandalism on a regular basis before its centrepiece was completely destroyed in a fire in 1989. It closed down a year later but the site remains a fascinating insight into Grimsby's more ancient past.

Archaeology graduates John Sills and Gavin Kinlsey dug at the site year on year since 1976. They uncovered pottery, weapons, huts and, most excitingly, four skeletons. The only known Iron Age chainmail suit was also found. The excavations revealed evidence of a mixed farming economy in Grimsby at the time, superseded by the production of high-status harness fittings. (*Grimsby Evening Telegraph*, 1986)

~ June 4th ~

1932: On this day, the king paid tribute to Grimsby fishermen for their heroism in rescuing the crew of the town's trawler *Howe*, which was wrecked at Bear Island in November the previous year. A bronze medal was awarded to George Harmer, deckhand of the stricken steam trawler, who attempted to swim ashore with a line. Other souvenirs were awarded to its crew. Mr Harmer made two attempts to swim through the surf from the wreck to shore, 40 yards away. Each time he was hauled back on board the wreck. (Grimsby Central Library)

1970: On this day, it was announced that the RAF station in North Cotes – home of the Bloodhound Mk 2 missile squadrons – was to be closed down. The shock news was delivered by the Commanding Officer, Wing Commander F.R. Davidson, who said that by the following March, the camp would be a ghost station.

The Ministry of Defence said no further use could be found for the station, which had served as an RAF base for fifty-six years and was one of the oldest in Britain. (*Grimsby Evening Telegraph*, 1970)

~ JUNE 5TH ~

1970: On this day, after being submerged by the tide for several hours, a coastguard Land Rover was finally dragged clear from sand on the Humberston foreshore, where it had been bogged down all night.

The Land Rover, from Donna Nook, got into trouble when it went to the rescue of people believed stranded on the Haile Sand Fort. A woman had reported seeing two people on the fort. The Inshore Rescue Boat was asked to stand by, but it soon became too dark to launch, and the falling tide made it useless to ask the Humber Lifeboat for help. The Land Rover followed the falling tide out but got bogged down in the soft sand. The driver went forward on foot and reached the fort after wading through water, waist-deep in some places, but no one was found.

At low tide on this day, a caterpillar tractor went to the partially sunken vehicle, attached chains and with the first pull, tugged it free. Covered in cloying mud, the Land Rover was taken by trailer back to the coastguard station. (*Grimsby Evening Telegraph*, 1970)

— JUNE 6TH —

1951: On this day, Bill Shankly was appointed as Grimsby Town FC's manager. He stayed for more than two years before resigning 'for personal reasons' on New Year's Eve 1953.

Shankly, affectionately known as Shanks, joined the Mariners from Carlisle. In his first season at Blundell Park, Grimsby Town won eleven games in a row – a club record – but just missed promotion.

Shanks took over the reins at Workington in 1954 after earlier saying: 'At one time I had visions of staying at Grimsby for the rest of my life, but that's football. Things change a lot.'

While Shankly failed to lead Town to promotion, the next-but-one manager, Allenby Chilton, hit the spot. He came from Manchester United to become the Mariners' first player-manager, and so successful was the team he moulded that they became the first club in Football League history to go from re-election one season to promotion the next. (*Grimsby Evening Telegraph*, 1951)

—–—

1978: On this day, *It's A Knockout* was staged at the old Cleethorpes Bathing Pool. The game was between Lincoln, Gainsborough and Cleethorpes. That year, Cleethorpes then went on to take part in a live BBC1 European finals at Lincoln Showground on August 23rd. (*Grimsby Evening Telegraph*, 1978)

~ JUNE 7TH ~

1960: On this day, shrimps had returned to the Humber after a seven-year famine. After struggling to earn a living all these years, Grimsby's two shrimp boats, the *Perseverance* and the *Unity*, were back in business landing bumper catches. (*Grimsby Evening Telegraph*, 1960)

1974: On this day, two brothers given up for dead by their mother after their drifting yacht was found in the North Sea were landed safe and well in Yarmouth by a Belgian trawler.

Michael Phillips and his 25-year-old brother John were plucked from their damaged yacht by the trawler. But although a radio message was sent by the trawler, delays meant that their family were not told they were safe until almost 10.30 a.m. on this day. Their mother, Gladys Phillips, of Cleethorpes, broke down and wept when she received a telephone call to tell her that her sons were safe. (*Grimsby Evening Telegraph*, 1974)

− JUNE 8TH −

1931: On this day, Grimsby and the surrounding area was severely rocked in the early hours by an earthquake. Although no one was even slightly hurt and no damage occurred, the shock received was equally as great as the shock given by Mother Nature.

It happened at about 1.25 a.m., when most people were asleep. A series of earth tremors, lasting about thirty seconds, sent people running into the streets in panic − thinking bombing was taking place. The tremors were accompanied by rumblings, described as being like heavy lorries in the distance or muffled thunder. Others said it felt like a train going by, or a bomb going off 25 miles away.

Skippers on trawlers at sea felt shockwaves and a great swell; it is thought the quake originated from underneath the sea.

People's imaginations were running riot, yet not everyone heard it. On Scartho Road, no tremor was felt at all − a stranger to the Richter Scale. (*Grimsby Evening Telegraph*, 1931)

– JUNE 9TH –

1937: On this day, it was reported that His Royal Highness The Duke of Gloucester had presented the Stanhope Medal – the Victoria Cross of the sea – to a Grimsby fisherman.

Noel Kinch had fought off a shark to rescue a shipmate, who went overboard the trawler *Northern Pride*. The gear was being shot when one of the crew was pinned to the rail. He went into the water with blood spurting from his back.

Mr Kinch went in after him, by which stage the shark had already bitten the man twice. Then it came back to attack them both. By the time the ship could pick them up, both had nasty wounds.

Meanwhile, the police were investigating a second mysterious outbreak of fire. Early in the morning, a lorry left parked in an alleyway in Scartho was set alight – just twenty-four hours after another lorry standing in exactly the same place had been badly damaged. The second incident was spotted at 12.30 a.m. by a woman attending an ill friend. She saw the cab of the lorry, which belonged to a haulier, was blazing.

The morning before, another haulier's lorry in the same alleyway was found ablaze at 3 a.m.; the cause was thought to be an electrical fault. 'There is a curious similarity between the two outbreaks', it was noted. (*Grimsby Evening Telegraph*, 1937)

~ JUNE 10TH ~

1985: On this day, John Cleese was in Grimsby filming a movie. Hit comedy *Clockwise* was partly filmed at Grimsby District General Hospital, and some locals got the chance to be in it.

For staff nurse Sue Tilley, it was just what the doctor ordered – a once-in-a-lifetime chance to appear in a big screen movie. She and several colleagues appeared alongside Cleese, and for Sue, it was a real tonic. Just a year earlier, she had been close to death after a horrific road crash. 'I feel reborn,' she said at the time. 'As a "welcome back", I was asked if I wanted to be in the film.'

Clockwise tells the story of a comprehensive school headmaster, played by Cleese, who has a race against time to get to a conference. Grimsby was week one of the eight-week filming schedule, and the cast were due to travel all over the country for the various scenes.

On this day, the crew spent the entire day filming in the town, coping with problems such as unexpected aircraft flying over. The hospital scene was to last only one minute and thirty seconds. (*Grimsby Evening Telegraph*, 1985)

‒ June 11th ‒

1848: On this day, businessman William Rowston unveiled a new attraction to draw in the crowds at his oyster booth on Cleethorpes seafront. Seals often visit the shoreline of the east coast, and in days gone by, some would be captured alive. William did just this ‒ and kept the seal on display at his oyster booth from this day until March 30th 1849.

The animal was domesticated like a dog, answered to the name of Billy and was loved by all who saw him. William fed Billy a diet of small fish in great quantities. But this was to prove poor Billy's downfall: his guzzling of so much fish, mixed with consuming seaweed, caused his death. (Edward Dobson, *A Guide and Directory to Cleethorpes*, 1850)

———

1947: On this day, Bill McVeigh, of Grimsby, riding a Triumph machine, won the first lightweight Clubman's TT race in the Isle of Man. His time was one hour, forty-four minutes and two seconds, and his average speed was 65.30mph. Bill, brother in a firm of haulage contractors, was a well-known rider at the Cadwell Park racetrack, in Louth, and at grass track meetings in Grimsby and Scunthorpe. In 1946, he came 15th in the Manx Grand Prix. (*Grimsby Evening Telegraph*, 1947)

− JUNE 12TH −

1933: On this day, an airfield between Holton-le-Clay and Waltham was officially opened under the stewardship of Lincolnshire Aero Club. During the early 1930s, enthusiasts formed the club and chose some meadowland between the two villages to build a clubhouse and two small wooden hangars.

Five years on, the RAF opened a flying school at the site to train pilots for the RAF Volunteer Reserve. This continued until September 1939, when it was closed upon the declaration of war. The facilities were used by the army until May 1940, when the RAF decided to lay concrete runways. A year later, the airfield opened as RAF Grimsby, a satellite to RAF Binbrook. It was used by the Wellingtons of 12 and 142 Squadrons. In December 1941, the 100 Squadron formed and operated there for most of the war. The first operation from Waltham was overnight on January 8th 1943.

At its height, the base was home to more than 2,400 personnel. During the conflict, 48 Wellingtons and 116 Lancasters from the base were lost.

The site was sold off in 1958 and is largely disused. (*Grimsby Telegraph Bygones*, 1996)

– JUNE 13TH –

1849: On this day, a poster appeared around Grimsby announcing A Grand Tea Festival. The authorities planned to mark the passing of the Grimsby Pastures Act with the festival, and tickets, costing a shilling each, were on sale. Tea would be on the table at five o'clock prompt, and the celebration also featured addresses and a performance from a musical band.

The event, which took place on Thursday, June 28th that year, was organised by the town's freeman and the widows of deceased freemen. It was held in the Preparatory Schoolroom, in New Street, to commemorate the passing of the act of Parliament entitled 'The Grimsby Corporation and Freeman's Arrangement Act', which received the Royal Ascent on May 24th of that year.

By the Act, the freeman and widows, paying Scot and Lot, were entitled to receive (after payment of expenses), an equal half-yearly distribution of all interest money, dividends and other revenue arising from their investments and freehold estate secured to them under the powers of the act. (Grimsby Central Library)

~ June 14th ~

1943: On this day, a terrifying butterfly bomb raid was executed on Grimsby. It began at about 1 a.m., when the sirens sounded. In the next half-hour, several 1,000kg blast bombs fell, with canisters containing 3,000 or more anti-personnel bombs and 6,000 incendiaries.

They fell on open land and in densely packed residential areas around Freeman Street, Victoria Street, Cleethorpe Road, the West Marsh and East Marsh and in north Cleethorpes.

Peter Dixon's Mill, the Bon Marche store and Weelsby Old Hall went up in flames; at one point, more than 300 fires were raging. Records show this raid caused 99 of the 196 deaths in bombings on the area. A further 184 were seriously injured and hundreds more slightly hurt.

Harold Blundell, 39, was one of three air-raid wardens killed when a bomb fell on a classroom at Canon Ainslie School. The school's caretaker also died. Fourteen men died in one incident in Victoria Street, and PC Walter Rouse was fatally wounded when a bomb exploded as he aided an injured man.

Incendiaries did the damage, but butterfly bombs killed. Canisters hung from trees and telephone lines, and lodged in gutters. The search for them went on for a month afterwards, and they claimed their last victim in 1945. But Grimsby scored a victory – security was so tight that the Luftwaffe never found out how successful the raid was. (*Grimsby Evening Telegraph*)

— JUNE 15TH —

1934: On this day, a gift of £15,000 towards the erection of a Grimsby Central Mission was made by an anonymous donor. The Superintendent Minister, the Reverend J.W. Mountford, said the princely gift came from 'a friend of missions' who preferred that his name should not be made public. It was known that the same gentleman had been instrumental in making possible the erection of a number of central mission halls in various parts of the country. The Grimsby Central Mission project was to cost £26,000 overall. It was built on the site of the Duncombe Street chapel and had seating for about 1,400 people. (*Grimsby Evening Telegraph*, 1934)

1959: On this day, the warden of the Grimsby Adventure Playground, Joe Benjamin, had received a £500 grant from the Nuffield Foundation to study similar ventures in Britain and on the Continent.

Joe, 37, who lived in Heneage Road, was to write a textbook of his findings. He described it as a 'wonderful opportunity to look at new techniques needed'.

He departed Grimsby the following month and the first stage of his tour was to take him to Bristol, where there were six playgrounds. He also planned to visit Liverpool and London, and later Denmark, where the idea originated. (*Grimsby Evening Telegraph*, 1959)

⁓ June 16th ⁓

1971: On this day, the submarine HMS *Artemis* was in Grimsby, waiting to sail the following day. She sank on July 1st and one Grimsby woman had predicted the vessel's demise.

Sandra MacDonald became friends with one of the sailors on board. The week after *Artemis* had sailed, Sandra had a dream. 'I saw a big grey wall – I thought it was a harbour – and I saw the submarine sink,' she recalled. 'In the dream, three men were trapped on board.' A week later, the sub sank – and three men were trapped on board, two of them Sandra's friends. When she sank, she was in just 30ft of water while moored at the HMS *Dolphin* shore establishment at Gosport, refuelling. She was raised five days later, decommissioned and sold for scrap.

The story was featured on the TV programme Arthur C. Clarke's *World of Strange Powers*. The *Artemis* was an Amphion-class Royal Navy sub, and first launched in 1946. (*Arthur C. Clarke's World of Strange Powers*; YouTube)

‒ JUNE 17TH ‒

2014: On this day, a teenager from a small village on the outskirts of Grimsby was at number one in the UK music charts. Ella Henderson, from Tetney, shot to fame on *The X Factor* TV show when she was just 16. Although she was beaten to the winning post by James Arthur, the young singer songwriter was snapped up by music mogul Simon Cowell's record label. Her debut single, 'Ghost', charted at number one, taken from her debut album, *Chapter One*. 'Ghost' was written by Ella, Ryan Tedder and Noel Zancanella, and she filmed the video in New Orleans.

It's not the first time Grimsby has tasted success on *The X Factor*. On this day in 2005, operatic quartet G4 – semi-finalists on the TV show – played a sold-out gig in the town. Band member Matt Stiff was a Grimsby lad and tickets for the gig sold out within a day of going on sale. It was the first show in the band's nationwide tour, following the release of their hugely successful debut album, which sold 245,000 copies in its first week and reached triple platinum status. G4 became so famous that Matt was name-checked in the comedy show *Little Britain* by actor Matt Lucas's infamous character creation, Vicky Pollard. (*Lincolnshire Echo*, 2014; *Grimsby Telegraph*, 2005)

~ June 18th ~

1937: On this day, Grimsby-born Freddie Frith won the Senior TT race on the Isle of Man, with an average speed of 88.21mph.

Freddie – or Frederick Lee Frith OBE – was popular in his hometown. Born in May 1909, he trained as a stonemason but declined to join the family business – a firm of funeral directors in Scartho – choosing instead to race.

He won the 1935 Junior Manx Grand Prix and then joined the Norton team for the 1936 TT, where he claimed the Junior TT title and finished second in the Senior TT as well as winning the 350cc European Championship. In fact, he was five times the winner of the Isle of Man TT, and had the distinction of being one of the few to win TT races before and after the war; in 1937, he set the first 90mph lap of the Snaefell Mountain Course. Freddie also has the honour of being the first ever 350cc World Champion: in 1949 he won all five events of the inaugural campaign.

During the war, he served at the Infantry Driving & Maintenance School stationed at Keswick. Sgt Frith taught officers how to ride cross-country in all weathers.

Many people will have visited his motorcycle shop in Victoria Street, which stocked Italian bikes. He retired to Louth, where he died in 1988. (*Grimsby Evening Telegraph*)

— JUNE 19TH —

1998: On this day, famous Grimsby artist Hai Shuet Yeung put the world's largest watercolour on display. His painting of 5,000 carp was insured for £1 million and was the highlight of the London Contemporary Art and Design Show at Kensington Town Hall. Measuring 200m in length by 1.5m wide, the work was executed on a single length of specially commissioned and sponsored Saunders Waterford art paper.

Mr Yeung, who had lived in Grimsby since 1969, worked on the painting – which was longer than a cruise ship – in the garage of his home in Scartho. Each fish represented one year since the dawn of civilisation in his homeland of China. It took him about a year to complete.

After the show it was divided into 100 sections to, in Mr Yeung's words, 'bridge the cultural gap'. Two sections went to museums in London and Beijing, seventy-eight more to museums around the world and twenty to private collectors.

When he first arrived in Grimsby, he would wait on customers at a restaurant during the day and paint at night, sleeping for a few snatched hours. In 1970, he sold his first painting for £40; by 1998, he could command thousands of pounds for his work. (*Grimsby Telegraph*, 1998)

— JUNE 20TH —

2009: On this day, the historic Leaking Boot pub was no more. The Cleethorpes landmark had been reduced to a pile of rubble following a devastating fire, sparked by arsonists. Thankfully the building, containing fifty-two bedrooms and bars, was unused at the time of the blaze, which caused part of the structure to collapse completely.

The pub was named after The Boy With The Leaking Boot, a famous statue in the resort. But to many, it was best known in its previous incarnation – Darleys, a popular nightspot famous for its live acts and sing-a-longs. One regular recalls a singer 'bashing a tray on his head whilst singing "Mule Train".'

It closed to the public in 2008 and was the location of a series of small fires until the one which destroyed it. Just weeks before the fire, transformation plans had been revealed by the site's owners. It was to become a boutique hotel and restaurant – a plan which was never realised. The building could not survive the damage and was demolished. (*Grimsby Telegraph*, 2009)

~ June 21st ~

1902: On this day, the Warwick revolving observation tower was built in Cleethorpes. This version was one in a long line of observation towers at such resorts as Great Yarmouth and Scarborough.

On March 9th 1900, a local newspaper confirmed its construction:

> At last, Cleethorpes is to have the much talked-of revolving observatory tower. The site of the structure, in connection with which a pavilion will be erected at the northern end of the Promenade ... The pavilion will stand on a site, which for the entire scheme is 60ft x 70ft ...

Standing 150ft tall and with a capacity for 200 people, the structure was a hit with tourists.

Boarding on to what looked like a gallery but was, in fact, a circular lift, passengers were carried as it revolved around the central pole. At the top, passengers stepped out on to a platform giving views over the Humber estuary and the Lincolnshire Wolds.

In its twilight years, the lift was fixed in one position, enabling flying boats to be hung from it. In 1911 it was decided that Cleethorpes no longer needed the tower. East Coast Amusements began to develop blueprints, and by the end of 1911 Wonderland had been built on its site. (*Grimsby Telegraph Bygones*, 1992)

~ JUNE 22ND ~

2006: On this day, the movie executives behind the smash-hit *Atonement* were in Grimsby discussing filming schedules. The major blockbuster, starring James McAvoy and Kiera Knightley, was partly filmed on Grimsby Docks.

Pride and Prejudice director Joe Wright turned the clock back to the Second World War, transforming the town's famous Ice Factory into the scene of a bloody battle between Allied and German soldiers at Dunkirk. Prior to filming, a bombed-out church was built as part of the set. With a replica stained-glass window, the structure took more than a week to complete.

Twenty-four-hour security had already been enlisted to guard the set, and when filming began, scores of locals were used as extras. The first clapper board eventually dropped in Grimsby in mid-August, and the extras had their hair cut in 1940s styles to add to the authenticity.

Night scenes of McAvoy and actor Daniel Mays walking through the streets were shot at Parker Street and Gorton Street and camera crews also used Gorton Street as a location to recreate 1940s wartime France.

The film went on to win awards and prove a hit at the box office. A deleted scene inside the Ice Factory, tracking past the machinery, can be seen on the DVD. (*Grimsby Telegraph*, 2006)

‒ June 23rd ‒

1349: On this day, Grimsby was in the grip of the Black Death. Lincolnshire was one of the worst-hit areas of England, as indicated in ecclesiastical records from the time. Records kept by the archdeaconry of Stow, which covered the north-west of the county, show that 57 per cent of the clergy had died from the bubonic plague, though in Grimsby alone, it was only 35 per cent.

The great pestilence, as it was regularly referred to, was noted to have struck between Palm Sunday and June 24th. Produced by Cistercian monks, *The Louth Park Chronicler* reported:

> In many places under a fifth part of the people were left alive. It filled the whole world with terror. So great an epidemic has never been seen or heard of before this time, for its people even the flood which happened in the days of Noah did not carry off so vast a multitude. This plague slew Jew, Christian and Saracen alike. It carried off confessor and penitent together.

(*The Louth Park Chronicler*; Grimsby Central Library)

~ JUNE 24TH ~

1970: On this day, tributes were paid to the Lincolnshire man who invented a widely used system of shorthand. Reginald John Garfield Dutton died at Norwich, aged 83. Mr Dutton created his system of 'Shorthand in 24 Hours' in 1918. (*Grimsby Evening Telegraph*, 1970)

1974: On this day, police were trying to trace a 3-year-old girl who ran away after being rescued when she fell into Grimsby's Alexandra Dock.

Twenty-year-old Michael Booth told how he had arrived at Corporation Bridge with the intention of going fishing when he heard screaming and saw a commotion. He spotted a girl in the water and dived in fully clothed. He added: 'The girl's older sister was screaming and was almost hysterical. She drew my attention, but after I had pulled the girl out, they both vanished.'

Mr Booth had difficulty climbing out of the water because of the steep side of the dock, and had to be pulled out by staff from a nearby department store. The ordeal happened on June 22nd, and on this day, the youngster still had not been traced.

A spokesman said, 'Mr Booth was not too well after being in the water for only a short while, and it is quite possible that the little girl may be ill without her mother knowing why.' (*Grimsby Evening Telegraph*, 1974)

— June 25th —

1959: On this day, the district's Medical Officer of Health, Doctor George Cust, delivered a warning to smokers, the lazy and 'those who are fat'. The biggest single cause of death in the Grimsby rural district in 1958 had been coronary artery disease, which killed twenty-four people (thirteen men and eleven women). The information was released in Doctor Cust's annual report.

He had found that the disease was more prevalent in men who were overweight, smoked cigarettes, took little exercise, or were under mental strain. Thin, easy-going pipe or non-smokers who took a reasonable amount of exercise appeared much less likely to contract the disease, he said.

In 1957, coronary artery disease was responsible for seventeen deaths, seven fewer than in 1958. (*Grimsby Evening Telegraph*, 1959)

1993: On this day, the heat was on at the Ice House, in Victor Street, where eight children collapsed in sweltering conditions. St John Ambulance workers were kept busy as the youngsters fainted and others suffered from the heat during a two-hour Festival of Voices concert. The inaptly named Ice House was turned into a cauldron by stage lights, a packed audience and a muggy evening. Six hundred children had been rehearsing for the evening show since the afternoon. (*Grimsby Evening Telegraph*, 1993)

– JUNE 26TH –

1993: On this day, it was revealed that a Grimsby man had left a fortune – almost £500,000 – to local and national animal charities in his will. The kind resident left instructions for the bulk of his £470,000 legacy to be divided between five organisations: the RPSB, a local animal sanctuary, the Animal Welfare Trust, the National Canine Defence League and the Battersea Dogs Home.

The Grimsby branch of the People's Dispensary for Sick Animals was bequeathed £3,000, while the Louth branch of the Cats Protection League and the Bransby Home of Rest for Horses each received £1,000.

Probate for the will, Ann Clark, said, 'He was an avid dog lover. He had a dog of his own which died shortly before his wife's death, and the will is really in memory of his dog.' (*Grimsby Evening Telegraph*, 1993)

2012: On this day, the Olympic torch descended Grimsby Dock Tower, in the hands of climber Alan Ellinson, as part of the nationwide relay prior to the start of the London 2012 Games. It was a very early morning start for residents who watched the flame appear over the parapet. It then went on a tour of Grimsby for two days. (*Grimsby Telegraph*, 2012)

~ JUNE 27TH ~

1638: On this day, Anthony Acham of Holborn promised that an annual rent of £5 – payable out of lands at Asterby and Goulceby – would be made to the mayor, aldermen and commonalty of Great Grimsby:

> … to be by them bestowed in wheaten bread at six times in the year amongst the poor people of the Town sixteen shillings worth and eight pennyworth of such bread to be distributed upon every last Sunday in every of the months of March, May, July, September, November and January yearly in the Town Hall of the Corporation so long as the world shall endure.

(Grimsby Central Library)

1959: On this day, a 70-ton cargo of bagged flour from Hull, aboard a Grimsby barge, was given the 'all clear'. Earlier, it was fumigated when some flour beetles were discovered. After receiving the result of a microscopic examination of a sample, the Grimsby Chief Port Health Inspector, Mr J.D. Syme, stated that the cargo would be allowed to discharge and no further action would be taken. (*Grimsby Evening Telegraph*, 1959)

~ June 28th ~

1959: On this day, the queen and the Duke of Edinburgh toured Grimsby Docks. The royal couple visited a seine netter during the tour, giving a seal of approval to this type of fishing. The invention of seine net fishing is credited to Jans Vaever in Denmark in 1848, but it was not until Germany invaded their country in the spring of 1940 that Danish fishermen came to Grimsby with their boats, establishing this type of fishing in the port. (*Grimsby Evening Telegraph*, 1958)

1974: On this day, Elton John released his album *Caribou*, which contained the track 'Grimsby'. It was written by Lincolnshire-born songwriter Bernie Taupin, a long-time collaborator with Elton. Taupin sometimes wrote about his youth, and 'Grimsby' was a tongue-in-cheek tribute to the port he would regularly visit with his friends. Elton's hit 'Saturday Night's Alright for Fighting' was inspired by visits to pubs and dance halls in Bernie's youth. (Claude Bernardin and Tom Stanton, *Rocket Man: Elton John from A-Z*, 1996)

– JUNE 29TH –

1839: On this day, the Manchester Order of Odd Fellows opened a lodge at the Leeds Arms, in Cleethorpes. It was called the Cleethorpes Fisherman's Rest No.1803 and consisted of five members. There were fifty-four by the year 1859, and in that year George Locking was the proprietor of the Leeds Arms. It was a hotel, and he kept horses and conveyances to let to visitors. (Edward Dobson, *A Guide and Directory to Cleethorpes*, 1850)

—–—

1903: On this day, a fire broke out at the pier head concert hall. The flames were spotted after the orchestra had left a morning concern. Despite valiant efforts from both Grimsby and Cleethorpes fire brigades, who were watched by huge crowds of onlookers, the building could not be saved.

A year later, the Railway Company bought the pier for £11,250, and a new pavilion was built in 1905. It was shortened during the Second World War in 1949, and in recent years became a nightclub.

In 2013, the iconic landmark was taken over by an organisation interested in bringing back its glory days, even looking at the possibility of restoring the pier to its original length. (Tim Mickleburgh, *Cleethorpes Pier and Promenade*, 2000; *Grimsby Evening Telegraph*, 1991)

— JUNE 30TH —

1959: On this day, despite recent heavy rain, there was still an urgent need for householders to economise with water. So serious was the position that loud speaker appeals were being considered. Leaflets urging people to stop using hosepipes, washing cars and swilling were distributed. The engineer and manager of the North East Lincolnshire Water Board, Mr C. Cooper, said, 'The rain has cut down the draw a little but the demand at Eskimo's factory, in Pelham Road, Cleethorpes, is causing us a great deal of concern.' He stated that one day the previous week, the factory used 600,000 gallons. 'I hope they will be able to give us a day a week off. We cannot give them what they want unless there is a lessened domestic demand,' he added.

Mr Cooper said that water supplies would be cut at night only as a last resort. The demand for water in Grimsby was exceeding 15,000,000 gallons a day – the highest the board had ever known. The cause was dry weather and seasonal increased demand. (*Grimsby Evening Telegraph*, 1959; Grimsby Central Library)

~ July 1st ~

1901: On this day, the actions of Grimsby fishermen sparked what has become known as the Great Fishing Dispute, prompting violent riots and widespread disorder. It was caused by the Grimsby Federated Owners' Protecting Society, which decided to replace the straight wage packet of fishermen with less wages and poundage, in other words, payment by results. Skippers were unaffected by this change. The men went on strike and the owners declared a lock-out – and there was a deadlock. This continued for weeks; the strikers were not paid and there were no benefits – the men lived on charity. In early September, the owners and men met again but there was a complete failure to agree. Through sheer frustration and anger, on the 18th and 19th, the men rioted, pelting stones at the police and windows in Riby Square. The Riot Act was read, restoring order, and the Earl of Yarborough agreed to mediate. More than three months after the dispute began, on October 7th, the first vessel sailed. There had been an agreement; the men accepting a return to work on the owners' terms, pending the result of an independent review by the Board of Trade. It was not until December 23rd that a settlement was finally reached. The owners' original proposal listed wages ranging from 15*s* to 30*s*, and poundage from 2*d* to 4*d* from deckhand to engineer. The independent review boosted wages to between 18*s* and 34*s*, and poundage from 1½*d* to 3½*d*, plus food, which had been left off the original offer. (*Grimsby Evening Telegraph*; verbal account by Peter Chapman)

– July 2nd –

1831: On this day, a drunken brawl in the Duke of York pub escalated into a fatal stabbing. Edward Hall, 22, had a drunken run-in with a landlord, called Mr Kempsley, and nearby resident Edward Button. Hall caused a disturbance at Mr Kempsley's pub, and Mr Button helped the landlord turf out the troublemaker.

A few days later, a witness heard Hall say, 'I'll kill Kempsley and somebody else!' as he sharpened a knife on a stone.

Nothing happened until July 2nd, when Hall went to the Duke of York with a friend, called Ratton. Hall was in high spirits and, according to witnesses, out to provoke Button. Button said, 'Hello! What do you want?'

'One bully has as much right here as another,' Hall replied, striking Hall in the face.

Button said, 'I'm ready for you any time!' and they fought, grappling on the floor. Button staggered to a chair, bleeding, and died. He had been stabbed in the chest.

Hall went outside to apparently throw away the knife, and went back in, denying he had a weapon – but an onlooker had seen the knife.

Hall was sentenced to hang at Lincoln. A reporter covering the trial said he 'looked forward to his approaching fate with calmness and resignation'. (Stephen Wade, *Foul Deeds and Suspicious Deaths in Grimsby and Cleethorpes*, 2007)

~ JULY 3RD ~

1943: On this day, an electrical short circuit on a Lancaster DV172 caused the entire bomb load to drop to the ground at RAF Binbrook. Within minutes, the 400lb 'cookie' and two 500lb bombs exploded, and the bomber disintegrated. (Grimsby Central Library)

1990: On this day, an adventurous puppy was recovering after firefighters had to lift an entire garden shed to rescue her. The tiny mongrel, which did not have a name, got trapped on her first day in her new home. She became over-excited while playing with her new-found friend, Labrador Ben, forced her head under the shed and couldn't get out. Ben alerted their owner by crying and whimpering. The uninjured pup had only been bought a few hours before the mishap.

Meanwhile, another local pooch was going through an ordeal. Vets performed life-saving operations on a puppy which swallowed a baby's dummy – twice. A dummy had already been removed from Ben's intestine by surgeons at the Blue Cross Animal Hospital. Just four days after he was allowed home, the Jack Russell was back on the operating table. This time the dummy had caused a complete blockage, and he would have died if it hadn't been removed. (*Grimsby Evening Telegraph*, Bomber Boys special edition, 1991)

~ July 4th ~

1941: On this day, the PS *Lincoln Castle* was brought to Grimsby. The coal-fired side-wheel paddle steamer ferried passengers across the Humber until 1978 – the last such vessel in regular service in the UK.

She was launched on April 27th 1940, named after the Norman castle at Lincoln, and delivered to Grimsby's Royal Dock on this day the following year, a sister to *Wingfield Castle* and *Tattershall Castle*, the latter now docked permanently on the Thames in central London. For years, she ferried day-trippers between the south and north banks of the River Humber, a regular sight on the water.

After finishing service, the 209ft long vessel was opened in 1989 as a floating restaurant in Alexandra Dock, Grimsby. Due to corrosion and seepage, she was closed in 2006, and by 2010, she was in an advanced state of deterioration.

It was announced that unless a new owner came forward, the PS *Lincoln Castle* would have to be scrapped. Despite a public outcry and valiant efforts by a campaign group to save and restore her, the historic vessel was broken up. (*Grimsby Telegraph Bygones*, 1998; www.grimsbytelegraph.co.uk)

~ JULY 5TH ~

1959: On this day, Waltham Flying Club – which had been formed only six months before –acquired a third aircraft. A £1,000 Auster four-seater had been bought by a club member who had made it available for the use of the club's sixty members, fourteen of whom had pilots' licences.

'Anyone could fly it after a little instruction,' explained assistant secretary Mr B. Pike. 'It is almost impossible to get hurt in it.'

The machine's performance was compared to that of a large car. With four people, it could achieve 15 miles to the gallon at 90 miles per hour.

The club's other machines were a two-seater Magister and a single-seater lightweight Dart Kitten, both privately owned.

Flying took place every weekend and on some evenings, weather permitting. The club hoped to shortly acquire the services of an instructor; a Canberra pilot at a nearby RAF station had offered to qualify so he could train club members. (*Grimsby Evening Telegraph*, 1959)

— JULY 6TH —

1915: On this day, a sample of chlorine gas was on display in Grimsby. An entry in resident H.S. Surfleet's diary read:

> The use of chlorine gas by the Germans against our troops in the trenches has aroused considerable curiosity on the part of the public as to the nature and appearance of the deadly vapour. A fair-sized sample of this chemical product may now be seen in the window of Messrs. J M Tierney Ltd, of Cleethorpe Road. It is enclosed in a gigantic glass bottle securely corked and sealed. Apparently this sample had been manufactured by one of the chemists employed in Hewitt Brothers' brewery.

(*Grimsby Evening Telegraph*, 1915)

1959: On this day, the *Grimsby Evening Telegraph* told how a galley boy who fell off a trawler was an experienced swimmer. Sixteen-year-old Alan Wakefield fell overboard from the Grimsby vessel *Northern Queen* in calm weather.

'I hope he doesn't do anything like that again,' said his mother, as she waited for him to return to his home in Hope Street after a short stay in Thurso Hospital.

Alan fell into the water 60 miles north-west of the Orkneys. The mate, Mr A. Favell, of Cleethorpes, and a trimmer, Mr A. Williams, of Grimsby, dived in after the teenager and pulled him on to a life raft. The ship, commanded by Mr F.O. Patterson, continued her trip to Icelandic grounds without further mishaps.

(*Grimsby Evening Telegraph*, 1959)

~ July 7th ~

1966: On this day, the Recorder of Grimsby, Mr W.A. Sime QC, was set to decide if two 'one-arm bandits' should be installed in the Mariners' Rest public house, in Albert Street. Grimsby Corporation had refused the installation of the machines – now a staple of most pubs – but the licensee, Thomas E. Ward, lodged an appeal.

A spokesman for the corporation said the proposal had been turned down because 'it was felt that the premises were not suitable, and that the machines would be undesirable and an annoyance to customers'.

At the time, fruit machines were allowed in Cleethorpes and also in clubs in Grimsby, but not pubs. The police were against the machines, which cost £360 each, because they thought it would 'cause rowdiness and unruly behaviour'. The recorder felt it his duty to inspect a similar machine, as there were thirty-six other applications awaiting the outcome of the appeal. (*Grimsby Evening Telegraph*, 1966)

1978: On this day, the comedian Ken Dodd visited Cleethorpes Zoo as the first of the summer season's guest entertainers. Ken, complete with his customary tickling stick, spent time chatting to fans. He was a repeat visitor to Cleethorpes, performing sell-out shows at the Memorial Hall which would go on for hours. (*Grimsby Evening Telegraph*, 1978)

- JULY 8TH -

1998: On this day, Grimsby man Roy Gibney won the National Lottery. Writing about his experience in *The Guardian*, Roy said:

> I was 44, living alone in a semi in Grimsby. It was a guaranteed £15 million that Wednesday, so I thought, 'All right'. I was in the bath when my brother started shouting out the numbers.
>
> The only number I saw drop was the last one – 36. I hit the door, hugged my brother … then silence hit the room. It was so strange – I'd won £7.5 million.
>
> Winning wasn't what I expected. I used to think I'd go off round the world. But you don't actually do it. I didn't want to move abroad – my mum's here, all my family is here, so why would I want to abandon everybody and find false friends?
>
> I found a house within two weeks of winning. When the swimming pool was put in, they asked what I wanted on the bottom. I said, 'I don't know.' They suggested Roy Gibney, the date and my numbers. I said, 'Slap it in'.

By 2003, Grimsby was officially Britain's luckiest town, with eleven major wins in the area since the first draw in 1994. Experts said the then population of 'Winsby', as the town became nicknamed, of 110,000 was two and a half times more likely to land a fortune. (*Grimsby Telegraph*, 1998; *Grimsby Telegraph*, 2003)

~ JULY 9TH ~

1959: On this day, Grimsby Town Football Club's 22-year-old right back, Bernard Fleming, asked to be placed on the transfer list. He was the fourth player to make such a request in recent weeks, the others being Jimmy Foll, Johnny Scott and Ron Rafferty. He said the main reason for seeking a move was that he wanted to better himself. He had been unable to command a regular first team place in the last two seasons despite outstanding displays on the pitch when making League appearances. Middlesbrough-born Fleming planned to get married by the following year.

'I must look to the future, and judging by the way things have worked out in recent seasons, I do not feel very confident about my position with the club,' he told the press. (*Grimsby Evening Telegraph*, 1959)

~ JULY 10TH ~

1914: On this day, the 1,456-acre Manor of Bradley estate was sold at auction. Bradley Woods, part of the estate, was purchased by Grimsby Corporation for £4,620, to be used for public amusement grounds. (*Grimsby Telegraph Bygones*, 1996)

1959: On this day, after nearly an hour's discussion in private, the Grimsby Highways Committee decided to recommend the town council to approve proposals made by the Grimsby branch of the Radio and Television Retailers' Association for the installation of 'piped' radio and TV in the town.

The council was to be asked by the Housing Committee to approve a ten-year initial concession to the association for the installation on council estates and to accept 7.5 per cent of the weekly rental collected from tenants. Subscribers would pay £5 at the outset, and a weekly service charge of 2*s* 6*d*. (Alan Dowling, *Grimsby: Making The Town 1800–1914*, 2007)

1914: On this day, TG Tickler & Co. – Grimsby's famous jam maker – bought land to plant further and extensive orchards to expand the company.

During the First World War, Tickler's jam tins were handily utilised. Once the contents had been consumed, the empty tins were refilled with explosives to make hand grenades. These were known locally as 'Tickler's Artillery'. (Grimsby Central Library)

1959: On this day, eighty employees at John Bull's rubber factory on the Pyewipe estate were back on the floor after having stopped work because of the heat. The management said everything was back to normal, and the union was monitoring the situation.

The men and women had claimed that the temperatures in the moulding and trimming sections, which were partly glass-roofed, rose to 100 degrees Fahrenheit. They walked out and went home, although a small number went back to work that day.

The heat wave being experienced in North Lincolnshire had dried up salad, raspberry and blackcurrant crops. Supplies were limited and the prices rose in reflection of this. (*Grimsby Evening Telegraph*, 1959)

‒ July 12th ‒

1906: On this day, the Kingsway, in Cleethorpes, was opened by Lady Henderson, the wife of a railway dignitary. The new sea wall was 2,000ft long, 18ft high and 7ft thick, creating more land and a secluded area in the resort. Lady Henderson used golden shears to cut a ribbon declaring this 'new' area of Cleethorpes open.

The band of His Majesty's Yorkshire Hussars led a parade, watched by crowds lining the route. Lady Henderson travelled in an open landau, accompanied by dignitaries, and attended a luncheon on the pier. For the public, three days of festivities were held. An 'improvement rate' of half a crown in the pound was levied on the properties on the Kingsway, a shilling in the pound on properties in the side streets and sixpence in the pound on a certain area of property in the rear. It is believed the cost of the scheme was about £22,000. (*Grimsby Telegraph Bygones*, 1995)

1946: On this day, first, second, third and fourth places in the Northern Counties' annual contest for the 'Airedale' Venus Trophy, held at Bradford, were won by Grimsby girls. The winner was Miss Irene Lee, of Weelsby Street, Grimsby. Second place was gained by Miss Gloria Baker, third Miss Penny Stephenson and fourth Miss Ann Hicky. (*Grimsby Evening Telegraph*, 1946)

~ July 13th ~

1870: On this day, a simple pantiled cottage and its central chimney stack which stood on the west side of Bargate, roughly where Westward Ho branches off, was sketched by artist James Jillott. Three years later, this quaint slice of Grimsby was torn down.

The cottage belonged to Tommy Wilkinson, the only Grimsby man, as far as records show, who fought at Waterloo. He's in the sketch, sitting beneath a tree, even though he died some years before Jillott, a schoolmaster, put pencil to paper. This wasn't the only bit of artistic licence Jillott used; what you cannot see in the pencil sketch is the huge hole in the back garden. Tommy had become obsessed that beneath his garden lay gold. He dug for years until infirmity halted his fruitless mining.

Jillott was the son of a baker. When nineteenth century prosperity came to the town, he made it his business to record for a grateful posterity, the old, rural, Georgian and pre-Georgian village. These works eventually passed to granddaughter Alice. To her, they were just old paper, so she used them to light fires. When she died, what remained passed to her second cousin, Edna, who steered them to the safekeeping of Welholme Galleries.

Many years later, the sketch of Tommy's cottage was found in a pile of rubbish, rescued, and added to the collection. (Alan Dowling, *Grimsby: Making The Town 1800–1914*, 2007; verbal account by Linda Roberts)

– July 14th –

2007: On this day, an empty space appeared where an iconic landmark in the borough had once stood.

The Winter Gardens, located on the seafront in Cleethorpes, was a venue the people of Grimsby and Cleethorpes were proud of. Not only did it boast appearances from bands like the Sex Pistols in its heyday, many couples met for the first time there, at its famous Melody Night. It was also the host venue for many Northern Soul gatherings.

The Winter Gardens began life as the art-deco style Olympia in 1934. It was constructed with compensation received by local railway worker George Eyre, following an accident which resulted in his legs being amputated. George's wife, Rose, owned the land. After the Second World War, it re-opened in 1946 as the Winter Gardens.

Bands that have performed there also include Queen, AC/DC, The Damned, The Stranglers, Genesis, Black Sabbath and Thin Lizzy. But it fell out of fashion and was demolished in the summer of 2007, despite a public protest. (*Grimsby Telegraph*, 2007)

~ July 15th ~

1955: On this day, the Cleethorpes Showboat officially opened. It started life as the Goodwin Sands lightship, and arrived in the resort in 1955 to be transformed into a floating restaurant, a fine attraction for the area. But the scheme proved controversial with the public, and never gained favour. It was made to look like a Mississippi showboat, something which stuck in the throat of local councillors. The beaching of the vessel took place the following April and proved to be a major operation. Crowds gathered to watch as the hulk of the old lightship, painted dark red, was hauled along the beach at high tide. It was beached at the north end of the promenade, and some councillors described it as a 'great monstrosity'. It left Cleethorpes in October, and spent the months of winter in Grimsby Docks. In April the following year, the Cleethorpes Showboat was stripped of its contents and sold off at a public auction. (*Grimsby Evening Telegraph*, 1955)

~ July 16th ~

1912: On this day, pioneering British aviator Gustav Hamel landed his aeroplane at Love Lane Corner in Grimsby, having achieved the first flight across the Humber in a stunt sponsored by the *Daily Mail*. He flew from Hull at 2,000ft to avoid sea mist, taking just sixteen minutes.

Born in 1889, Hamel was prominent in early aviation history and was taught to fly in France at the age of 21, two years before his Humber flight. His best-known exploit was a flight between Hendon and Windsor in eighteen minutes, delivering the first official airmail to the Postmaster General. Among the delivery was a postcard he had written en-route.

On January 2nd 1914, Hamel flew with Miss Trehawke Davis, and she became the first woman in the world to experience looping the loop.

He went missing over the English Channel on May 23th 1914, while returning from Paris in the new Morane-Saulnier monoplane he had just collected. In July, the crew of a fishing vessel found a body in the Channel. They did not retrieve it but the description matched that of Hamel. No trace of the aeroplane was ever found. (Grimsby Central Library)

– July 17th –

1939: On this day, snatching her three-month-old baby girl from her pram, a Grimsby woman rushed, choking from her house through clouds of soot and flying debris when the house was struck by lightning during a fierce thunderstorm. Her husband and their two other children dashed after her into the street. Slates were torn from the roof and carried 30 to 40 yards. (*Grimsby Telegraph Bygones*, 1989)

1959: On this day, Grimsby was in the midst of a printing dispute over wages which saw the *Evening Telegraph* publishing emergency news bulletins only. As a result of the dispute, falling demand for newsprint forced the management of the town's famous paper mill, Peter Dixon and Son Ltd, to cut down the working week from six days to five. It had 700 staff at the time. A director of the company, Mr A. Dixon, said, 'We have had to do this because of the trouble in the printing industry. Unfortunately, our main output is newsprint for the provincial Press. We still have small orders for emergency editions.'

The five-day week, he said, would remain in place until the mill closed for the annual fortnight's holiday, from July 19th to August 3rd. 'If the strike is still on when everyone comes back from the holidays, then it will be a very short time indeed for everyone,' Mr Dixon added. (*Grimsby Evening Telegraph*, 1959)

~ July 18th ~

1909: On this day, an unusual instrument was used to batter a man to death in an ill-lit and squalid alley. The weapon, a three-pint iron kitchen pot, provided the nickname for one of the most 'celebrated' of all Grimsby's Edwardian murder scandals. And the three brothers who committed what came to be known as The Saucepan Murder were lucky to escape the death penalty.

Their victim, Alf Day, had been living with the brothers' only sister for four years, and the brothers disliked Alf intently. On this night, Alf Day strode along the Newmarket Street footbridge. Unbeknown to him, he was watched by Alfred Ridlington, crouched in a yard off Burgess Street, holding a saucepan. In the street, Percy Ridlington was ready to give his brother the tip-off, and Thomas Ridlington loitered too.

It was about 10,30 p.m. when Alfred struck Alf over the head. The brothers beat him and then left. Alf died within twenty-four hours, and the Ridlingtons were soon arrested. They were tried for murder, and the jury took an hour to return a verdict of manslaughter. Percy and Alfred received fifteen years' penal servitude, Thomas three. (Stephen Wade, *Foul Deeds and Suspicious Deaths in Grimsby and Cleethorpes*, 2007)

– July 19th –

1928: On this day, Edward, Prince of Wales, visited Grimsby to open the new Corporation Bridge. The prince stayed at Brocklesby Hall, the home of the Earl of Yarborough, who was Lord Lieutenant of Lincolnshire.

The visit began early, arriving at the Nuns Corner Cenotaph at 8.30 a.m., where he was met by a civic party, including the mayor, Councillor K. Osmond. There, Edward laid a wreath on the Cenotaph step.

By 8.45 a.m., the prince was travelling along Hainton Avenue and Freeman Street to the Fish Docks, where he inspected a guard of honour. He also looked over a trawler on the Pontoon. He then visited Grimsby Coal Salt & Tanning Co. Ltd's net-braiding department and visited the Grimsby Ice Company.

He went on to the Queen Mary Fishermen's Hostel, in Riby Square, and by 11.45 a.m., he opened Corporation Bridge. The steamship *Marple* passed through the open bridge before it was closed again by the prince, who also unveiled a tablet on the east side of the structure. He then visited Peter Dixon's Paper Mills before lunch at the town hall.

By 2.45 p.m. he was on his way to Armstrong Street School, where he laid the foundation stone with a silver trowel. He then went to People's Park Children's Home and at 4.50 p.m., caught the train back to London. (True North Books, *More Memories of Grimsby*, 2001)

1924: On this day, Vivean Gray was born in Cleethorpes. She went on to become an actress and play one of the most iconic characters in the Australian television soap opera Neighbours – Mrs Mangel.

Throughout her early life, Vivean lived in England but moved to Australia after struggling in the acting profession here. She played the role of gossipy Nell Mangel in *Neighbours* for many years but left the soap after receiving abuse from fans who could not separate fact from fiction. In the show, her character moves to St Albans in England. In reality, Vivean returned to England and retired.

She also played Ida Jessup in *The Sullivans*, another Australian TV soap opera, for its entire run. (www.comedycentral.co.uk)

1957: On this day, idle buses and coaches were seen in picket-lined garages, and long queues at railway stations. This was the picture for most of Lincolnshire, and indeed, around the rest of the country. Lorries, vans and private cars were carrying people to work, and many towns and villages were left isolated as a big bus stoppage brought public transport to a halt.

In the local area, there was a stoppage of 1,500 men employed by the Lincolnshire Road Car Co. Ltd. About 100,000 workers employed by private companies went on strike in support of their claim for a £1-a-week pay rise. (*Grimsby Evening Telegraph*, 1957)

~ JULY 21ST ~

1955: On this day, the story of transport in Grimsby saw the opening of a revolutionary chapter when the very first of the one-man operated buses went into service.

In the beginning, the new buses only operated on the number seven route but gradually all buses were operated by the driver only. At the end of 1955, a bus driver was earning £7 19s a week; a conductor £7 14s; a mechanic £7 10s 3d; and a cleaner £7.

In about September, six trolley buses were sold for £85 each and seven double-decker buses were bought at £4,390.

With the amalgamation of Grimsby and Cleethorpes Transport in January 1957, it was decided to close the depot in Pelham Road, Cleethorpes. At the time, records show transport staff consisted of: 'Officials, office staff, inspectors etc, 30; craftsmen, 24; others, 257'. That same year, Belgrave Autos bought from the new committee five motor buses, seven trolley vehicles, one canteen van and one break down tender, for a grand total of £1,036. (*Grimsby Evening Telegraph*, 1955)

— JULY 22ND —

1912: On this day, King George V and Queen Mary boarded the royal train at King's Cross, London, and travelled north to open the new £2.6 million dock at Immingham. Built by the Great Central Railway, the first sod had been cut on July 12th 1906 by Lady Henderson, the wife of GCR's chairman. Up to 3,000 men were employed throughout construction, during which they lived in a shanty town called Humberville, nicknamed Tin Town by its inhabitants. Six million tons of earth was excavated and 700 miles of sidings laid.

The king had also agreed to tour Grimsby on the official opening day, and 100,000 people turned out to catch a glimpse of them. The train arrived at Grimsby Town station at 12.47 p.m. to a ceremony led by Lord Heneage, the High Steward of Grimsby. The mayoress presented a bouquet of flowers, arranged by Pennells, to the queen, and the couple journeyed through the streets to Grimsby Dock station, stopping to watch 10,000 schoolchildren sing the National Anthem.

They re-boarded the train and arrived in Immingham at 2.20 p.m. to a salute fired by the Royal Field Artillery. They were taken aboard the *Killingholme*, where the king pressed an electric signal to open the dock gates, and the steamer sailed in. It made a twenty-minute circuit of the dock to cheering crowds, and the royal couple then attended a reception in a pavilion erected inside the No.xxs 2 transit shed. (*Grimsby Telegraph Bygones*, 1996)

– JULY 23RD –

1936: On this day, the foundation stone of Carr Lane Council School was laid. It cost £31,250 to build and was officially opened on April 8th the following year, by Alderman J.H. Curry. He had stern words for parents:

> The teachers lay the foundation and if the parents won't help them to build on that foundation, which is a solid one, it is not their fault or the school's, or the Education Committee, but of careless, neglectful and thoughtless parents. If they sought a monument to education, let them look round Carr Lane School.

In 1949, it was said to have the most modern canteen in Grimsby. In 1950, a primary section was opened, providing 300 more places for youngsters in the borough. It later became known as Havelock School, and then Havelock Academy. (Edward Drury, *The Greater Grimsby Story*, 1990)

———

1983: On this day, a beautiful rose was blooming in the village of Ulceby – destined for the Princess of Wales. Flower grower Louie Ehret and his wife planned to present the princess with the delicate white rose fern when she paid a visit to the region in the following days. Called White Weekend, the variety was so new it had yet to be catalogued. (*Grimsby Evening Telegraph*, 1983)

~ July 24th ~

2004: On this day, the *Grimsby Telegraph* reported on the closure of Nunsthorpe Maternity Hospital as staff left the old building in Second Avenue to move to a new state-of-the-art unit. It was the end of an era for the town's midwives and nursing staff.

The hospital had been established on the estate in the late 1920s, using converted council houses. It was incorporated into a new building which opened in 1933, and was where thousands of Grimbarians took their first gulps of air.

Nunsthorpe, known locally as The Nunny, was designed before the war as a garden city in the suburbs of the western part of the town. It takes its name from the nuns who inhabited the priory of St Leonard, which stood on Nuns Corner. For centuries, the land where Nunsthorpe stands was farmed using the open field system of agriculture. Now, there are more than 2,400 properties on the estate, mostly former council homes. (*Grimsby Telegraph*, 2004)

~ JULY 25TH ~

1989: On this day, *Memphis Belle* was being filmed at RAF Binbrook, featuring a cast of extras made up of locals. But it was a drama of a different kind at the airfield which also made history.

One of the five historic B17 Flying Fortresses being used to make the movie crashed into a cornfield. The French-owned plane burst into flames and all ten on board escaped in the nick of time.

The film, set during the Second World War, was released in 1990 and tells the story of an American bombing raid in Europe. RAF Binbrook, which had closed on August 22nd 1987, was chosen as the location for filming because it had a similar layout to the original Memphis Belle base in Brassingbourne, Cambridgeshire. Alterations were carried out, including disguising modern buildings and the construction of a Second World War control tower. Grimsby locals answered the call for extras in an advert in the local newspaper. (*Grimsby Evening Telegraph*)

~ July 26th ~

1983: On this day, Princess Diana opened Grimsby District Hospital. She greeted thousands of people who turned out to see her. Among them was wheelchair-bound Doreen Richman. She said it was the most memorable day of her life because the princess kissed her on the cheek. Mrs Richman waited for six hours in Town Hall Square, hoping for a glimpse of Diana as she went on a walkabout in the town centre. She recalled: 'She stopped in front of me and held out her hand. She leaned towards me and gave me a kiss on the cheek and asked me how long I had been waiting. It lifted my spirits.'

Hospital gardener Mick McArthur was mobbed by reporters when he gave Diana a 'big, sloppy kiss'. He recalled how the site was swarming with security, so he used his inside knowledge for a sneak entry. 'I went right up to the front door, placed my bike next to me and I just stood there and she waved at everybody.'

Mr McArthur then had to wait while the Princess went into the hospital, exiting an hour later. She walked straight towards him, perhaps recognising his distinctive bike, which he had built himself. 'She just held out her hand and I kissed it. It was a big sloppy kiss!'

After her death in 2007, the hospital was renamed after Diana. Previously, protocol had not allowed the name-change. (*Grimsby Evening Telegraph*, 1983)

⹃ July 27th ⹃

2013: On this day, 92-year-old Sidney Lewis was proudly holding a medal commemorating his role in one of the longest continuous military campaigns of the Second World War. The modest pensioner was given the Arctic Star Medal, awarded by Russia to British servicemen in recognition of their bravery.

Mr Lewis, from Immingham, was badly hurt when the Battle of the Atlantic was at its height in 1943. It began in 1939 and lasted until the German surrender in 1945, and involved protecting convoys travelling mainly from North America and going to the UK or the Soviet Union.

'We often did the Murmansk run to Russia in bitterly cold weather,' he said. 'We rescued 661 men at Dunkirk. Two men on board were killed by aircraft fire and we witnessed cargo ships being sunk around us.'

On September 26th 1943, the ship he was serving on, the *Intrepid*, was sunk by German bombers in Lexus harbour. 'There was a man on fire,' he recalled. 'I was thrown overboard but got picked up by a Greek guy in a fishing boat.' On him had been two precious photographs: one of his wife Madge, the other of his ship. 'A padre came to the hospital to tell me they had picked the photographs up in the sea – it was remarkable!' he added. (*Grimsby Telegraph*, 2013)

1959: On this day, some dodgy building work from 150 years before caused a problem for a firm of Grimsby contractors. The front of Noble's confectionary shop, in Victoria Street, had to be shored up while the workers remedied the negligence of workmen of the early 1800s.

The contractors had been rebuilding the Scotch Wool shop premises and setting the front back by several feet. However, when the old front wall was demolished, it was discovered that the main beam supporting the front of Nobles had never been properly set in the dividing wall. The beam was inches too short and the job had been 'cobbled up' by setting a block in the wall and resting the end of the beam on it. The result? Lacking the support of the demolished brickwork, the wall of Nobles began to move.

'We knew it would cause trouble and we have been watching it all along,' said Mr Thompson, one of the directors of the building firm. 'So when it moved about a quarter of an inch, we were ready for it.'

Temporary support girders were put in and the wall was shored up. The old brickwork below the beam was, on this day, being removed and rebuilt 5ins in, under the end of the beam – where it should have been in the first place. (*Grimsby Evening Telegraph*, 1959)

∼ July 29th ∼

1957: On this day, Shirley Bloomer, the British, Italian and French hard courts champion, Britain's number one and a Wightman Cup veteran at the tender age of 23, returned to her home town of Grimsby to do something she hadn't done for years – play tennis.

She opened three hard courts at the Ross Group Sports Club before playing an exhibition match, which Shirley won 6-3, 6-3. To mark the occasion, both Shirley and her opponent were presented with gold wrist watches.

Shirley was born in Grimsby in 1934. She won three Grand Slam titles during her career and was the second ranked singles player in the country in 1957. She was a member of the Grimsby Town Tennis Club, which was located in College Street.

In 1959, she married Chris Brasher who helped pace Roger Bannister to running the first sub-four-minute mile in 1954. They had three children, including their daughter Kate, who played on the women's professional tennis tour in the 1980s. (*Grimsby Telegraph Bygones*, 2001)

~ July 30th ~

1961: On this day, Grimsby trawlerman Walter George wrote another heartfelt letter to his wife. His letters, which have been preserved by his family, are a fascinating snapshot of one man's life at sea. On this day, the letter, postmarked Harstad, read:

My own darling, I am writing this in some of the worst weather that I have experienced for a long time. Goodness knows when we shall start fishing. So, if we are a long time this trip, don't get downhearted or worried darling it is just part of the game.

We never seem to get used to it though do we? It will have taken us nearly six days to get to Harstad and we are calling as seawater has got into the fresh-water tanks and contaminated them. I may have a look round for a pair of those sealskin gloves that I bought before dear. How is the new telly going dear, everything OK? I don't suppose we joined the ranks of the idle rich this week did we? It would be nice if we could though.

In a later letter, Walter wrote:

My darling, I think each time I stay at home the going away is a little harder and this time I would have given anything to have stayed home with you. I know this, love grows as one gets older and my fondest dream is the time when I shall say to you 'I am not going away again darling'.

(Stan N. Allen, *Hello My Darling*, publication date unknown)

~ July 31st ~

1948: On this day, Cleethorpes' miniature railway had started to roll over a 300-yard track from the Boating Lake to the bathing pool slipway. The mayor, Councillor Frank Broddle, drove the first engine, a steam-driven miniature of the *Flying Scotsman*, under the critical eye of his 2-year-old grandson, Peter. The first passenger service began following months of work to lay the track under the supervision of Mr W. Botterill, of Botterill's Miniature Railways. (*Grimsby Evening Telegraph*, 1948)

1972: On this day, a huge search was launched off the Lincolnshire coast after a holidaymaker reported seeing a jet plane crash into the sea. An RAF helicopter and the emergency services joined in the operation, which was called off when a check was made with civilian and military airfields up and down the entire country.

One theory was that the 'plane' may have been mistaken for a missile falling from a jet using the bombing range at Theddlethorpe. Later, a sighting of what was thought to be a life raft turned out to be a piece of driftwood. (*Grimsby Evening Telegraph*, 1972)

~ August 1st ~

1877: On this day, the Yarborough Hotel was the setting for an election riot. Years after the scenes on Valentine's Day in 1862, history repeated itself, this time when Liberal Alfred Watkin was elected as Grimsby's new MP, following the death of John Chapman.

It was not a result everyone accepted. Watkin had provided transport for voters in outlying districts, whom some claimed had no business voting at all. When he went to the hotel to give his victory speech the crowd booed and shouted at him. Eventually over 1,000 people had gathered. There had been much drinking, and stones were thrown through the hotel windows.

A twenty-four-strong mob broke into the bar. Inside, Watkin and his team were armed with stair rods, pokers, fire irons and a pair of pistols. In the refreshment room, the gang drank 30 gallons of ale, a barrel of whiskey and half a barrel of port. The police were outnumbered, and a constable was knocked out during the mayhem.

The army was called in, arriving the next morning to find the mob had vanished – leaving 200 broken windows and furniture reduced to scraps. The hotel was later repaired and a stone was put on display in the Town Hall as a reminder of a remarkable day. (Grimsby Central Library)

∼ August 2nd ∼

1939: On this day, work commenced on the conversion of three Grimsby trawlers which have been purchased by the Admiralty. They were the *Dalmatia*, *Waveflower* and *Crestflower*.

Messrs J.S. Doig Ltd, of Grimsby, put in a tender for the conversion of a number of trawlers to Admiralty requirements, which was accepted. A number of additional hands were engaged by the firm to carry out the work. (*Grimsby Evening Telegraph*, 1939)

1950: On this day, damage estimated at £2,000 was caused by a torrential freak hailstorm. For half an hour, sheets of hailstones as big as moth balls battered down on the crops. Nearly 200 acres of wheat, barley and oats at a rural farm several miles from Grimsby was destroyed, the grain stripped as cleanly as if it had been threshed by a machine. In all, 90 per cent of the crop had been damaged. The farmer also discovered that four of his sheep had been killed by lightning. (*Grimsby Evening Telegraph*, 1950)

1997: On this day, the GY900 *Jubilee Quest* was launched, at a cost of £1 million. It was the first new trawler in Grimsby for ten years. (*Grimsby Telegraph*, 1997)

AUGUST 3RD

1837: On this day, Peter H. Haagensen was born. It was his interest in travel that made him journey from Norway to Grimsby, where he became a well-known businessman. In 1841, he became the Norwegian/Swedish Consul and looked after union interests within trade. He and his wife Janna, living at Spring Villas, a large house in Bargate, had four children.

Janna sadly died and Peter lost most of his fortune, probably through bad investments. He moved to Bournemouth and died there in May 1919. But he was buried in Laceby, at the highest point of the cemetery under a grand marble memorial, and his funeral was a big occasion.

Peter's son Frederick achieved fame as an established artist, staying in Italy for a time. He counted Queen Mary, Lady Chalmers of Chelsea and Princess Alice of Athlone among his admirers. The British Museum and the Victoria and Albert Museum exhibited some of his work in the 1930s.

In 1977, which was the centenary of Frederick's birth, a collection of paintings were displayed in Grimsby and in other towns. His wife, Audrey, made sure they were exhibited in Norway too. Peter's memorial became a tourist attraction in Laceby, and the Haagensens were never forgotten. (Laceby History Group, *The Chronicles of Laceby*, 1980)

– August 4th –

1904: On this day, Sidney Park in Cleethorpes was officially opened to the public. It was described by the press at the time as 'a fair garden, an old English garden such as Tennyson would have delighted in, filled with the colours of a multitude of summer flowers, the air fragrant with the perfume of the rose'. (*Grimsby Telegraph Bygones*, 2003)

1978: On this day, Grimsby lumpers answered a special SOS from a local trawler firm – almost certainly saving a £30,000 catch from rotting. They took the unusual step of agreeing to a Friday night/Saturday morning landing to clear 500 kits of fish from a Belgian trawler.

The *Atlas*, from Zeebrugge, should have landed that morning but her place in the queue was taken by a Grimsby trawler, which had a priority call on labour. Her agents tried desperately to contact the Belgian skipper to tell him not to come to Grimsby, but without avail. At one point, it looked like the Atlas would not be landed, meaning the catch would have gone rotten and ended up as fishmeal. An urgent appeal to the lumpers committee was answered when thirty volunteers agreed to land the ship late that night.

Her entire catch, which included 400 kits of plaice, was bought by one of Grimsby's biggest fish merchants, E.A. Bates Ltd. (*Grimsby Evening Telegraph*, 1978)

～ August 5th ～

1977: On this day, a 6-year-old boy was recovering from a horrific experience – which all began with a tickle under the arm. Charles Hargreaves was climbing railings to take a shortcut home through Sydney Park when a friend tickled him. Charles slipped and impaled his arm on the railings.

He was trapped for half an hour before firefighters and ambulance workers managed to cut him free. He was taken to Grimsby General Hospital by ambulance, where he had almost twenty stitches put into the wound on his left arm. After two hours at the hospital, he was allowed home – but not empty-handed. Charles left with the piece of railing as a gruesome souvenir of his ordeal.

He had a much-needed rest and the following morning told a local reporter: 'I'm all right really, but I'm not going to climb any more fences.'

His mother, Sylvia, added: 'He was so brave; I'll never forget this as long as I live.' (*Grimsby Evening Telegraph*, 1977)

~ August 6th ~

1951: On this day, Effie Lewis celebrated her 68th birthday – three days after marrying the love of her life. Hers and Frederick Parker's love story lasted half a century.

Mr Parker was introduced to Effie at the turn of the century, and, even though he was already married, the young girl stole his heart. When Effie was 21, in 1906, they embarked on a unique affair – through books. They both worked for the Britannic and through this, they bonded for life.

They declared their love for each other through inscriptions in books, given to each other as gifts. By 1933, the friends had become a familiar sight in Grimsby, doing their rounds together, a most old-fashioned couple, although Mr Parker's attentions were criticised.

In 1950, Mr Parker's wife died. In August 1951, he wed Effie at Old Clee Church – she a spinster no more, he no longer a widower. Their library of love came under one roof in Hainton Avenue, and they spent two years and one month together.

On an early autumn day in 1953, Effie said goodbye to 79-year-old Mr Parker. She continued to live in Hainton Avenue until she died, surrounded by their books, in December 1968. She was 83. (*Grimsby Evening Telegraph Bygones*; verbal account by Peter Chapman)

– August 7th –

1967: On this day, a stowaway from a far-off isle made an unexpected arrival in town – in a box of bananas. He was discovered when the box, from Jamaica, was opened in Whitewood's grocer's shop in Park Street, and although only 5ins long, he caused quite a stir. As yet unidentified, the stowaway was a millipede.

Leslie Whitehead, who owned the shop, said:

> Everyone gave it a wide berth because we weren't sure whether it was dangerous. It was about as thick as a man's finger and covered with black scales. It gave my wife and daughter the shivers every time we mentioned it, so we decided to take it to the zoo.

(*Grimsby Evening Telegraph*, 1967)

1978: On this day, a giant structure – resembling a rocket being towed to its launch pad at Cape Canaveral – crawled laboriously from Immingham Dock to Lindsey Oil Refinery. The 370-ton column, measuring 130ft long and 40ft in diameter, was thought to be the biggest load carried on Britain's roads. It was accompanied on its journey by a 270-ton regenerator and a 125-ton boiler, to be used by the refinery as part of a £7 million conversion project. (*Grimsby Telegraph Bygones*, 2008)

~ August 8th ~

1964: On this day, a local man was cleared by the courts of being drunk and disorderly. A policeman had been called to a laundry in central Grimsby and found the man in the pressing room. He had visited the premises to enquire about a suit but had become insulting. He refused to leave, so was ejected. The officer could smell alcohol on his breath and was 'unable to make sense of anything he said'.

However, he was cleared because he had only drunk two pints, and his speech was slurred because he lost his teeth in the Mediterranean during the war and had never had them replaced. (*Grimsby Telegraph Bygones*, 1994)

1983: On this day, the bravery of a docks gatekeeper was recounted on the front page of the *Grimsby Evening Telegraph*. An 8-year-old boy was only seconds away from drowning in dangerous currents at the entrance to Grimsby Fish Docks.

The small boy had been on the decking of the flood gate but tripped and fell into the dock and was being carried out into the estuary by a current of about 2 knots.

He was spotted by Paul Daniel, 29, who stripped off and dived in. The boy, who was floating face-down in the water when he was rescued, spent time in hospital before being allowed to go home to Doncaster. (*Grimsby Evening Telegraph*, 1983)

~ August 9th ~

1937: On this day, Grimsby's *Visenda* was the next vessel to make the headlines. The 455-ton trawler, measuring 162ft, was boarded by a party from an Icelandic coastguard cutter, off the south coast of Iceland, and her skipper, Martin Olsen, was charged with fishing inside Icelandic waters.

One coastguard officer was left on board the *Visenda*, and the trawler was ordered to follow the cutter into harbour. Skipper Olsen claimed that he had laid his buoy by cross bearings, on grounds he had fished many times before, and he was certain it was half a mile outside the territorial limit. The Icelandic coastguard captain claimed he had seen the *Visenda* pass inside the buoy and the skipper was promptly arrested.

Olsen knew the odds were against him in an Icelandic court so he set off at 13 knots – still with the Icelandic officer on board. The coastguard knew they wouldn't catch up with her, so put out a radio message for Olsen to give the vessel up. The call was ignored and nothing was heard from the *Visenda* for eight days, apart from a brief message to the owners of the vessel, reporting that all was well.

It transpired that the coastguard officer pleaded to be put on board an Icelandic ship instead of being taken to Grimsby. He had recently married and did not want to leave his bride. Duly deposited, the *Visenda* had resumed fishing off the east coast of Iceland and no further action was taken. (Harry C. Hutson, *Grimsby's Fighting Fleet*, 1990)

1973: On this day, it was announced that the sale of Grimsby council houses could be suspended. Faced with a dormant waiting list and a dwindling range of houses at its disposal, the Grimsby Estates Committee asked the council to take the action by October that year. Committee chairman Councillor P.R. Bemrose said, 'There has been a drop in the number of council houses coming back into the pool for re-letting and this fact, together with the general waiting list, which is dormant, calls for immediate action to preserve the number of council homes at the disposal of the committee.' (*Grimsby Evening Telegraph*, 1973)

2001: On this day, celebrity couple Christine and Neil Hamilton were arrested after being falsely accused of a sex crime by a mother-of-four from Grimsby. Nadine Milroy-Sloan was later jailed for three years for perverting the course of justice. Prior to her jailing, the Hamiltons fought back publicly, brought a libel and slander case and were paid undisclosed damages. The famous publicist Max Clifford, who represented Milroy-Sloan, withdrew 'highly offensive' comments about the issue. Mr Hamilton, an ex-Tory minister, and his wife had never met the woman.

The ordeal didn't put them off from visiting Grimsby. At a social function where Mrs Hamilton was a guest speaker, she told a local reporter: 'Despite those tough times, we've had fun over the years.' (*Grimsby Telegraph*, 2006)

1945: On this day, Irene Walker walked up the aisle at St Mary's, in Grimsby, to meet her husband-to-be, Jack Barrett – a perfect example of love on the coupon.

Tradition demands that every bride should have something borrowed on her wedding day, but Irene just about borrowed everything! Her dress had already seen two weddings, and was to see at least three more. The bridesmaids' dresses were on loan from Jack's relations in London and the cake was decidedly 'black market'.

Irene grew up in Hope Street, worked in the laundry at Scartho Road Hospital and met Jack at a dance. She had been engaged to an airman at one time, but went to a fortuneteller with a friend, who told her she hadn't yet met the man she'd marry. 'And when you do,' she was told, 'you will carry red roses.'

'That was in the March,' said Irene. 'I met Jack in May, he proposed in June and we were married in August. And I carried roses.'

At the time, Jack was in the Royal Navy, working in stores at Immingham, and what civilians couldn't buy, the navy could usually get its hands on. So the couple's reception, at rooms in Pasture Street, was a success.

'We managed to get half a barrel of beer and just half a bottle of gin,' recalled Irene.

The couple, who went on to have four sons and one daughter, progressed to running a family wine business in Victor Street. (*Grimsby Telegraph Bygones*, 1985)

~ AUGUST 12TH ~

1946: On this day, there was a sale at the Augusta Street Barracks. Unwanted Civil Defence items went under the hammer, and scores of people flocked to the barracks to buy items which were otherwise unavailable or out of their usual price range. The war was over but it was difficult to get hold of some of the basic necessities for setting up a home. Furniture, mattresses and bedding were still strictly rationed, which explains why a sale was so successful.

Easy chairs, for example, had a 'controlled price' of £7 10s, one and a half times as much as a labourer on the fish docks earned in a week. So it explains why two dozen easy chairs – described as being somewhat worse for wear and a bit battered – quickly sold out at 17s 6d each. A total of twenty-six camp beds were sold for £1 each, and canvas beds for 5s. Six mattresses went for 27s 6d, feather pillows at 9s a pair (no more than one pair per buyer was allowed) and blankets were sold for just a few shillings each. (*Grimsby Telegraph Bygones*, 1985)

~ August 13th ~

1946: On this day, squatters moved into the old RAF camp at Waltham – starting a squatting movement across the area.

The end of the war brought with it a housing crisis, the like of which Britain had never seen before. The homes bombed and damaged were a major factor, but the war also coincided with the end of the useful life of thousands of back-to-back properties. The replacement of those had begun in the 1930s but the shortage of manpower and building material in the post-war years, together with the wedding rush and baby boom, created an almost impossible situation.

Within weeks, Waltham's old RAF base was home to more than three dozen families, some of whom stayed for almost four years. The family who started the squatting movement were stopped from moving their furniture into one of the huts off Ings Lane by the local miller, who owned the land and realised that if they moved in, his chance of getting it back was slim. The husband and wife, who had both served in the forces, left. By the following night, dozens of people had converged there with their possessions, determined to move in.

Each hut was sufficiently large to accommodate two families, and the authorities decided not to impose their powers of eviction. (*Grimsby Telegraph Bygones*, 1985)

~ August 14th ~

1930: On this day in 1930, a report was released containing information about an accident at Grimsby railway station on July 15th which had resulted in some passengers being sent to hospital. The report into what happened was published by the Ministry of Transport for public consumption.

The original document was a bound volume and comprised of five pages detailing the particulars. Now, the Office of Rail Regulation keeps an electronic version of it. It read:

> While the 7.33am up passenger train, Sheffield to Cleethorpes, was standing at the up platform, the 9.50am up passenger train from New Holland to Cleethorpes ran into the rear of it. Three of the company's servants were injured, but only one, the guard of the New Holland train, left duty. Fifty-two passengers complained at the time of shock or injury, of whom only seven were detained in hospital. Fifteen other passengers subsequently made complaints in this respect, making a total of 67 in all.

(Office of Rail Regulation)

~ August 15th ~

2012: On this day, preparations were underway to unveil Dudley the donkey, a new statue on Cleethorpes seafront, in memory of former Mayor Gladys Nuttall.

The late Gladys, affectionately known to children as The Donkey Lady, and her husband Buster offered donkey rides along the beach for many years. After she passed away in 2011, aged 85, the sculpture of one of her donkeys, Dudley, was commissioned in her memory.

Her friends and family gathered for the official unveiling ceremony of the statue, created by local artist Donnas Peterson, and the explanatory information board and cast-iron plaque, made by Fowler and Holden.

At the time, her son John said, 'Donkeys are in our family's legacy, and it is unbelievable to get something that looks so good. It is the best tribute my mum could get and I wish she could be here to see it.' (*Grimsby Telegraph*, 2012)

~ August 16th ~

1951: On this day, Grimsby woman Brenda Fisher swam the English Channel – becoming a world record-breaker in the process.

She was born in 1927, the daughter of a Grimsby trawler skipper, and learned to swim at the age of 9. She found she had a talent for speed swimming, but developed an interest in distance swimming, under the tutorship of Herbert McNally.

On this day, she became the twenty-third swimmer of the English Channel from France to England, completing in a record women's time of twelve hours and forty-two minutes – seventy-three minutes faster than the previous women's record set by Jenny James. She won the first prize – £1,000 from the *Daily Mail* who sponsored the race.

She went on to swim the Channel again in 1954 (as part of the Billy Butlin Cross Channel International Swim) and was the first woman ashore. Two years later, she won the 29-mile River Nile swim in the fastest recorded time, followed by the 32-mile Lake Ontario swim. This epic journey, from Niagara to Toronto, took Brenda eighteen hours and fifty minutes. She beat the record held by Marilyn Bell by two hours and six minutes – the third person in history to complete the swim.

Brenda, who was married to footballer Paddy Johnson, retired and became a swimming teacher. (*Grimsby Evening Telegraph*, 1951)

~ August 17th ~

1868: On this day, more than 50,000 people gathered to witness the first launch of the twelve-oared lifeboat, *Manchester Unity*. It was named after its sponsor, The Loyal Fishermen's Rest Lodge No. 1,807 of the Manchester Unity of Odd Fellows. A branch had been established in Cleethorpes about thirty years before. A lifeboat station had been constructed in Cleethorpes following requests from locals, and almost immediately, the Life Boat Inn was opened nearby, by the enterprising Charles Day, proprietor of the Queen's Hotel in Itterby. In its lifetime at Cleethorpes, the boat was launched twenty-four times and saved thirty-five lives. It and the station were transferred to Grimsby in 1882. (*Grimsby Telegraph Bygones*, 2006)

1883: On this day, the jewel in Grimsby's crown – People's Park – was officially opened by the Duke and Duchess of Connaught. The 27 acres had been presented to the people of Grimsby by MP Edward Heneage, and the Corporation spent £6,000 transforming it into parkland for all to enjoy. It included a 2-acre ornamental lake, a pavilion for refreshments, a bowling green, a cricket ground, tennis courts and a bandstand, much of which still exists today.

To mark the 80th birthday of Queen Victoria, the Queen's Observatory was built there. It measured 50ft tall and had a balcony atop a climb of eighty steps. (Ivan E. Broadhead, *Portrait of Humberside*, 1983)

— AUGUST 18TH —

1874: On this day, Fred Longmate, a wholesale grocer, was bitten by an errant dog. He wrote to the *Grimsby Observer*, explaining the remedy administered after his ordeal.

I was bitten by a mad fox terrier in six places. I went dizzy, the wounds were cauterised and I suffered excruciating pain. The huntsman at Brocklesby Hall, a Nimrod Long, said a remedy in the hands of Mr Smith, of Ulceby Skitter, had been handed down as a family heirloom and so I went to Ulceby, where my wounds were washed with vinegar and warm water for an hour. I was then told to take a dose of nearly a gill of thick, warm brick dust, skilly flavoured with beer and ugh, I did not know what to do. After persuasion, I drank and was then given an onion to run my hands and face with. Next I was told to fast for 12 hours, have no tea or milk, but I could drink beer and have a mutton chop. My wounds were then dressed again with a kind of brick dust after being washed again in vinegar, and I was charged one guinea.

(*Grimsby Observer*, 1874)

~ AUGUST 19TH ~

1940: On this day, almost a year after the declaration of the Second World War, four high-explosive bombs fell in the Wellowgate area of Grimsby – claiming the first civilian casualty in Grimsby.

At 10.24 p.m. the previous night, the sirens sounded and most people went to their shelters. The North family, of Abbey Drive West, was among them. Fred made sure his wife Ruth and daughter Barbara were safely in the shelter with his two neighbours. Then he walked to the front gate to see what was happening. Seconds later, a single German raider dropped a stick of bombs.

The first bomb hit Treadgolds laundry and the second hit the home of Nat Blau, in Abbey Drive East. The third hit Fred's home, killing him instantly. The fourth caused considerable damage to other homes in that area. Fred was to be the first of more than 180 Grimsby men, women and children who died in air raids. (Edward Drury, *The Greater Grimsby Story*, 1990; *Grimsby Telegraph Bygones*, 1997)

~ August 20th ~

1983: On this day, the first broadcast of Radio Caroline from on board the Grimsby vessel the MV *Ross Revenge* was made. A commercial trawler, she was bought in August 1963 by Ross Fisheries and registered as GY 718.

In the 1970s, she was involved in the famous Cod Wars, and in 1976 she gained the world record for the biggest catch when she landed 3,000 kits – about 218 tonnes – of Icelandic cod at Grimsby. It sold for a record price of £75,597. But it was when she became home to the pirate radio station that her fame truly began.

In the early 1980s, she was kitted out as a radio ship, complete with 300ft antenna mast and 50kW transmitter. It was the tallest radio mast ever fitted to a ship.

Broadcasts began on this day in 1983; the final pirate broadcast took place in November 1990. She ran aground at Goodwin Sands a year later, but was salvaged and maintained by the Caroline Support Group, a group of supporters and enthusiasts.

In August 2004, she was used for legitimate Radio Caroline while berthed on the Thames at Tilbury, funded by the UK National Lottery. Restoration work on the *Ross Revenge* has been ongoing. (www.offshoreradio.co.uk.)

– August 21st –

2000: On this day, a freak tornado up to 100ft high swept down the Humber. The giant twister sucked up water from the river as it swirled in a northerly direction for about fifteen minutes, narrowly missing land.

The gaze of hundreds of locals and visitors turned seaward as the funnel cloud touched the Humber Estuary, forming a towering tornado over the mouth of the river. The Humber Coastguard kept an eye on the natural phenomenon, which was dying down and resurfacing on a regular basis as it made its way along the coast. A twister can cause problems at sea, particularly if it strikes vessels. Luckily, the Humber's tornado caused no harm at all.

One eyewitness said, 'At first I thought a plane had gone down; then I realised it was a water spout. It was all frothy at the bottom and went up, as black as your hat.' The tornado was the peak of bizarre weather conditions, which included ferocious hail storms, prolonged thunder and lightning strikes, and thick fog – all within twenty-four hours. (*Grimsby Telegraph*, 2000)

~ AUGUST 22ND ~

1935: On this day, Haydn Taylor swam the Channel. Born in Sheffield, he became a dentist in Cleethorpes, but he was equally well-known for his feats of endurance in the water. He set off on this day from Cap Grisnez, near Calais, at 1.35 a.m. and arrived just west of Dover at 4.23 p.m. The crossing, of fourteen hours and forty-eight minutes, was, at the time, the eighth fastest ever recorded.

Hadyn was also the first man to swim the River Humber. A keen athlete, he served with the City Battalion in the First World War and was wounded on the first day of the Battle of the Somme. He died in 1962. (*Grimsby Evening Telegraph*, 1935)

1998: On this day, lone sailor Derek Tuke's attempt to sail from Grimsby to America for his daughter's wedding ended in a dramatic rescue in stormy seas off the Lincolnshire coast. The 65-year-old mariner was just five days into his ambitious voyage when his 18ft yacht developed mechanical problems in bad weather near Norfolk and was forced to turn back to port. He was rescued off Spurn Point. He had been confident of arriving in Ohio by October 30th for the wedding, even turning down a Concorde flight to get there. (*Grimsby Telegraph*, 1998)

2013: On this day, a 13-year-old boy faced the wrath of his mother after police officers told her he was responsible for a spate of attacks on the donkeys on Cleethorpes beach.

The animals had for years provided pleasure rides to children along the sand, and rested at night in a field nearby.

There was public uproar when it was reported that youngsters had been seen assaulting the donkeys. They were seen wrestling two of the animals in headlocks and kicking them in the face and hitting them with pieces of wood. They even gave them beer to drink. (*Grimsby Telegraph*, 2013)

1967: On this day, it was revealed that Britain's first training trawler could be operating out of Grimsby by the end of next month – if the scheme got the go-ahead from the port's fishing chiefs. The *Ross Mallard* had recently been converted to carry ten trainee fishermen. Now Ross Group had offered to charter the vessel to the Grimsby Fishing Vessel Owners' Association. (*Grimsby Evening Telegraph*, 1967)

~ August 24th ~

1948: On this day, the *Grimsby Telegraph* reported on the gifting of Weelsby Woods to the public. The beauty spot was donated to residents by Fred Parkes, one of the wealthiest fishing magnates in the town's history. He was chairman and managing director of the Boston Deep Sea Fishing and Ice Company, and gave almost 150 acres of the wooded Weelsby old Hall Estate which was, at the time, on the outskirts of the town.

The gift was on agreement that: the lands hall be preserved perpetually as an open space; that no trees shall be felled or lopped 'except where absolutely necessary'; that no buildings, other than shelters and public conveniences, shall be erected on the land.

The woods and parkland were part of a 1,574 acre estate bought by Mr Parkes in 1942. He sold 36 acres on the north side of Weelsby Road as a housing site, and 22 acres in the Love Lane corner area. (*Grimsby Evening Telegraph*, 1948)

~ August 25th ~

1922: On this day, a famous Grimsby landmark met an unexpected and incredibly dramatic end. The Hippodrome Theatre was erected in the 1890s at the east end of Newmarket Bridge, on Railway Street in Grimsby. Formerly the Grimsby & Cleethorpes Circus Co. Ltd, it was pre-fabricated and clad in iron sheets but decorated inside.

By 1909, it was showing a form of cine-variety entertainment known as bio-tableaux; when films were screened, it became known as the Picturedrome, and the Hippodrome when live shows were staged.

On August 25th 1922, the Hippodrome was gutted by fire – the film showing at the time was called *The Vital Spark*. It was eventually demolished, and the site was later used as commercial premises.

In the early 1900s, Grimbarians were somewhat spoilt for choice when it came to entertainment. There was the Prince of Wales Theatre in Freeman Street, the Tivoli Theatre in Duncombe Street, the Palace Theatre of Varieties in Victoria Street North, and the Empire Music Hall in Lower Spring Street. Then came more – the Picture Playhouse in Kent Street, the Strand on the corner of Hamilton Street and Park Street, and the Paragon Picture Pavilion in Corporation Road. (www. grimsbytelegraph.co.uk; www.rodcollins.com)

~ August 26th ~

1976: On this day, a Grimsby man fled from his burning bungalow in his underclothes and watched helplessly as the uninsured building was razed to the ground. Fisherman James Love, of Victor Street, had bought the £3,000 holiday home on the Humberston Fitties chalet park only a few months before. It had just been fitted with £1,000 worth of carpets.

The Fitties has an interesting history. According to research, the first known reference to an actual bungalow there was made in 1921, but it had long been used for camping. The advent of the First World War saw the military take over the area. The 3rd Battalion of the Manchester Regiment trained recruits for active service, helped wounded men recover and guarded the coastline between Cleethorpes and Tetney Lock. Trenches were dug and soldiers would practise bayonet fighting and musketry. To relax, every Sunday evening, the battalion band gave concerts on the pier and played sports.

After the war, the campers returned to the area, pitching tents to enjoy what summer had to offer in the resort. In later years, many campers recall playing in the trenches and dug-outs created by the military during the conflict. (*Grimsby Evening Telegraph,* 1976; verbal account by Peter Chapman)

1946: On this day, Waltham showed how grateful it was to its sons and daughters who served their country during the Second World War. When they returned home, they were each presented with £4. There was £4 too for the men who had defended Waltham in the village's Home Guard unit.

All the money had been raised by a special Welcome Home committee. Their fund wound up on this day, and had raised £108 through dances, whist drives and other social events. Home Guard men received the cash and the balance was handed over to the Welcome Home Fund.

The real celebrations were on September 19th, when most of the village's ex-servicemen and women, together with friends and family, gathered at Ross Hall for the official welcome back to the village.

A total of 172 men and women received their £4 gift – not far short of an average week's wage – and entertainment was provided by the Ranco Dance Band. Tributes were paid to the seven men who did not return, and their names were inscribed on the village's war memorial. (*Grimsby Evening Telegraph*, 1946)

August 28th

1962: On this day, Sub-Officer Walter Frederick Robinson answered a call to a fire aboard the *Shearbill*, a Grimsby-registered steam trawler berthed in the Fish Dock. He soon found himself walking into a potential death trap to save the life of a young colleague who hadn't been long in the fire brigade. He recalled:

> The chief decided it would be an experience for him to go down into the hold. I was at the top when, suddenly, I heard a thud. I looked through the smoke and all I could see was the young lad's boots on the floor. I had to crawl over him to turn him round and get him to the foot of the ladder, during which I lost my breathing apparatus.

As he heaved the 6ft tall, heavily built unconscious fireman, called Stephen Nicholson, through the only exit, Walter realised he could become trapped in the smoke-filled engine room. 'They got him out, and somebody hauled me out. The chief put his arm around me and said, "I'm proud of you". Then the lights went out!'

Walter was awarded the British Empire Medal for gallantry in April 1963. (*Grimsby Evening Telegraph*, 1962; www.grimsbytelegraph. co.uk)

~ August 29th ~

1935: On this day, heavy thunderstorms caused chaos in Grimsby. As the storms broke over the town and the wider district, two houses were struck by lightning and a 2ft hole was torn in the roof of No. 9 Reporto Avenue, the home of Mrs F.C. Bridges. At No. 17 Garner Street, the home of Joseph Freshney, a hole was ripped in the outer wall, scattering plaster and brick into the house and igniting a gas pipe, which was extinguished by Mr Freshney's daughter. The cellar of the Red Lion Hotel, in Freeman Street, was flooded, and at the Prince of Wales Theatre, water poured from the roof through the floor of the gallery, into the circle. (*Grimsby Telegraph Bygones* 1996; verbal account by Stuart Russell)

1969: On this day, treacherous and wild weather struck yet again. Wind and tide damage at Cleethorpes spelled disaster for beach traders, who could only stand by and watch as their stalls were demolished and washed away in the high tide. Amusements, including the big wheel and helter-skelter on the sand, were threatened and the children's dodgems were ruined when the foundations were washed away. (*Grimsby Evening Telegraph*, 1969)

~ August 30th ~

1971: On this day, a Bible taken from the body of a Cleethorpes soldier on the battlefield at Granderaux, France, in 1916, turned up at his home in Lovett Street – fifty-five years after his death.

It belonged to Private Lee Grimble, of 15 Platoon, D Company, 8th Gloucester Regiment, and when he was killed on November 26th 1916, the Bible was collected by a German soldier. After handing in Private Grimble's other documents, the German, who by now was 81, kept the Bible at his home. But by a strange twist of fate, Mr J. McIntosh, of Renfrewshire in Scotland – who had no connection with the Grimble family – met the ex-soldier while he was on holiday in Germany.

While the two men exchanged war talk, the German produced the YMCA-issued Bible and asked Mr McIntosh to send it back to the address in Cleethorpes which had been printed on the back.

Quite why the German veteran had kept it with him all this time is unclear. But it was to be a happy reunion as the house in Lovett Street was still occupied by a Grimble – Herbert, the British soldier's brother. (*Grimsby Telegraph Bygones*, 2005)

~ August 31st ~

1976: On this day, the construction of the Humber Bridge was delayed by three months, and the estimated cost of the entire project increased by £3.5 million. The clerk of the bridge board, Mr Haydon Glen, said that the predicted cost of the scheme, calculated precisely to that very day, had risen to £54,386,000 thanks to inflation. That compared with £50,900,000 estimated at the end of February. The super structure was officially opened by the queen on June 24th 1981, in debt to the tune of £151 million.

Passenger ferries crossing the river ceased on the same day, three of the most famous ferries being the paddle steamers *Lincoln Castle*, *Tattershall Castle* and *Wingfield Castle*.

The bridge remained a structural wonder, with its world record-breaking span of 1,410m. It lost the record some years later to a bridge in Japan, which spanned 1,990m long.

When it first opened, it was being used by about 700 vehicles a day. By 1997, that had increased to 19,000, and had tallied up an impressive 60 million crossings. Despite the bridge making a substantial operating profit every year, the income was never enough to cover loan charges. That is until recently, when the government agreed to wipe some of the outstanding debt. (*Grimsby Evening Telegraph*, 1976)

— September 1st —

2003: On this day, former staff of Peter Dixon's paper mill were preparing to gather together and mark thirty years since its closure.

The family enterprise of Peter Dixon and Son (Holdings) Ltd was among the finest and most respected Grimsby companies, and the country's third largest producer of newsprint. At the height of its success the firm was one of Grimsby's largest employers (certainly the largest employer on the West Marsh in its day) and is remembered fondly by those who worked there. Nearly every family living nearby had a relative who worked there or who had a large roll of Dixon's greaseproof paper in the pantry.

Scottish Peter Dixon had been making paper since 1866. In 1871, his son Joseph joined the firm, earning 8*s* a week, and founded the mill in Grimsby. It operated successfully for decades, and was floated on the Stock Exchange in 1958. It was the subject of a £4 million expansion in the early 1960s and suffered a devastating fire in 1970. It survived for three more years, closing down in 1973, with the loss of more than 800 jobs, after months of speculation, negotiation and rising debts. Grimsby's MP at the time, Antony Crosland, called it a 'national disaster'.

Since its closure, former staff regularly organised reunions to talk over old times and fond memories. (*Grimsby Telegraph*, 2003)

~ SEPTEMBER 2ND ~

1873: On this day, Freeman Street Market opened. The freemen of the town laid out the East Marsh area of Grimsby for construction in 1959, and an area was mapped out for a market on Freeman Street, but nothing came of it. By the 1870s, residents were demanding that a market was created.

There had been an ongoing row between the Corporation and the freemen about an acre of disused land in the East Marsh, which both said they owned. The Pastures Committee proposed that the Corporation should sell the land and use the proceeds to construct a market square on the designated land in Freeman Street. In return, the freemen offered to let go of any interests or rights they had. The plan was accepted, and the sale of the land netted £862. This cash paid for the market square's construction, and on this day, the market officially opened. (*Grimsby Telegraph Bygones*, 2001)

1978: On this day, the former Oxford Cinema burned down. Built in Oxford Street, Grimsby, in 1920, you could be admitted to the Oxford for a penny, and you were given an apple or an orange as you entered. For a time, there was no floor; the wooden benches were placed on dry soil. It was not until the cinema was renovated as the New Oxford in about 1930 that a proper floor was installed. Known locally as The Ocky, it did not remain long and the final curtain was in November 1931. (Stuart Russell, *Memory Lane Grimsby*, 1999)

– September 3rd –

1945: On this day, all butcher's shops in Grimsby were closed and would not be opening until the following morning. Practically all of the butchers had gone to Blackpool to witness the installation of the Mayor of Grimsby, Alderman C.W. Hewson, as president of the National Federation of Meat Traders. Although some of the local traders had not made the journey west, all of them agreed to close for three days. (*Grimsby Telegraph Bygones* 1940s edition, 1985)

1963: On this day, two police officers and Grimsby's Deputy Chief Fire Officer won a battle in the early hours … a battle of persuasion enacted 150ft above the ground.

A man was threatening to jump from the control box of a crane, and for more than three hours, the rescuers perched precariously while they talked to him. The crane towered above some multistorey flats being built in Albert Street. At the height of the drama, the watching crowd below had swelled to 3,500 people. To disperse them, officers covered a detective in a coat and bundled him into a car. Convinced the man had come down, the crowd left. The decoy worked, and the man eventually came down to safety, relatively unharmed. (*Grimsby Telegraph*, 1963)

~ September 4th ~

1961: On this day, residents of Grimsby who used the Grimsby-Immingham Tramway found themselves paying higher fares. Earlier in the year, the tramway had been granted a reprieve from closure by the Eastern Area Board of the British Transport Commission. A reduced service, limited to peak periods, was also imposed during September 1961, but tickets could also be used on the buses. A statement read: 'The Area Board ... will do its best to ensure that the real difficulties of financing and maintaining the tram service are overcome, so that the necessity to return with a proposal for closure earlier than now envisaged can be avoided.'

Grimsby's Town Clerk, Mr F.W. Ward, said, 'Now that we know the days of the light railway are numbered, the council will renew its efforts to persuade the Minister of Transport to make an early start on the direct road between Grimsby and Immingham, which has become even more urgent with this news.' (*Grimsby Evening Telegraph*, 1961)

1959: On this day, there was relief in the homes of two families. They and the police had been out all night, searching for two missing young boys – but the children had merely been camping out, sleeping on old bags placed over leaves on the grass. They were fine but had not asked their parents because they thought they wouldn't have been given permission. (*Grimsby Telegraph Bygones*, 1986)

— September 5th —

1959: On this day, The Plaza, in Cleethorpe Road, closed its doors after twenty-five years of trading. It had replaced an earlier cinema, The Premier, which had been destroyed by a fire in the 1930s. The Plaza became an electrical warehouse for some time and is now home to a theatre. (Stuart Russell, *Memory Lane Grimsby*, 1999)

1963: On this day, an 8-year-old boy was nursing a broken arm – after falling the 20ft from underneath the pier pavilion, on the promenade, on to the beach below. The accident happened while he was playing on the beach with his older brother. He wandered off and decided to embark on a climbing expedition underneath the pier. On one of the pipes he slipped and fell to the ground below, escaping a more serious injury. Thankfully, the tide was out.

An eagle-eyed passer-by spotted the incident and raised the alarm. The boy was treated at hospital and posed, grinning, for the local newspaper cameraman with his arm in a sling. (*Grimsby Evening Telegraph*, 1963)

1973: On this day, a 60-year-old woman died after being found injured in the forehold of the Grimsby trawler *Rhodesian*. The trawler, lying at the North Wall, was due to sail later that day for the Faroes. A police investigation was launched but sadly the findings are untraceable. (*Grimsby Evening Telegraph*, 1973)

~ September 6th ~

1904: On this day, Agnes Turner was murdered by her husband, George. He was a Cockney, and fell for Agnes, a wayward girl with an illegitimate child. They married in London in 1901 and came to Grimsby, where George found work as a deckhand.

When George was away, Agnes accompanied other men, settling for a fisherman called Brown. Finding his house empty when he came home from one trip, George traced Agnes to a house on the West Marsh. Brown was not there and the meeting was surprisingly amicable, the couple taking supper with Agnes's daughter and her sister, Annie.

The couple went to sleep, with Annie downstairs. However, at 7 a.m., George called to Annie, telling her that he had killed Agnes. Annie found a policeman, who gave George mustard and water to counter the laudanum he had taken to kill himself.

At his trial, the judge said George, 23, was a kindly, generous man. George said he'd pleaded with Agnes to give Brown up, but she refused, suggesting they live together when Brown was away, but that George find somewhere else to live when Brown was home. He drank the laudanum in front of her, but Agnes still said she liked Brown better. George then caught Agnes by the throat and 'held her tighter than I thought'.

He was convicted of manslaughter and given seven years' penal servitude. (Stephen Wade, *Foul Deeds and Suspicious Deaths in Grimsby and Cleethorpes*, 2007)

~ SEPTEMBER 7TH ~

1908: On this day, a snapshot of life in 1908 is provided by a local newspaper. In the pages of the *Grimsby Evening Telegraph*, the Yarborough Hotel was advertising lunches at half a crown, while the owners of a five-bedroom house in Littlefield Lane were asking £375 for the property and visitors to Cleethorpes were paying 8*s* a week for apartments.

The Prince of Wales Theatre and The Palace were showing drama and variety respectively. The Highways Committee were discussing trams which frequently blocked traffic in Freeman Street. Fishing was very poor and some trawlers were making only about £7 profit per trip. And unemployment was rife; pawnbrokers extensively advertised their services. (*Grimsby Evening Telegraph*, 1908)

1936: On this day, another Grimsby fishing vessel came to grief on the treacherous coast of Iceland. The *Trocadero* was wrecked at Grondavik on her outward journey to the Greenland fishing grounds. The *Trocadero* carried a crew of fourteen, of whom thirteen were from Grimsby, and all were rescued by means of the life-saving apparatus. (*Grimsby Evening Telegraph*, 1936)

~ September 8th ~

1956: On this day, townsfolk were enjoying the last day of the Grimsby Docks Centenary Exhibition. It was the largest fishing exhibition ever seen in Britain, featuring two trawlers, an RNLI lifeboat, two Royal Navy ships, and warships from Belgium, Poland, Holland and Sweden. The highlight was Donald Campbell's *Bluebird*. Campbell held eight world speed records in the 1950s and 1960s, and officially opened the event on September 1st. (*Grimsby Evening Telegraph*, 1956)

1979: On this day, a pet Siamese cat had been killed and hung from the handle of a local gamekeeper's door – sparking fears that it may be a kind of curse. The cat, belonging to a local family, had disappeared earlier in the week, as the harvest was coming to an end. They thought the cat was out hunting, but they were distraught to learn of his macabre end. It was not unknown for corpses of animals to be left on doorsteps in this manner by travellers as a warning. (*Grimsby Evening Telegraph*, 1979)

~ SEPTEMBER 9TH ~

1914: On this day, the Mayor of Grimsby sent out an appeal for men to fight in the First World War. This was the beginning of the Grimsby Chums – the name given to the Pals battalion of Kitchener's Army raised in and around Grimsby.

It began with the headmaster of Wintringham Grammar raising a 250-strong group of former pupils. When others expressed a wish to join, the process was handed to the town council, and men from as far away as Boston were accepted. When it was taken over by the army, it was named the 10th Battalion, The Lincolnshire Regiment.

The battalion first saw action in the Battle of the Somme. On the first day, the Grimsby Chums were in the first wave attacking the fortified village of La Boisselle. The only officer to make it into the German trenches was Second Lieutenant Harold P. Hendin, who led five men to the German reserve trench and held off a series of German counter-attacks before having to retire. Overall, the Chums suffered 502 casualties that day; 15 officers and 487 other ranks. Only two of the officers came back unwounded, and only about 100 men. (Peter Chapman, *Grimsby's Own: The Story of the Chums*, 1991)

— September 10th —

1953: On this day, a Grimsby yachtsman and his friend were landed at the Royal Dock, in the early hours, having been saved from certain death by pure chance. The men were dramatically plucked from the River Humber after clinging for twenty minutes to their capsized sailing dinghy a mile and a half off the Cleethorpes coastline.

In rough, wind-tossed waters, the pair – both non-swimmers – had kept close together, gripping to the side of the upturned boat with their fingers. One sent signals of distress towards the shore by waving his free arm.

Just as hope seemed to be fading, they were spotted by a War Department tug coming from Grimsby to Bull Fort. The vessel was making an unexpected non-routine trip, so it was only by chance that the men were rescued. (*Grimsby Evening Telegraph*, 1953)

1976: On this day, police and local authority workmen patrolled parts of the area, as the town prepared for a possible repeat of the flooding which ruined dozens of homes earlier in the year. Despite the combination of strong winds and a high tide the evening before, the sea defences stood firm; there was only minor structural damage and no reports of flooding. (*Grimsby Evening Telegraph*, 1976)

— September 11th —

1999: On this day, the Hon. Alexandra Shackleton officially named a Grimsby ship. She renamed former Norwegian ship the *Polar Queen* in honour of her famous grandfather, Ernest Shackleton, at a ceremony attended by dignitaries.

The RRS *Ernest Shackleton*, based in Grimsby, was replacing the British Antarctic Survey's *Bransfield*, which for thirty years sailed out of the port on her long trek to those in hospitable polar waters.

Grimsby-born Captain Stuart Lawrence, who had received an MBE for his services to Antarctic expeditions, was to continue at the helm of the vessel, taking vital supplies to Antarctic stations. He had already completed one voyage on the *Shackleton*, which would have been renamed in 1998 were it not for licensing problems in the Falkland Islands.

Miss Shackleton told how she had been present, as a young girl, at the naming of the first RRS *Ernest Shackleton*, also owned by the British Antarctic Survey: 'my grandfather would have been the first to the South Pole but turned back because he could not guarantee the safety of his men. In a letter to my grandmother, he wrote: "Darling, I thought you would rather have a live donkey than a dead lion".' (*Grimsby Telegraph*, 1999)

— September 12th —

2007: On this day, one of the largest fires ever seen in Grimsby broke out. It was such a spectacle that people brought deckchairs to the cordon, settled down and handed out sandwiches and hot drinks among themselves, in a prime spot to view any action.

Arsonists – suspected to be six local lads – had sparked the blaze at the enormous Birds Eye factory, in Ladysmith Road. The building, which towered over the neighbourhood, had been empty since 2005, when Birds Eye moved out, with the loss of 650 jobs. It had been making fish fingers there since 1929 and was a landmark brand in the town.

At its height, about eighty firefighters tackled the blaze, which broke out shortly after 7 p.m. Several explosions went off and nearby residents were asked to leave their homes. They were taken to the King George V sports stadium nearby, but allowed to return once the flames were under control.

Although a cordon was put in place, the emergency services could not prevent the public from gathering. The atmosphere became jovial, with cheers and rounds of applause when parts of the building melted and collapsed. Following the fire, the construction was demolished and the site has stood empty since. (*Grimsby Telegraph*, 2007)

~ September 13th ~

1995: On this day, indie pop band Blur gave a whole new meaning to Cleethorpes rock. Hundreds of fans screamed, clapped and cheered as their heroes stormed through a dazzling ninety-minute set at Cleethorpes Pier.

Their appearance was part of a UK-wide end-of-pier tour, and fans couldn't believe their luck. They had queued for hours to catch a glimpse of the stars, and their luxury coach finally arrived at 4 p.m. Police horses were dispatched to make sure the gig-goers got safely inside the pier, but they were not needed, with young and old making their way in peacefully.

The four-times Brit Award winners proved to Cleethorpes just why they were the country's best, and Blur's performance there was a family affair for lead singer Damon Albarn. His cousins and his aunt, the Drings, of Market Rasen, joined the crowd at the biggest night of the year so far. The family had a farm near Market Rasen, which had long been a retreat for Damon from the spotlight. The young star had also been known to frequent public houses in Louth when staying at the farm. (*Grimsby Telegraph*, 1995)

~ September 14th ~

2002: On this day, Grimsby artist Colin Carr passed away, aged 73. His unique paintings, full of character and often containing a small black cat, are popular among collectors and have sold for thousands of pounds.

Mr Carr was born in Grimsby in 1929 and brought up on the Nunsthorpe Estate. He studied at Grimsby School of Art, and was the editor of *Lincolnshire Life* and art editor of *This England*. Hundreds of editions of the latter contain prints of his work. Married to Olive, the keen antiques collector became known for painting Lincolnshire scenes and did most of his work in the 1970s and 1980s.

His talent is represented in several public and private collections. Margaret Thatcher had one, and he was once presented to the queen and the Duke of Edinburgh, when one of his paintings was presented by the Chief Constable of Lincolnshire to the royal couple at the opening of the county's new police headquarters. (*Grimsby Telegraph*, 2002)

2009: On this day, the relatives of two Grimsby-area soldiers killed in active service received the Elizabeth Cross from the queen. Her Majesty presented the new honour to relatives of six soldiers killed during operations in Afghanistan and Iraq. These included the families of Trooper Robert Pearson, of Grimsby, and Trooper Kristen Turton, of Holton-le-Clay. (*Grimsby Telegraph*, 2009)

— September 15th —

1947: On this day, an outbreak of infantile paralysis – later known as polio – claimed lives. The outbreak saw the first use in Grimsby of the 'iron lung', a breathing aid necessary to keep badly affected patients alive.

The epidemic began in July, when the *Grimsby Evening Telegraph* reported briefly that five people were being treated at Grimsby Corporation Hospital; four from Tetney and the other from Spilsby. Within a fortnight, there were eleven confirmed cases and one suspected case. Three were holidaymakers who had been staying at Cleethorpes.

The number had risen to fifteen by August 15th and the situation was far from under control. A housewife at RAF Binbrook was the next confirmed case, and the base was effectively sealed off, with shops and cinemas closed. In the Grimsby area, all swimming pools had to close, and by August 25th a second iron lung had to be rushed from Lincoln to Grimsby for one desperately ill patient.

The first death occurred on August 27th and the second on September 3rd, by which time there were thirty-four cases. The third death occurred on this day, when three of the twenty-two cases still in hospital were on iron lungs. By October 8th, the total number of cases since the outbreak began was seventy-seven. (*Grimsby Evening Telegraph*, 1947)

— September 16th —

1966: On this day, a wooden cross was placed on the grave of an unknown Grimsby fisherman where he lies, in a bleak and lonely cemetery. This windswept and barren corner of Iceland's grim west coast is his last resting place.

All that is known of him is that he was a crewman on the ill-fated trawler *Jeria* – GY 224 – lost in a severe gale on January 22nd 1935. The 349-ton vessel sank without a hope for any of her thirteen-strong crew. Lashed by gales and mountainous seas, her hull was swept clean, the bridge, funnel and lifeboat being lost. Her engines were out of action and the lights failed. Helplessly she smashed on to the rocks and was totally wrecked.

The unclothed body of this sailor was washed ashore at Latrabjarg a few days after the disaster. The only clue to his identity was a signet ring. Appeals in England have failed to produce a clue so that relatives could put down a plaque to mark the loss of their loved one. Instead, on the evening of this day, the son of an Icelander who originally discovered the body placed the cross there as a mark of respect. (*Grimsby Evening Telegraph*, 1966)

— SEPTEMBER 17TH —

1969: On this day, a horse-riding instructor and three children died in thick fog on Cleethorpes beach, a tragedy etched in the minds of many.

The search began after Mary Tasker, and 8-year-olds Margaret Heaton, Susan Fellowes and Linda Darnell failed to return from a ride along the beach. A thick blanket of fog had descended during their ride and the tide came in, cutting them off from the shore.

More than 100 police officers with tracker dogs were joined by forty RAF men, firemen, coastguards and members of the public, watched over by a helicopter from RAF Leconfield, to comb a 6-mile stretch of coastline between Grimsby and Tetney. The fog was so thick in places that the search party had to hold a rope in order to stay together.

After an all-night hunt, the bodies of 41-year-old riding school instructress Mrs Tasker and all three girls were found. All but one of the horses also died.

At the time, the then police superintendent described the incident as 'a terrible tragedy – the worst we have ever seen'.

Mourning parents and devastated residents pledged to do all they could to prevent suffering in this way again, and the Cleethorpes Vigilantes Inshore Lifeboat Service was established, helping anyone in difficulty in the water. It is now no longer operational. (*Grimsby Evening Telegraph*, 1969; www.grimsbytelegraph.co.uk)

— September 18th —

1856: On this day, a committee was appointed to further the interests of ratepayers in Grimsby. The move was agreed during a meeting held at the Oddfellows Hall, and the main aim of its members initially was to identify Municipal Election candidates who would support their aims. The Ratepayers Committee would then sponsor the candidates. The resulting four candidates went on to victory in the elections of 1856/7 and 1857/8.

Overall, the committee's task was to keep rates to a minimum and to monitor the workings of the council.

One of their successes was to fight the imposition of a district rate: it was later declared illegal. And under pressure from hawk-eyed members, the council took a much more considered approach to how they utilised their finances. The council's accounts were published for the first time in August 1857. Members regularly complained about the authority, claiming town clerk George Babb was incompetent.

The committee was made up of: five labourers, four seamen, four joiners, four boot repairers, two shopkeepers, two sawyers, two blacksmiths, a carter, a cow keeper, a rope maker, a painter, a teacher and a coal merchant. There were others whose trades could not be traced, and the majority of members lived mostly in the new dock area of town. Some were linked to the Temperance movement and the Primitive Methodists. (Grimsby Central Library)

~ September 19th ~

1974: On this day, a famous Grimsby home décor shop had a weasel in their Wedgwood. The tiny creature got into the premises of Lee's, in Victoria Street, Grimsby, through a 1in crack under a door, and was proving to be an extremely tricky customer. It performed an impromptu show in the window of the shop for passers-by.

The owners said they thought the animal then took refuge at the rear of the china department. The weasel thwarted all attempts to lure it into a baited cage: the management put food down, which disappeared – along with the weasel – into a store room.

'Most of us naturally find this amusing,' said a spokesperson, 'but one member of staff has been horrified by the episode.' Upon the story making it into the local newspaper, the weasel was unavailable for comment.

Meanwhile, there was a tricky situation of a different kind not too far away on Grimsby Docks. Three fitters had been sent to Coventry by their colleagues. They would not work with, speak to or eat with the trio because they had refused to take part in a national strike which lasted merely a few hours. (*Grimsby Evening Telegraph*, 1974)

— September 20th —

1878: On this day, the first meeting was held about the formation of a football club in Grimsby. It took place in a room above the Wellington Arms, in Freeman Street, attended by members of the Worlsey Cricket Club, some weeks after the summer season had ended. The idea was to form a football club to occupy winter afternoons until cricket began again. It was called Grimsby Pelham, Pelham being the family name of the Earl of Yarborough, a local landowner who became the club's patron.

Sir John Astley was elected as president, with John Wintringham serving as vice-president. S. Huxley, a player, became secretary, and schoolmaster Charles Horn was the club's first team captain.

Grimsby Pelham was, of course, the foundation for Grimsby Town Football Club. Its formation was announced in the *Grimsby News* on September 27th, with a practise game held eight days later. Its first true match was on November 2nd, away to Britannia and Brigg, and the team lost 2-0. The first home game, at Clee Park against the Brigg club, was again a loss, this time 4-1. Forward Arthur Mountain goes down in history as scoring the club's first goal.

Two victories during the first part of the second season saw the committee change the name to Grimsby Town Football Club.

The team was made up of professionals and gentlemen with business interests, and all matches were friendly; it would be years before points could be won. The playing record for the season of September 1879 to May 1880 read: 'Played 15, won 6, drawn 3, lost 6, goals for 23 goals and against 15.' (Dave Wherry, *We Only Sing When We're Fishing: Grimsby Town FC The Official History 1878–2000*, 2000)

— September 21st —

1967: On this day, it was documented that the meteorological office at RAF Manby received a report of a mysterious light over the East Coast. But there was nothing sinister in the sighting: it was thought to be caused mainly by a lot of 'shimmer' in the air, caused by currents of air rising over the sea. There was also a point of light above the shimmer – possibly Venus or a star – and because of this, the shimmer appeared to be moving. (Met Office)

1971: On this day, the latest craze among youngsters – whirling balls on a string called Clackers – was banned by the headmaster of Welholme Junior School, in Grimsby, for safety reasons. Mr A. Coleman informed parents that Clackers were strictly forbidden after five children, he said, were killed by the toy in Malta. (*Grimsby Evening Telegraph*, 1971)

1987: On this day, the owner of a Grimsby takeaway came within inches of death when two masked robbers blasted at his shop with a double-barrelled shot gun. Ah Choi Wong was in the kitchen of Wong's Bamboo Chinese Takeaway, in Waltham Road, when the shot left a fist-sized hole in the wall just inches above his head. No one was injured and the gunmen left empty-handed. (*Grimsby Evening Telegraph*, 1987)

1948: On this day, the Grimsby Education Committee announced that the biggest school building programme in the history of the town was to start the following year. It would involve five new schools, costing an estimated £400,000; a girls' secondary school in the Chelmsford Avenue area, a boys' secondary school at Highfield, two primary schools at Carr Lane and a nursery at Nunsthorpe. In addition to this programme for 1949, four primary schools were already under construction in the Yarborough Road district. (*Grimsby Telegraph Bygones*, 1940s edition, 1985)

1984: On this day, a New Waltham housewife told how a ten-minute dog walk ended with her dream home in flames. School caretaker Ann Miles decided to give her golden labrador, Busby, and poodle Totty a spot of lunchtime exercise. She returned to find her bungalow – on which she and her husband Frank had just spent £10,000 – ablaze. Ann said:

> I was only gone ten minutes. I lit the gas fire with a piece of paper and put it in the litter bin. It must have been still smouldering. When I came back, I turned the corner and smelt burning. As I came down the street, I saw smoke pouring from the roof. I dared not enter the house, so I thought I'd look through the window. But all the windows were red hot.

(*Grimsby Evening Telegraph*, 1984)

~ September 23rd ~

1916: On this day, at midnight, fourteen bombs were dropped on to Scartho by a German zeppelin airship – luckily no one was killed.

One of the bombs landed in the middle of St Giles' churchyard and the spot is marked today by a monument presented by J. Grantham, who also donated the clock in the church tower.

During the First World War, fishermen from Grimsby were called up for service in large numbers, mostly to the Royal Naval Reserve, but some to the Trawler Reserve. Again, we turn to a church to commemorate their efforts: a memorial lamp was dedicated to their memory in St Andrew's Church in 1926. (David Kaye, *The Book of Grimsby*, 1981)

1947: On this day, the Minister of Labour, George Isaacs, paid an hour's visit to Grimsby, when he toured the Grimsby Employment Exchange. His visit, it was emphasised, was of a purely informal nature. This was the first time that a Minister of Labour had visited Grimsby. (Grimsby Central Library)

1963: On this day, Alan Green, the Minister of State, Board of Trade, opened the Great Grimsby Exhibition at the Duke of York Gardens. There were more than seventy stands including frozen foods, crime prevention demonstrations, vending machines, electrical trends, holidays at home and abroad, as well as various demonstrations. (*Grimsby Telegraph Bygones*, 1996)

— September 24th —

1987: On this day, British Telecom in Grimsby was at the centre of a fraud probe. A team of special investigators had been interviewing installation and fitting staff at the telephone exchange and six people had been suspended. It was believed that British Telecom had discovered discrepancies in its stores.

One worker said, 'We are being treated like criminals.' Another furious worker stripped to his underwear after being interrogated and declared: 'I'm ashamed to wear the uniform.' The man walked away from his grilling at the company's office on the Pyewipe Estate wearing just underpants, vest and socks. Identifying himself only as Mr Warburton, he said he had been exonerated following the interviews. (*Grimsby Evening Telegraph*, 1987)

2003: On this day, Cleethorpes-born Jane Andrews lost her High Court appeal against her conviction for murdering her boyfriend. She achieved even more notoriety for being the former aide to Sarah Ferguson, one of the Duchess of York's most trusted members of staff. In 2001 she was jailed for life for killing her wealthy boyfriend Thomas Cressman after he refused to marry her. The daughter of a joiner and a social worker from Cleethorpes, she worked for the Duchess of York for nine years as her dresser, joining her on royal duties both at home and abroad. (*Grimsby Telegraph*, 2003)

⟶ September 25th ⟵

1849: On this day, a service of thanks for the deliverance from an outbreak of cholera was held in Grimsby's parish church. Throughout the course of 1849, there had been a severe epidemic across the entire country.

Hull was badly affected. In comparison, victims in Grimsby were relatively low. Eight people died but there were additional deaths of seamen on vessels which did not belong to the port.

The church service was attended by the Mayor of Grimsby and councillors, all dressed in their civic robes, and every single pew was filled with people. Dissenters formed a reasonable part of the congregation, and even the aisles were filled with thankful worshippers. (Edward Drury, *The Old Grimsby Story*, 1984)

1959: On this day, the Blue Cross Animal Hospital was opened in Grimsby. It was one of only four in the UK, the others all being located in London. The current site, in Nelson Street, was opened in 2005. (*Grimsby Evening Telegraph*, 1959)

1987: On this day, Grimsby's Chegwin family had a double celebration on the way. Not only was Rose and Ronnie Chegwin's celebrity niece, DJ Janice Long, expecting her first baby, but their famous nephew Keith Chegwin revealed that he was to become a father. Janice and Keith's aunt and uncle lived in Ladysmith Road. (*Grimsby Evening Telegraph*, 1987)

1933: On this day, six men, including a local journalist and a leading Grimsby shopkeeper, watched the first television pictures ever shown in the town.

Fred Wood – whose Bull Ring premises are well-remembered – turned down the lights in the sitting room of a home in Grimsby and twiddled with the knobs of his Baird mirror drum television receiver. 'Unfortunately,' wrote the nonetheless impressed reporter, 'the atmospherics were at their worst.'

However, shortly after 11 p.m., the demonstration began and on the receiver's small screen appeared the head of a pierrot. 'It looked like a badly focused photograph,' wrote the journalist:

> but the demonstrator (Mr Wood) made some adjustments to the motor of the receiver and the image became more sharply defined. The mouth of the image moved and it would have been perfectly obvious that the pierrot was singing even had there been no song issuing from the wireless receiver to prove it.

Then a pierrette appeared on the screen and began to dance.

> The demonstration was the first locally of this apparatus. Those who witnessed it will, in the course of a few years when television has become commonplace, look back perhaps with a smile and contrast what development has been brought to hand. The pictures were little more than singing shadows, but they represent the beginnings of scientific achievement with immense potentialities.

Mr Wood was the first man to sell wirelesses in Grimsby. (*Grimsby Telegraph Bygones*, 1999; Grimsby Central Library)

— September 27th —

1957: On this day, the new police headquarters in Victoria Street, which still exists today, was officially opened. To make way for it, old properties were demolished. The Gospel Mission and Hyden the printers stood on the site, as did the Animal Clinic and Abbott's shop. Mr Abbott would regularly be seen in his gun shop sporting tweed breeches, leather leggings and a tweed hat. One of Grimsby's popular pubs, the Nelson Tavern, was located on the corner of Grime Street, but was also torn down to build the new station.

When it was formed in 1846, the Grimsby Borough Police force had just one officer and three men.

By 1870, it had one head constable, two sergeants and nine constables, to serve a population of about 12,000 people. In 1946, Peggy Grimstead became the first policewoman to be appointed. She went on to become the town's first female police sergeant, in July 1951.By 1955, it had 165 men and women, with nine specialist departments. And in that year, crime was in the news.

It was certainly gruesome but the rope which hung Dr Crippen proved a real crowd-puller when Grimsby Borough Police staged an exhibition. It also featured the cablegram from the SS *Montrose* telling of Crippen's attempt to escape, as well as the false arm, dark glasses and folding ladder used by burglar and murderer Charles Peace. (*Grimsby Evening Telegraph Bygones*, 2002)

1980: On this day, the final passenger trains were run between Grimsby and Louth. A number of special trains made the journey, organised by the Grimsby Louth Rail Group, following the withdrawal of passenger services by British Rail. The journey on this day was from Louth to York, and then back again, and they had to stop at each of the eight level crossings between the towns for the crew to open and close the gates – a time-consuming activity one can only imagine taking place nowadays.

The last special journey was on December 20th 1980, when a special was run from Louth to Grimsby Town, and back again.

The line was the first section of the Great Northern Railway, which was opened on March 1st 1848, and closed to passenger traffic by British Rail in October 1970. The line to all traffic was closed on December 28th 1980. (*Grimsby Evening Telegraph*, 1980)

‒ September 29th ‒

1536: On this day, the Abbey of Wellow was dissolved. The last abbot was Robert Whitgift, the uncle of the future Archbishop of Canterbury. He and his ten canons signed a document acknowledging Henry VIII's supremacy over the Church. In return, Whitgift was granted a yearly pension of £16, while his canons shared £8 10s. The lead and bells were sold off, fetching £202 16s.

The open fields of Grimsby prior to dissolution covered 640 acres, of which Wellow Abbey had the largest holding, of 250.

The nunnery of St Leonard – which boasted 72 acres of arable land and 66 acres of pasture – stayed open for another three years, dissolving on September 15th 1539. The last Prioress, Margaret Ridsdale, was granted a pension of only £4 per annum. The site of the nunnery is the present site of the Grimsby Institute, at Nuns Corner. (Grimsby Central Library)

1888: On this day, the last victim of a smallpox epidemic was discharged from hospital in Grimsby. Since August 1887, a total of 254 cases were admitted to hospital for treatment. The total number of deaths from the disease was twenty-five. (Grimsby Central Library)

— September 30th —

1970: On this day, a real powerhouse of a lady slipped quietly away from Grimsby to be put through her paces. The *Lady Elsie* weighed 640 tons, had a 30ft beam and was capable of handling the biggest of customers quite nicely. She was one of a family of three of the most powerful tugs in the UK and she showed her owners – J.H. Piggott and Son Ltd – just what she was capable of during her acceptance trials in the Humber.

Lady Elsie had cost £280,000 but she was able to sail into Immingham, and moor off the oil jetty construction at Tetney. Her accommodation was second to none, and she had first-class kitchen facilities. She went into service at Immingham, joining her sister tug, *Lady Sarah*.

Lady Elsie's vital statistics were: 190ft overall length, 30ft beam, 16ft 16ins drain, gross tonnage 640 and a 4,000 horsepower engine capable of a 40-ton stationary pull. She was sold to a Spanish owner in 1990. (*Grimsby Evening Telegraph*, 1970)

~ OCTOBER 1ST ~

1947: On this day, part of a newsreel being shown at a cinema was deleted – after three people fainted at the footage. Others in the audience at The Ritz buried their faces in their hands and moaned when the newsreel showed a man being pierced with a sword. Mr W. Connolly, the cinema manager, told the local newspaper:

> The three who fainted were a woman aged about 50 and two young men. They had to be carried out. Two ambulance men, who were on duty in the theatre, revived them. A good many more started moaning and groaning, and covering their faces. I immediately decided to cut this part of the film. It had made me feel a little bit queer too.

The film showed a Dutchman, who had studied the methods of Indian fakirs, submitting to sword thrusts in the chest and stomach with apparently no ill effects. The manager of the Queen's Cinema, in Alexandra Road, Grimsby, where the newsreel was due to be screened the following day, also decided to delete the feature. Less than an hour after seeing the newsreel, a Chesterfield cinema manager collapsed in his office and died later in hospital. (*Grimsby Telegraph Bygones*, 1940s edition, 1985)

~ OCTOBER 2ND ~

1958: On this day, the widow of the man who gave the Doughty Bequest to Grimsby travelled from London to officially open the Doughty Museum, in Town Hall Square. The museum, formerly the Corporation Grammar School for Girls, became the permanent home of a large collection of model ships, maritime paintings and valuable china.

Mrs M.V. Doughty, the widow of William Vere Doughty, was escorted around the building by the mayor and mayoress, alderman and Mrs M. Larmour. Mr Doughty spent his youth and early years in Grimsby before later moving to Hertfordshire. He was the son of Sir George Doughty, local businessman and former Liberal MP for Grimsby.

When he died at Ickleford Manor in 1941, he bequeathed his vast collection to the people of the Borough of Grimsby, on condition that it was displayed for free. For many years it wasn't possible, but the school was eventually converted. (*Grimsby Evening Telegraph*, 1953; *Grimsby Telegraph*, 1958)

1962: On this day, a Grimsby soldier, 21-year-old Lance Corporal Kenneth Atkin, of Cleethorpe Road, was in hospital at Luneburg, West Germany, after being stabbed after a fight between British soldiers and Italians. Lance Corporal Atkin, who was stationed at Osnabruck, was not seriously hurt. (*Grimsby Evening Telegraph*, 1962)

— OCTOBER 3RD —

1883: On this day, a wealthy woman starved to death – within ten months of coming to Grimsby.

Thirza Briggs married the son of a chemist, Charles Frederick Joseph Beaumont Briggs, in Chislehurst. Briggs, his wife and his widowed mother – who had a reputation for public drunkenness – moved to Grimsby on Thirza's insistence, where she had distant relatives. They took a house in Cleethorpe Road at Christmas in 1882.

Briggs was not, like his father, a proper chemist. On arrival, he obtained a peddler's licence to sell medicine door-to-door. His wife was wealthy and of private means when she married him, but she relinquished it to Briggs. Her £200-a-year income and a £1,000 railway investment now belonged to him.

By now they had a daughter, and Thirza became thinner and thinner. A friend used to feed her daily, and Thirza told her she never had enough food. Her only meal was breakfast, and that was only because she got up before her husband and mother-in-law. When her mother-in-law found out, she locked up the food.

When Thirza became ill, Briggs did not send for a doctor. On October 3rd, she died, pitifully thin and bruised. Death had been due to want of food, said doctors.

Briggs was found guilty of manslaughter and sentenced to twenty years' penal servitude. His mother was acquitted of any crime. That would have been the end of the matter. But Briggs was let out six months into his sentence, after the case was scrutinised in *The Lancet*, where an expert said the doctors had been wrong in their conclusion. (*Grimsby Telegraph Bygones*, 1999)

— OCTOBER 4TH —

1934: On this day, the *Grimsby Town* was the first trawler to sail into the new Fish Dock when it was officially opened by Sir Henry Betterton, chairman of the Unemployment Board.

It had taken almost four years to complete, at a cost of nearly £1.75 million. The *Grimsby Town*, a new steam trawler, sailed through the lock pit, severing a ribbon to symbolise the opening of the dock to fishing craft. (*Grimsby Telegraph Bygones*, 2003)

———

2002: On this day, Great Grimsby's outspoken Labour MP of many years, Austin Mitchell, changed his name to Austin Haddock. The deed poll stunt was in honour of National Seafood Week, and hoped his name change would boost trade for local trawlermen. But he did admit he would eventually revert to his given name because his family thought he was 'mad'.

Austin, who was in Blackpool for the Labour Party conference at the time, said:

> I got in a cab and the driver said, 'If you're Mr Haddock, you don't need a taxi to get to the conference centre – just hop in the sea and swim'. The idea is to encourage people to think fish, cook fish, eat fish and buy fish. If they do that, it's good for the industry and good for Grimsby.

(*Grimsby Evening Telegraph*, 2002)

~ OCTOBER 5TH ~

1571: On this day, sixty ships on the coast between Grimsby and New Holland were wrecked during a high tide. It was not the first, or the last, time the Lincolnshire coast felt the effects of flooding: there are references to such natural disasters as early as 1178. The 1571 flood devastated the low-lying land. It was caused by two factors – heavy rainfall over the whole of the south of England, swelling all the main rivers, and a storm surge down the North Sea. It was the onshore wind which led to the multitude of shipwrecks, and huge numbers of livestock were drowned. Records say 20,000 cattle and at least 3,000 sheep were lost on the North Sea coast alone. Just outside Grimsby, shepherd Spencer and his flock of 1,800 sheep drowned when the sea burst through the walls, constructed of earth, along the shoreline.

Hollingshead's *Account of Damage Done In The County of Lincoln, By The Tempest of Wind and Rain* records that the village of Mumby Chapel (north of where Chapel St Leonards is now) survived, but with just three houses. A ship had smashed into one of the homes, and the mariners climbed on to the roof, saving a mother they found there. Her husband and child perished. (Grimsby Central Library; *Grimsby Telegraph* archives)

~ October 6th ~

1947: On this day, Grimsby was suffering from a plague of giant rats. Many uncleared bomb sites in the town were teaming with vermin. The worst-affected area was the town's North East ward – Victoria Street, King Edward Street and Burgess Street – and parts of the Humber ward.

It was so bad that in one house visited by a councillor, a baby's cot had to be surrounded by candles to stop rats nibbling at the bedclothes. And the mayor told how he caught a 16in rat in his back garden and Councillor W.J. Molson told how he had visited a home and found the occupant plastering a hole in the skirting board made by rats the previous night. .

In and around King Edward Street, health officials found a labyrinth of rat runs and tunnels. Councillor Molson said he had walked through the area one night and had been horrified to see rats every 5 or 6 yards. 'One good thing,' he said, 'was that most of them were being chased by cats which fortunately abound in the area.'

Chief Sanitary Inspector Mr H. Parkinson said the main problem was the old and inadequate sewers. In one cleaning exercise, 5,000 rats had been killed in a matter of days. (*Grimsby Evening Telegraph*, 1947)

~ October 7th ~

1915: On this day, Ivy Lilian Wallace was born in Grimsby. She is best-known for writing the Pookie series of illustrated children's stories.

Ivy began drawing as a child, and her encouraging parents thought she might grow up to become an artist. When she left school, she joined Felixstowe Repertory theatre as an actress and at the outbreak of the Second World War she joined the British film industry to make educational films.

It was while carrying out support work for the police that she first thought of Pookie, a winged rabbit. She was manning the police switchboard and began doodling, drawing a fairy sitting on a toadstool with a little rabbit in the foreground. She decided fairies were 'two a penny' and so rubbed out the fairy and gave the rabbit wings. She wrote: 'This is the story of Pookie, a little white furry rabbit, with soft, floppity ears, big blue eyes and the most lovable rabbit smile in the world.'

So confident was she in her work that in 1946 Ivy took a train from Grimsby to London to present her manuscript to publishers. She arrived at the offices of Williams Collins Ltd without an appointment but the response was unenthusiastic.

A few weeks later she was contacted by William Hope Collins and asked to attend the Glasgow office. Borrowing some money from her brother, she travelled to Scotland and not only did William accept the book, he fell in love. They married in 1950 and lived in the Scottish Borders, having two daughters. Ivy died in 2006. (*The Daily Telegraph*, 2006)

1935: On this day, the first Bishop of Grimsby, the Right Reverend Ernest Morell Blackie, was formally inaugurated. In June 1937, he was appointed as Dean of Rochester, and preached his last sermon at St James' parish church on November 7 that year. (*Grimsby Evening Telegraph*, 1935)

1985: On this day, footballer Les Wood was thanking his friends – who saved him in a heart-stopping drama on the pitch.

Mr Wood, aged 35, was halfway through a game when he collapsed and stopped breathing. Fellow players rushed to his aid when they realised he was in trouble during the Yarborough United Stallingborough match in Grimsby's Sunday League. He was taken to hospital immediately and treated for a ruptured spleen, and on this day, was hoping to be discharged.

United manager Chris Holt said:

> At half time, Les had complained of feeling winded after a knock in the first half. Then about five minutes into the second half, he was chasing after the ball when he suddenly stopped running. He went off the pitch and the game continued until we noticed him lying on the grass clutching his chest. He stopped breathing. We listened to his chest and could not get a heartbeat. I'm just glad Les is recovering. I just hope this is the end of accidents for this season.

And the game? United crashed to a 6-1 defeat. (*Grimsby Evening Telegraph*, 1985)

~ October 9th ~

1901: On this day, operations began at Grimsby Ice Factory. The continuing expansion of the fishing industry naturally resulted in an increased need for ice. This was imported from abroad and by 1895, 73,390 tons had been brought in – a rise of 132 per cent since 1880. Although some factories had begun to manufacture ice, they simply could not produce the volumes those overseas could.

An amalgamation of the Great Grimsby Ice Company and the Grimsby Co-operative Ice Company was formed, and representatives identified a site adjacent to No.2 Fish Dock to construct a new factory capable of producing 300 tons of ice daily. And so operations began on this day, and Grimsby Ice Factory became a Victorian institution.

It was modernised between 1930 and 1933, changing from steam to electricity-driven compressors. At its completion in 1933, it was capable of producing 1,110 tons of ice a day. A new compressor room was constructed in the 1950s and other modifications took place – all around the time Grimsby became known as the world's premier fishing port.

But the decline of the industry which followed ended its usefulness. Ice was no longer needed in such vast amounts and it closed in July 1990. Now the disused Grade-II listed building is owned by Associated British Ports. (Garry Crossland, *A History of Grimsby Ice Factory*, 2011)

1552: On this day, a widow called Catherine Mason granted a perpetual annuity of £7 to the mayor and burgesses of Grimsby. The money, issued out of lands in Guelceby, Asterby and Scamblesby, was for the finding and maintenance of a schoolmaster to teach children grammar and Latin. The Free Grammar School was located in Chantry Lane, for sons and daughters of freemen. (Anderson Bates, *A Gossip About Old Grimsby*, 2011)

1968: On this day, a report was made public that revealed more than 200 council house tenants in Grimsby were 'seriously thinking' of buying their home. The Estates Committee heard that inquiries were coming in at a rate of between twelve and twenty a day. Requests were from all over the town – the Weelsby Estate, the Willows, Grange and the St Michael's Road area.

The rules were that people could only buy one house – the one they were occupying – and that if they were to let it out, it was at a rate fixed by the council, to last for five years. After that, homeowners could do as they wished. (*Grimsby Evening Telegraph*, 1968)

~ OCTOBER 11TH ~

1922: On this day, no one saw Thomas Hayter and Annie Ostler take their last steps as they walked, hand in hand, on to an empty stretch of beach between Cleethorpes and Skegness. No one saw them as they faced each other to make their tender farewells, nor saw Thomas remove the sawn-off shotgun from beneath his coat, shoot Annie dead and then turn the gun on himself. It was a lovers' pact, and their footprints in the sand were certain proof of their final moments.

Thomas, a mechanic in Grimsby, lived in North Thoresby with his wife and infant child. Their digs was with the village cobbler, Albert Ostler and his wife, who were Annie's parents.

Mrs Hayter fell ill and despite devoted care, she was taken, with her child, to Grimsby's hospital, where they died. Widowed Thomas, 43, left his lodgings to a new home nearby, and it was from there on this day that he said he was going to Grimsby to catch the London train. Later, he and Annie, 21, were found dead at Sutton-on-Sea, a wedding ring on Annie's finger.

The inquest was straightforward, but there was a twist. Thomas was recognised in a newspaper report in the London Press – by a woman claiming to be his wife. She said they had married in 1917 and had a child, but Thomas had deserted her. Had he been to London and, refused a divorce, married Annie bigamously? The truth will never be known. (*Grimsby Telegraph Bygones*, 1999)

~ OCTOBER 12TH ~

2002: On this day, the current HMS *Grimsby* stopped off in port. The town's adopted ship is a £30 million mine hunter.

Its previous incarnation sank in the Mediterranean in May 1941. The 900-ton sloop was escorting supplies ship SS *Helka* when both came under attack from enemy aircraft. Both vessels were sunk 40 miles north-east of the Libyan coast, and eight crew members of HMS *Grimsby* were lost. The silver from the ship was later discovered in an officers' mess in Aden and was put on display in Grimsby Town Hall as a tribute to those who died.

The only other HMS *Grimsby* was a Scottish trawler built in 1896 and requisitioned by the navy in the First World War. Now, a yellow mini-submarine is just one part of the kit of the vessel – one of the world's most advanced mine hunters. Measuring 52.5m, it was the third of seven Sandown class vessels ordered by the Ministry of Defence. Built by Southampton shipbuilders Vosper Thorneycroft, HMS *Grimsby* has a displacement of 470 tonnes and room for forty crew, and it is equipped to deal with mines of all types. (*Grimsby Telegraph*, 2002)

~ October 13th ~

1832: On this day, the Countess of Yarborough laid the foundation stone of the Grimsby workhouse. Shortly after it officially opened, a public inquiry was held into allegations of cruelty to inmates.

A small boy had been in a cell for three weeks, another for two weeks and one for one week – they had all been placed in solitary confinement. One boy was discovered with no stockings or shoes on his feet, and another, a 10-year-old, was sitting picking oakum. One boy, also in solitary confinement, was placed in a room in bad weather with no heating. All he had to lie on was an iron bedstead with a sack on it. The boy's back was black and blue with bruises, and a visiting guardian, Mrs Osborne, 'gave words of comfort'.

Tales of neglect litter Grimsby's history. For example, a father and mother appeared in court in 1883 charged with beating their 6-year-old child. The youngster was said to swear, chew tobacco, kick the monitors at school and spit in teachers' faces. The parents were acquitted, however, and the child was sent to an industrial school. (*Grimsby Telegraph Bygones*, 1998; Grimsby Central Library)

━ October 14th ━

1854: On this day, Queen Victoria officially opened the Royal Dock. Her Majesty and Prince Albert arrived on the royal yacht from Hull, inspected the new dock and ascended the hydraulic tower. Reaching out into the River Humber, the dock took six years to complete, first opening to commercial traffic in 1852.

Fishing and Grimsby had been closely linked since medieval times, but it was not until the arrival of the railway in 1848 and the subsequent construction of a series of docks that Grimsby's reputation as a prime fishing port on the East Coast was established.

The Manchester, Sheffield and Lincolnshire Railway Company wanted an eastern terminus next to the North Sea, and Grimsby was well-placed for such a development. It already had a dock with potential for expansion so, in 1845, the directors acquired the Old Dock from the Grimsby Haven Company.

In the spring of 1846, the firm employed James Rendell and his engineer, Adam Smith of Brigg, to begin work on the new dock. (David Kaye, *The Book of Grimsby*, 1981)

~ October 15th ~

1947: On this day, Rodney Lynn Temperton was born in Cleethorpes. He went on to become a songwriter, record producer and musician, famous for writing songs performed by the King of Pop, Michael Jackson.

Music was a big influence in his life from an early age. In an interview, he said, 'My father wasn't the kind of person who'd read you a story before you went off to sleep – he used to put a transistor radio right on the pillow, and I'd go to sleep listening to Radio Luxemburg and I think that had an influence.'

The young Rod went to De Aston School, in Market Rasen, and enjoyed playing the drums. He began his working life in the office of a frozen food company in Grimsby, but soon became a full-time keyboard player in several dance bands.

In 1974, he saw an advert in *Melody Maker* and became a member of the band Heatwave. Four years on, Rod left the band and moved to Beverley Hills to write. A year later, Quincy Jones recruited him to write three songs – including 'Rock With You' – on what became Michael Jackson's first solo album in four years, *Off the Wall*. In 1982, Rod wrote for the album *Thriller*, including penning the title track. (*Grimsby Evening Telegraph*)

— OCTOBER 16TH —

1998: On this day, a Grimsby-born ship's captain told the queen he could not collect his MBE at Buckingham Palace – because he was sailing to the Antarctic. Stuart Lawrence, then aged 54, was captain of the British Antarctic Survey ship *Bransfield*, which set sail from Grimsby's Royal Dock at 3.45 a.m. on this day.

The skipper of the Grimsby-based ship, which was carrying supplies and crews for the survey's Antarctic bases, was due to be awarded his MBE several days later. 'I had to tell her Majesty I could not make it and we have decided to go in the spring,' Stuart explained.

He was awarded the MBE in the Queen's Birthday Honours List for his services to the Antarctic expedition.

1998 was his twenty-eighth season on the *Bransfield*, which also had Grimsby men Mark Jones and Mark Hines in her catering department. The newly refurbished ship set out in what were expected to be the worst gales to hit the East Coast for years. 'It will put a few people back in their beds, I expect,' said Stuart. 'The winds are more an annoyance than anything else.'

On the massive trek south, the ship was due to stop at Montevideo, Uruguay and two of the Falkland Islands before continuing to the Antarctic stations. Stuart was looking forward to witnessing a giant iceberg, more than twelve times the size of the Isle of Wight, which had recently broken off the Antarctic ice shelf. (*Grimsby Evening Telegraph*, 1998)

~ October 17th ~

1898: On this day, the Grimsby to Manchester passenger train was approaching Wrawby junction, near Barnetby, when tree trunks on a goods train from the opposite direction slipped and sliced through the roofs of the passenger train coaches. Nine people died and twenty-six were injured.

The passenger train was the 16.45, consisting of a brake van, three passenger carriages and a rear guard's van. The goods train, which had left Grimsby earlier that day for Doncaster, had forty-four wagons loaded with tree trunks of up to 42ft. They were so heavy it took fifteen men to lift even one of them.

The following day, the *Grimsby Evening Telegraph* offered an examination of the scene:

> To-day's scene at the place of the lamentable accident to the Manchester express is one of sad desolation, and discloses even more emphatically than was the case yesterday the dire extent of the disaster. The train, with the exception of the brake van, has been shunted under the goods shed, and is indeed a pitiable object. Some of the telescoped carriages, which can hardly be recognised as having been the comfortable compartments of the Great Central Railway, present a sickening aspect. After making a closer examination of the wrecked compartments, everything conforms the impressions originally gained that the passengers who escaped with their lives have done so under miraculous circumstances.

(*Grimsby Telegraph Bygones*, 2004)

1863: On this day, Marcia Amelia Mary Lane-Fox was born, the eldest daughter of the 12th Baron Conyers and his wife, Mary.

On August 5th 1886, she married wealthy local landowner Charles Pelham, the 4th Earl of Yarborough. She was the eldest co-heir of the Duke of Marlborough and the Duke of Schomberg, and was the seventh Countess Fouconberg and Conyers in her own right. Upon her marriage, the young woman brought 153 quarterings into the Brocklesby clan. They had four sons, and the title continues today within the Brocklesby family, the current earl contributing greatly to local life.

In 1920, the countess was appointed an OBE in recognition of her role as Commandant of Brocklesby Park, her husband's ancestral home, which had been used as an auxiliary hospital during the First World War.

When she died on November 17th 1926 of sleeping sickness, her titles were inherited by her eldest surviving son, Sackville. She was laid to rest in the mausoleum within the woodlands of the 28,000-acre Brocklesby Park estate, which was originally laid out in the 1770s by Capability Brown. (Grimsby Central Library)

— OCTOBER 19TH —

1936: On this day, brothers George and Jim Orsborne appeared at the Old Bailey charged with the theft of the *Girl Pat* trawler.

What began on April 1st that year goes down in history as one of Grimsby's most famous incidents. The ship, owned by Marstrand Fishing Company and skippered by George, set sail for the Dogger Banks. However, instead of going north, he went south to Dover – and vanished to Africa.

In fact, George illegally took a detour which saw him voyage to a series of far-flung places, navigating with his son's school atlas. George and Jim were arrested by the pursuing government in June, off Georgetown, Guyana, and returned to England for trial.

The 70ft seiner, abandoned at Dermerara, had been painted in white and re-named *Kia Ora* by her errant crew. It was rescued by a syndicate. Such was the interest in the saga, 500 people applied for crew positions.

George was given eighteen months' hard labour and Jim twelve. The former wrote five books about his journey and became a celebrity – a hero rather than rogue, the whole episode probably a jaunt despite a rigorous defence during his trial. After the war, George was convicted of gun-running and died in the 1950s. (*Grimsby Evening Telegraph*)

— OCTOBER 20TH —

1972: On this day, the Grimsby trawler *Aldershot*, holed in a collision with an Icelandic gunboat, slipped into a secret repair yard after getting a rough reception from angry demonstrators in the Faroes capital.

She was being made ready to return to the Icelandic grounds that very evening, after the 3ft gash in her stern was sealed up. However, the 427-ton trawler was met by demonstrators chanting 'Britons go home' as she put into Thorshaven the evening before. The crew tried to tie up at the quay but were prevented by the crowd from getting the lines fast.

The *Aldershot* then went alongside another Grimsby trawler, the *Northern Sun*, which was taking on fuel – but the demonstrators cut the oil hose. The line was later restored and the *Northern Sun* left for Grimsby with more than 1,200 kits of fish from Iceland.

'We have always had a friendlier reception from the Faroese than the Icelanders, and I am sure that officials in Thorshaven are embarrassed by what has happened,' said a representative from Aldershot's owners, Consolidated Fisheries. The incident shows how seriously the territorial fishing limits issue was for Grimsby during this time. Trawlers had begun working in pairs, with one fishing while the other stood guard, to prevent the gunboats from cutting the warps. (*Grimsby Evening Telegraph*, 1972)

‒ October 21st ‒

1966: On this day, the Lincolnshire Aircraft Preservation Society, formed six months earlier to save some of Britain's vintage flying machines, bought its first aircraft. It was a battered Percival Proctor of the type used by the RAF during the Second World War. Unlike the Hurricane and Spitfire, it had no real claim to fame and was used as a trainer or general transport. The newly purchased Proctor was kept at a farm at Grainsby, near North Thoresby.

The society planned to restore the plane, and eventually the group wanted to open its own museum for the public to view exhibits. Its young and enthusiastic members were keen to take on an old hangar in one of Lincolnshire's abandoned airfields.

The society had spent the last few months holding fundraising events to buy old aircraft, although many people placed no value on them and would often give them away to scrap merchants. It was this type of person the members were anxious to get in touch with before too many vintage planes ended up as scrap. (*Grimsby Telegraph Bygones*, 1999)

1969: On this day, the Humber Hovercraft service closed for the winter. It had replaced the steam boats which took passengers from the north and south banks, and although established with such high hopes eight months previously, there were concerns for its future.

The *Minerva* and *Mercury* linked Hull Pier and Grimsby Docks, but suffered frequent mechanical failures. It was, of course, to be many years before the Humber Bridge opened.

The *Grimsby Evening Telegraph* reported:

> It is not putting it too strongly to suggest that if it failed to emerge again in the spring, it would be something of a national tragedy. For Britain has long been the pioneer, the innovator, in engineering and modes of transport, and too often the criticism has been that we fail to nurture the fruits of our inventive genius. It would be sad, indeed, if that accusation were levelled again and we lost the commanding lead held for some years in this field. This enterprise was the world's first estuarial hovercraft service and its benefits were quickly felt. Despite snags and setbacks, the potential of the hovercraft still seems to us enormous. The £150,000 sunk into the venture so far is small when weighed against the potential.

The service was sadly short-lived; it did not reopen. (*Grimsby Evening Telegraph*, 1969; Grimsby Central Library)

~ OCTOBER 23RD ~

1499: On this day, bull-baiting was on the council's agenda. The sport was extremely popular. In Grimsby, bull-baiting had taken place for centuries and was pursued with such an appetite that it was made the subject of official regulation. Records show that, on occasions, pepper was forced into the bull's nose to enrage the animal and make the entertainment even more lively. If this failed to cause anger, it was not uncommon to pour hot spirits or flash gunpowder on to the beast, or lacerate fleshy parts of the bull's body with knives and pour nitric acid into the wound.

In Grimsby, it became the subject of regulation by magistrates to increase its importance and to prevent the possibility of it falling out of favour. At the beginning of the reign of Henry VII, butchers found the requirement to provide bulls for the entertainment of the masses not only troublesome but inconvenient. As a result, they sought to evade the requirement, but it was made essential by an edict from the mayor and burgesses of the town. On this day, the edict was incorporated into a code of ordinances 'for the better government of the borough'. (Ivan E. Broadhead, *Portrait of Humberside*, 1983)

~ OCTOBER 24TH ~

1957: On this day, Her Royal Highness Princess Alexandra opened the YMCA hostel in Grimsby.

It was in 1906 that a group of young businessmen, feeling there was a need for club facilities with a Christian background, founded the Young Men's Christian Association in Grimsby. Among the founders were Alderman Thomas George Tickler, the Mayor of Grimsby and the Boer War plum and apple jam manufacturer, who declared the opening of the YMCA in 1907.

An appeal for funds was launched and enough was raised to purchase 39 Heneage Road and soldiers billeted in the area were invited to parties there. By 1917, the group took over a temperance hotel and converted it into a hostel for soldiers and sailors. As the organisation's property portfolio grew locally, so did its reputation.

In the 1920s, football became important, with YMCA teams winning many trophies.

Further hostel extensions were added and, on this day, No. 43 Heneage Road was officially opened by Princess Alexandra.

The hostel was soon overflowing, so the group rebuilt the YMCA in Peaks Lane, where it stands today, thanks to a 4-acre gift from a businessman. It was officially opened in 1972, open to men and women. (*Grimsby Evening Telegraph*, 1957; *Grimsby Telegraph* archives)

⚊ October 25th ⚊

1953: On this day, Judy the pony was saved from the slaughterhouse. The 14-year-old brown-coloured animal was destined for death until sixty-four schoolchildren stepped in to rescue her. The youngsters were all members of the Animal Defenders' Corps, which had been formed for only three weeks and was the third branch to be established in the country under the auspices of the RSPCA.

An officer spotted Judy, measuring about 12 hands high, being led down a lane in Waltham and learned of her fate. She had been bought for slaughter by Mr R. Vermeersch, a butcher who famously sold horse meat during the war from his very own horse meat shop in Cleethorpe Road. Mr Vermeersch told the group it could buy Judy over a period of two years. On this day, half of the amount – part of which came from the children's pocket money – had been paid.

A field was loaned as a home for Judy at a modest sum, and she became the group's pet, spoiled somewhat by the huge number of then un-rationed sugar lumps fed to her as treats. All that was asked of the docile pony was that she gave children rides at weekends – and she duly obliged. (*Grimsby Evening Telegraph*, 1953)

～ October 26th ～

1937: On this day, Robert Guy Pulvertaft was celebrating the birth in Grimsby of his daughter, Elizabeth Clare. Known as Guy, he was born in Cork in 1907 and went on to study medicine at Cambridge, but it was in Grimsby where he developed his specialist interest in hand surgery.

He came to the town in 1937, when he was appointed consultant orthopaedic surgeon for the hospitals in Grimsby, Scunthorpe and Louth. During his time in Grimsby, he treated many patients for hand injuries – usually men who had sliced themselves cutting fish in the factories. He was so interested in this area that he dropped his general orthopaedic practice to develop hand surgery.

He moved from Grimsby in 1947 and took a job at Derbyshire Royal Infirmary, where he established a specialist unit to treat injuries and disorders of the hand. In an obituary in the *Journal of Hand Surgery*, one of his colleagues wrote:

> As all hand surgeons are aware, this was, and still remains, one of the most challenging fields of surgery demanding the highest degree of technical skill, dedication and the endless patience only possessed by relatively few surgeons. Guy possessed all these qualities.

At the time of his retirement from the NHS in 1972, he was appointed a Commander of the Most Excellent Order of the British Empire, and spent several years paying prolonged visits to leprosy hospitals in Ethiopia and setting up Hand Centres in Kuwait. His life is honoured by a library, opened after his death in 1986 in Derbyshire Royal Infirmary. (www.pulvertaft.co.uk)

— October 27th —

1938: On this day, weird happenings at Holton-le-Clay so frightened women and girls in the village bordering Grimsby's outskirts, that they were too nervous to go out at night alone. The manifestations took the form of flying bottles and bricks, with stones and pebbles landing on roofs and flying through windows. A Mr Lamb, of Tetney Lane, received a severe wound on the temple from a flying stone, and Arthur Thompson was confined to bed as a result of his experience. Miss Atkinson, living nearby, fainted when as shower of stones descended on her bungalow roof.

Villagers formed parties to discover the cause of the trouble; the fact they took torches and weapons with them showed they expected to discover something more substantial than a ghost. One villager went out with a double-barrelled shotgun and although he fired one or two shots, he contracted only thin air. Mr J. Brocklesby claimed to have seen a figure in some bushes while on watch with his fierce Labrador. A couple of bottles floated through the air soon afterwards.

The trouble occurred between dusk and 10pm, and only on fine nights, and lasted weeks. The 'ghost' was not caught. (*Grimsby Telegraph Bygones*, 2001)

∼ OCTOBER 28TH ∼

1939: On this day, the Grimsby trawler *Lynx II* became the port's first war casualty. Over the next six years she was to be followed by another 119 fishing boats from the port.

The *Lynx II* was built in 1906 and a veteran of the First World War. She was sunk by a U-boat 90 miles off Scotland after she had gone to the aid of the Hull trawler *St Nidan*. *St Nidan*'s crew had been ordered into the boats by the U-boat commander, but they managed to fire flares. These were seen by the *Lynx II* and her skipper, Arthur Cressey, steamed to investigate. They managed to send an SOS before the U-boat surfaced again – this time ordering the *Lynx II*'s ten-strong crew into the boats too.

An armed party went on board the Grimsby trawler and placed charges in her engine room. The crew was later landed safely at Stornoway.

Not so fortunate was the crew of the 345-ton *Wigmore*, which left Grimsby three weeks later. She disappeared – along with the sixteen men on board. It is believed she was the victim of a U-boat some 25 miles off the Scottish coast. (*Grimsby Telegraph Bygones*, The War Years, 1984)

~ October 29th ~

1949: On this day, the explosion of a firework in a garden in Hart Street, Cleethorpes, caused a catalogue of damage. It smashed thirteen windows, blew bundles of wood from the scullery into the yard, knocked the pendulum off a clock in the living room of the house next door and brought down soot from chimneys some distance away.

Fourteen-year-old Richard Newland, who had stood well back after lighting the firework, collapsed after limping into the house, dazed, with his leg bleeding from cuts and his trousers torn.

Richard had bought a box of fireworks a few days before and decided to let a few of them off for the benefit of his uncle, who would not be around on November 5th. The first two went off normally, but the third went with a crash and a bang ... and a whole lot more! Even a shaving brush and soap, which had been in the pantry window of the house, were blown into the garden. (*Grimsby Telegraph Bygones*, 1940s edition, 1985)

1958: On this day, the first steps towards the abolition of the 11-Plus examination were being taken in Grimsby. A pilot scheme was being introduced that year, to operate against the current system, and then both results analysed. One of the features of the new system was that greater weight should be given to the teacher's knowledge of the child being examined. (*Grimsby Evening Telegraph*, 1958)

– October 30th –

1926: On this day, Grimsby Town FC played a goalless Second Division match at home at Blundell Park against Chelsea, before a crowd of 12,423 fans. Little did the spectators at the unremarkable fixture know that the programme from that match would go on to make a world auction record in 2002.

The programme, called *The Mariner*, went under the hammer at Sotheby's, in London, making £3,760 as part of a lot of four brochures – more than five times the pre-sale estimate. It was so valuable to collectors because it was printed before the war, in the year of the General Strike. The programme contained a cartoon of an old fisherman smoking a Woodbine and there was an advert for the Empire Coliseum.

Sotheby's would not disclose the identity of the winning bidder, but it was certain the mystery winner was a Chelsea collector. Auctioneer Graham Budd said, 'I thought the programmes would go for quite a lot but I never envisaged they would be for this much.' He said the only Grimsby Town programmes worth more would be pre-war fixtures against Manchester United. (Dave Wherry, *We Only Sing When We're Fishing: Grimsby Town FC The Official History 1878–2000*, 2000)

~ OCTOBER 31ST ~

1943: On this day, a motor gunboat – *Gay Viking* – docked at Immingham. She was one of the five MGBs allocated by the Admiralty to run between the Humber and the Swedish port of Lysekil, where they would load and bring back machine tools, ball bearings, components and other materials essential to the war effort. Each boat was provided with a defensive armament of 20mm Oerlikons and machine guns. (Grimsby Central Library)

—— ·——

1949: On this day, more than sixty villagers from nearby cottages in Barnetby were recovering after helping fight a serious fire which broke out at Low Farm. The *Grimsby Evening Telegraph* took up the story on the front page: 'They formed a chain to bring water in buckets from the hydrant to the scene of the fire before the brigades arrived. Stacks of wheat and oats due to be threshed and ricks of clover in and around the crew yard were totally destroyed.'

Mr F.W. Lowish, owner of the farm, told the paper: 'But for the marvellous job done by the villagers, our house and all the buildings would have been destroyed.'

The blaze was discovered by neighbours and completely burnt out the crew yard. Two boys, who had been seen lighting matches in the yard, were thought to have been responsible.

(*Grimsby Telegraph Bygones*, 1940s edition, 1985)

~ NOVEMBER 1ST ~

1950: On this day, Weelsby Woods was officially given to the public but it wasn't until May 1952 that it was officially opened, in a ceremony presided over by the Mayor of Grimsby, Alderman J.A. Webster.

The land was once the grounds of Weelsby Villa and Victorian maps of the area display a manor house to one side of the park, and to the other side a plantation, a pheasantry and a large pond. During the First World War, the woods were a training ground for locally recruited soldiers. In the Second World War, it became a camp for Italian prisoners of war. Prisoners were held in single-storey buildings, most of which remained standing for many years afterwards.

The army was still in possession of much of the area in 1950, and the opening ceremony was slightly marred by a decision by the army to ban the public from its disused camp by the entrance gates. The mayor was sarcastic, criticising the decision and saying that the 'most terrible consequences to national defence' would occur should officers let even an inch of the empty camp be walked through by the public. But the ceremony must have still been quite a sight – the mayor did the honours by driving along the paths on a decorated horse-drawn cart. (*Grimsby Evening Telegraph*, 1950)

⚊ November 2nd ⚊

1936: On this day, Grimsby resident Harry Shimeld exercised his vote but ended up in hospital with a fractured ankle after a head-on crash in a candidate's car.

Harry cast his vote in the morning but discovered he had missed his train to work in Hull. He found a friend, Mr W.D. Antill, a candidate for the Alexandra ward, who offered to run him in his car to New Holland so he could catch the boat across the Humber. They missed the boat and the pair returned home. At Love Lane Corner, Mr Antill's car skidded and collided head-on with a tree.

Harry suffered a fractured right ankle and other injuries to the leg, as well as his face. Mr Antill escaped with minor injuries to his arm and face, bruises and shock. Harry was taken to hospital by ambulance. The road at the time of the accident was wet and slippery, and there were many dead leaves on the surface from the trees at the corner. The front bumper and axle of the car were pushed back by the impact.

Meanwhile, 99-year-old Mrs Kirby reportedly arrived at Flottergate Polling Booth in a bath chair to cast her vote. She walked unaided to cross and post her ballot paper in the Grimsby municipal elections. (*Grimsby Evening Telegraph*, 1936)

— NOVEMBER 3RD —

1889: On this day, Sequah, an American quack doctor, came to town and pitched in Freeman Street Market, where large crowds gathered to see him. He had two remedies which he sold in considerable quantities.

One was an embrocation claimed to be effective in cases of rheumatism, the other was known as Prairie Flower and was said to be a herbal medicine from a secret Indian formula.

Sequah also extracted teeth for free. The operation was carried out in front of his caravan in full public view. One report said it provided a 'certain amount of amusement for onlookers'. (*Grimsby Telegraph Bygones*, undated; verbal account by Stuart Russel)

———

1949: On this day, wrapped and sliced bread was on sale again in Grimsby for the first time since the war – and there was a big demand for it. Mr T. Hewson, secretary of the Master Bakers Association, said most of his members who had the machinery had taken advantage of the relaxation in the regulations.

Meanwhile, on the same day, the most up-to-date canteen in Grimsby served its first meals. The canteen was at Carr Lane School and Miss J. Batty, Grimsby school meals organiser, explained it had taken about a year to install the equipment. (*Grimsby Evening Telegraph Bygones*, 1940s edition, 1985)

~ November 4th ~

1896: On this day, Jimmy Slater was born. He was a Yorkshire lad and started performing in seaside concerts just before the First World War. His debut was in Cleethorpes at an event called The Barn-Stormers, in which he appeared in drag. During the conflict, he honed his stagecraft entertaining the military, and after was recruited to the cast of Splinters, a successful revue which toured Britain throughout the 1930s.

During this time, he produced his own Super Follies at Cleethorpes and Skegness on an open-air stage on the beach. Dripping with gorgeous costumes and beautiful girls, it went on to tour the country.

Jimmy himself continued performing well into the 1960s and was a pal of the Grimsby-born comedian Freddie Frinton. A true star of variety, he was in demand as a panto dame; he once took over the role of an Ugly Sister in panto at Cleethorpes Pier in 1975 when the actor fell ill. He was in the audience at the time and spotted by a cast member. Within minutes, he was costumed up and on stage, ad-libbing through the script.

By this time, he had built up so many costumes he was running his stock as a supply business and continued to do so after retiring from the limelight, all from his home on the Fitties, where he lived with his sister Annie. He died aged 100 in January 1996. (*Grimsby Telegraph Bygones*, 2001)

— NOVEMBER 5TH —

1939: On this day, the 655-ton HM trawler *Northern Rover* was expected back at Kirkwell, in the Orkneys, but failed to return. She was the first former Grimsby-based vessel enlisted into Admiralty service to be sunk by U-boat action. German built, she was one of fifteen such vessels and certainly the largest that sailed from Grimsby before the war. All fifteen were registered in London and initially fished from Fleetwood.

While at sea, fishing in the Arctic in October 1937, the fleet was ordered to return to Grimsby with their catches. The *Northern Rover* made it to port on October 11th and then went off again, fishing off Spitzbergen.

She was requisitioned in August 1939 and converted by the Admiralty into an armed boarding vessel. She was to be used for contraband control duties on the northern patrols, based at Kirkwell, in the Orkneys, with several Grimsby men on the crew. On October 30th, she intercepted a Norwegian vessel and escorted her to the harbour, immediately resuming her duties in the water.

On this day, she was due back to harbour, but was posted as missing when she failed to arrive. Her status remained as missing until June 1945, when German records captured by the British revealed that the U-59 had sunk an armed patrol trawler shortly before midnight on October 30th by firing a torpedo. The position of the sinking corresponded with the area the *Northern Rover* patrolled. (Harry C. Hutson, *Grimsby's Fighting Fleet*, 1990)

~ NOVEMBER 6TH ~

1997: On this day, Grimsby ghost hunter Robin Furman was investigating reports of apparitions at Thornton Abbey. Robin's large house in the centre of town is said to be haunted by a nun, and he achieved fame in the 1980s as a ghostbuster and parapsychologist. With his group, Ghostbusters UK, he was filmed for television and wrote a book about his experiences way before *Most Haunted* came along.

From spirit lights and poltergeists to alien sightings, Robin and his team have an enormous casebook going back many years. On this day, he was at the abbey in North Lincolnshire, following up the report of a sighting of Henry VIII and his court in the grounds. That summer, a group saw a number of people they assumed were in fancy dress – but they later discovered they had been alone all along. Robin said he did not know if it was a sighting of the infamous king, but reports of strange, unexplained organ music are common at Thornton Abbey. (*Grimsby Telegraph*, 1997)

~ November 7th ~

1938: On this day, a Grimsby pilot played his part in achieving a world record. Pilot Officer M.L. Gaine was the signals officer for the RAF unit of three planes which set out on November 5th from Ismailia, in Egypt, in an attempt to break the world long-distance flight record – by flying non-stop to Australia.

The three Vickers Wesley bombers took off on a route across India, the Bay of Bengal, Borneo and across the Timor Sea to Darwin. Signals were transmitted from the planes every half hour over the 7,162-mile journey, which took about fifty hours – smashing the record of 6,306 miles set by Russians who flew from Moscow to California in 1937.

Grimsby's pilot officer, who flew in plane one, was born in October 1910 and educated at Wintringham Secondary School, entering the RAF in September 1926 as an aircraft apprentice. He trained as a wireless operator-mechanic and passed out of the electric and wireless school at Cranwell in August 1929 as a leading aircraftsman. He was selected for pilot training in September 1931, and was promoted to sergeant pilot in August 1932. He served with the No. 100 (Bomber) Squadron until January 1938, when he joined No. 33 (TB) Squadron, at Singapore. In February 1938, he was granted a permanent commission as pilot officer.

His mother, at home in Welholme Road, said, 'My son was always pretty confident that they would pull it off, so his confidence has been justified.' (*Grimsby Evening Telegraph*, 1938)

‒ November 8th ‒

1951: On this day, it was revealed that Grimsby had built 1,449 council houses since the war. (Grimsby Central Library)

———

1978: On this day, a £2 million scheme to develop the old Cleethorpes Zoo area into a sports centre was publicly announced. Where once elephants were put on show in a ring would be four squash courts, and two dolphin tanks would be transformed into a fish breeding area and model boat pond. A third tank could be used for model yachts. Councillors agreed in principle to create, among other facilities, a new indoor swimming pool, sports hall, athletic and cycling tracks, an arena for equestrian events and a grand stand.

A special meeting had been held to request more detailed plans and a costing schedule so a final decision could be made. The report also suggested that, due to the realignment of Kings Road, the line for the miniature railway attraction on the seafront could be extended.

Cleethorpes Zoo and Marineland was founded by Pentland Hick and operated as a satellite zoo to Flamingo Land. It boasted dolphin displays and was famous for its sea lion shows. The zoo closed in 1977 and on its site now stands a theme park, with sporting facilities further along the seafront. (*Grimsby Evening Telegraph*, 1978)

~ November 9th ~

2008: On this day, for the first time in history, a Carpathian Lancer laid a wreath at Grimsby Cenotaph on Remembrance Sunday. The regiment holds a special place in the hearts of many people in the region. The Carpathian Lancers have roots in Grimsby, and even camped in Weelsby Woods at the end of the Second World War.

In 1939, when Germany invaded Poland, a number of soldiers escaped their stricken country and – via the Carpathian Mountains – gathered in the Middle East. The Polish Army had thirty-three horse cavalry regiments, which called themselves the Carpathian Lancers. After service under Allied command in North Africa and enhancing their immense reputation through their part in the Italian campaign at Monte Cassino, the Lancers returned to Britain. At the end of the Second World War, the regiments were brought to Grimsby for demobilisation, but as their nation was now occupied by communist Russia, nearly 1,000 men stayed and settled in Grimsby.

On this day, Sergeant Thomas Kopij laid the wreath in memory of past comrades and all those who gave their lives for their countries. He had been released from his base in the Polish city of Poznan for seven days to attend, and stayed with one of the last remaining original lancers, former architect George Palejowsji, at his home in New Waltham. (*Grimsby Telegraph*, 2008; verbal account by Peter Chapman)

~ November 10th ~

1944: On this day, Grimsby soldier Ken Hale spent what should have been his wedding day in a prisoner-of-war camp. Ken was all set to marry his sweetheart Barbara at St James' church, but war put paid to that. Ken worked in the Royal Artillery and was transferred to the 1st Airborne. He was captured at Arnhem in the abortive Market Garden operation that September. It wasn't until Christmas that his family back in Grimsby – and his anxious fiancée – heard that he was in a PoW camp.

Barbara, who served with the Wrens, recalled: 'The first I heard that he was safe was in Lord Haw Haw's Christmas message. Then a few days later, we got a card from him.'

The couple had met at Robert's milk bar, in Pasture Street. Ken, a dockworker at the time, was secretary of the Clarion Cycling Club and had called in with fellow cyclists. Barbara had slipped out for the evening.

Ken was finally released by the Russian Army on April 3rd 1945 – 'they treated us more roughly than the Germans had', he said – and a fortnight later was back in Britain, weighing just over 8 stone.

The wedding was rearranged for May 5th and they honeymooned in Blackpool, costing £12 for the both of them for a week. They went on to have six grandchildren. (*Grimsby Telegraph Bygones*, 1940s edition, 1985)

~ NOVEMBER 11TH ~

1924: On this day, Lilian Maycel Lilliman left her lodgings in Fraser Street, Grimsby, taking neither hat nor coat. Almost immediately after returning home, never saying where she had been, she visited her mother nearby. She felt, she said, very ill, and the following day, a doctor was called. As soon as he left, she had a miscarriage. Despite the constant attention of the doctor and her family, she died on November 20th, aged 23.

It transpired that Mrs Lilliman feared – without any foundation – losing her lodgings if she had a baby. A post mortem examination revealed she had been the victim of an abortionist.

The doctor explained that she'd suffered an internal perforation, by an instrument improperly used by someone who had anatomical knowledge. 'Injury,' he said, 'had been caused by an instrument. It was impossible for the injury to have been caused naturally.'

No such instrument was found at her home, but there were pills she had not been prescribed and that were also not legally recognised. Despite the lack of information, the inquest jury returned a verdict of murder against some persons unknown. The case remained unsolved. (Stephen Wade, *Foul Deeds and Suspicious Deaths in Grimsby and Cleethorpes*, 2007)

⤙ November 12th ⤚

1883: On this day, Thomas Sleight faced the scrutiny of a court after being arrested the day before for being drunk and disorderly – a claim he adamantly denied. The Grimsby cordwainer's submission on the ill treatment he received at the hands of his father-in-law, Thomas Lumley, was printed in the *Grimsby News*:

> On Sunday, during the day, I had three gills of ale: at four o'clock, I was by Lumley dragged to prison, on a charge of being drunk and disorderly. Thomas Lumley swore that I was drunk, having my coat off to fight. Berry swore I was not drunk when he took me into custody. John Richardson swore I was not drunk, nor had any coat off to fight. Thomas Newby, junior, said that in jest I knocked his hat off, for which I apologised, and we shook hands, and the affair ended.

Despite the evidence, Thomas was fined 5*s* and ordered to pay costs – and on any default of payment to sit in the stocks for six hours – so he appealed against it. He said he would sit in the stocks if 'the unlawful decision be carried into effect'.

'I hope as many of my friends as conveniently will attend my sitting in the stocks,' he added. Documents do not reveal if Thomas got his wish. (*Grimsby News*, 1883)

~ November 13th ~

1991: On this day, a little-known pop group performed in front of youngsters at Toll Bar School, in New Waltham. The good-looking young men went by the names of Gary Barlow, Robbie Williams, Mark Owen, Howard Donald and Jason Orange and, as Take That, went on to dominate the music world for years to come.

Take That were the biggest boy band of all time, the subject of posters plastered on bedroom walls up and down the country. In commercial terms, the band sold more records than any English act since the Beatles, reaching number one in the charts seven times. And although the teenagers who watched them perform all those years ago had no idea of their soon-to-be fame, they still cheered as the five hunks danced and sang for their entertainment.

At the time of the performance, Robbie was just 17 years old. Wearing a baseball cap and matching jacket, a baseball shirt and baggy white trousers with knee-pads, he break-danced for the crowd of screaming teens. Mark hid his slight frame under a huge sweatshirt, while Howard showed off his rippling abs and washboard stomach by undoing his spotty shirt. Gary sported peroxide blond hair, a look he lost as time went on. (*Grimsby Evening Telegraph*, 1991)

— NOVEMBER 14TH —

2002: On this day, Green Goddesses were on the streets of Grimsby during a firefighters' strike. Soldiers were experiencing their second day of manning the engines, following a night without major incidents. They attended five car fires, two garage fires, one kitchen fire and a blaze in an empty house on a Grimsby estate. Elsewhere wasn't so fortunate during the firefighters' forty-eight-hour walk-out: three people died in house fires.

Green Goddesses is the nickname given to the rather archaic-looking Bedford RLHZ Self Propelled Pump, in other words, fire engines originally used by the Auxiliary Fire Service and latterly by the British Armed Forces. The distinctive vehicles, painted green, were built between 1953 and 1956. The strike in 2002 was the first time some generations had seen them. Indeed, residents would often line the streets to watch the engines in action when on a call-out.

The strike action, taken over a pay row, eventually ended on November 30th. The Green Goddesses remained in action on the streets throughout that time, with members of the public applauding the army's dedication while acknowledging the firefighters' right to strike. (*Grimsby Evening Telegraph*, 2002)

— NOVEMBER 15TH —

2009: On this day, a furious rant by a Grimsby Town Football Club fan became an internet sensation. Known only as Poojah, the supporter laid into his 'hopeless' team, unable to contain his bitterness anymore, as his side languished at the bottom of League Two.

He launched a savage attack on the players in an open letter posted online. Poojah claimed he had passed kidney stones which had brought him greater pleasure than his team's performance. Within days it had received more than 100,000 hits and was then picked up by sporting sites in America, Australia and South Africa.

Such was its success, the letter was rumoured to be nothing more than a publicity stunt. Whatever it was, it got attention. In it, Poojah described his 'absolute astonishment and disbelief at the sheer magnitude of your complete lack of talent to carry out the job for which you are paid'.

He penned:

> I am not aware of any swear words or other derogatory phrases in my current vocabulary which come close to a description of your performance – and I use the term loosely – but you have reached a level of inadequacy and ineptitude neither I nor modern science has considered possible.

(*The Telegraph*, 2009)

~ November 16th ~

1949: On this day, many people in Grimsby had probably never heard of Flour Square, a somewhat obscure little street off Cleethorpe Road, near the Royal Dock Chambers. But there began a scheme which would result in the saving of thousands of man-hours through prompt attention to dock workers injuries and illnesses.

A building in the square was converted into a National Dock Labour Board clinical centre, and was staffed temporarily by two nurses and a doctor. It was the first of its kind in Grimsby, though other centres were established in ports all over the country. (*Grimsby Telegraph Bygones*, 1940s edition, 1985)

1977: On this day, an attempt was made to rescue a stricken puling rig which sank into Cleethorpes beach the day before, and had spent most of the night under water. A large crane was called in to lift the 35-ton machine, which buried itself in sands near Wonderland.

Sub-contractors had just begun sinking the first piles into the beach north of Wonderland for what would be the resort's new stretch of sea defences. (*Grimsby Evening Telegraph*, 1977)

1978: On this day, there was a £600 windfall for each of the 150 Grimsby bakery workers who had lost their jobs earlier in the year when Glenton's bakery, in Ladysmith Road, closed. A tribunal in London ruled that the workers who were made redundant were entitled to a protection award. (*Grimsby Evening Telegraph*, 1978)

~ November 17th ~

1987: On this day, Olympian Gladys Carson, who won the bronze swimming medal in the 200m breaststroke at the 1924 Paris Olympics, died. Her son, David Hewitt, of Grimsby, told her story for a local paper.

Gladys, who was born in Leicester in 1903, had two older sisters who were also good swimmers, and all three became known as the Swimming Sisters. Gladys's sporting career began when she was small. Such was her natural talent that, aged 18, she won the breaststroke championship of All England with a time of three minutes, twelve point four seconds.

Her prowess ensured her a place in the Olympic team. Aged 21, she was funded by the British Olympic Association to travel to Paris to compete in the 1924 Olympics, which featured in the 1981 film *Chariots of Fire*. In Paris, Gladys was advised on everything, from how to behave on the train to how to get to the Folies Bergère!

On July 18th 1924, Gladys competed in the finals of the women's 200m breaststroke, coming third with a time of 3 minutes, 35.4 seconds, winning the bronze medal for Britain.

She is buried in Hogsthorpe, on the Lincolnshire coast. (*Grimsby Evening Telegraph*, 1987; Grimsby Central Library)

~ NOVEMBER 18TH ~

1893: On this day, records describe that Grimsby's lifeboat, the *Manchester Unity*, was launched to aid an unknown steamer in distress. A dredger and several lighters were blocking the entrance to the dock basin, so the lifeboat could not get out to sea.

In the resulting confusion, the lifeboat was dashed hard against one of the piers, not only causing damage to the vessel but also plunging Coxswain Charles Risdale Barr overboard. Tragically, he was crushed to death between the boat and the pier.

A smaller *Manchester Unity* rowing boat was provided in 1894 and was replaced by a larger boat, powered by oars and sails, in 1904. This was launched sixteen times and saved seven lives before the station was closed in 1927. (Ivan E. Broadhead, *Portrait of Humberside*, 1983)

1982: On this day, Grimsby's Della Dolan was crowned Miss United Kingdom. The title is held by the highest-ranked contestant from the UK in the Miss World pageant. The presenters of the show, held at the Royal Albert Hall in London, were Peter Marshall and Judith Chalmers, and entertainment was provided by The Three Degrees. (*Grimsby Evening Telegraph*, 1982)

– November 19th –

1927: On this day, Grimsby's Singing Postman was born. Allan Smethurst came to the nation's attention thirty-eight years later, in February 1966, when he appeared on *Top of the Pops* singing his self-penned song, 'Hev Yew Gotta Loight Boy?'

At the time, Allan worked in Grimsby as a postman, earning £12 a week, and would hum the tunes of his own creation as he did his rounds, all in his native Norfolk accent. He recorded 'Hev Yew Gotta Loight Boy?' and it was picked up by the BBC, so he gave up his job to pursue fame as the Singing Postman. That year, he won the Ivor Novello award for best novelty tune.

All his songs were based on his childhood in Norfolk, but he had lived in Grimsby since the Second World War. By 1970, Allan was penniless. He suffered severe stage fright and developed arthritis, which affected him playing the guitar. Allan lodged at Grimsby's Salvation Army from the 1980s, leading a quiet life. It was there he died from a heart attack in December 2000.

'Hev Yew Gotta Loight Boy?' had a small comeback in 1994, when it was featured on a TV advert for Ovaltine. (*Grimsby Telegraph* archives)

— November 20th —

1927: On this day, the first petrol bus ran in Grimsby. It went via Riby Square, Cleethorpe Road, Humber Street, Victor Street and Wellington Street. (Grimsby Central Library)

1958: On this day, John Charles Emslie, a pile-boring machine operator, descended an 87ft borehole to try to save the life of a workmate. He and Walter Shoebridge were working on a new bridge joining the Isle of Sheppey to the mainland of Kent, when Walter fell. John found him with his head and shoulders buried in wet sand, and brought him up on the hook of a crane.

He received a Queen's Commendation but nearly missed the presentation at the Ministry of Labour. The day before, he was working on an extension to a Grimsby brewery when he injured his spine in a mishap. Doctors wanted him to stay in hospital for three weeks, but he wanted to go to London, so he was put in plaster. He did not arrive at the Ministry until the ceremony was over because of difficulties walking. But the Minister went through the ceremony again, telling John: 'I have read of your gallantry towards your workmate with very great admiration indeed.'

Two years previously, John, who lived in Durban Road, was awarded a Royal Humane Society certificate for a similar rescue at Tower Bridge, London. (*Grimsby Evening Telegraph*, 1958)

— NOVEMBER 21ST —

1944: On this day, a fearless Keelby bomber pilot who survived being shot down over the sea during the Second World War was officially presented with his Distinguished Flying Cross by King George VI at Buckingham Palace. The medal, with its distinctive purple and white striped ribbon, was made of solid silver.

Flying Officer George Bertram Willerton, who was born in Keelby in 1917, was awarded four other medals for his courage. The citation read:

> Flying Officer Willerton was captain of a Liberator aircraft set on fire when attacked by five Junker 88s while on an antisubmarine patrol over the Bay of Biscay. The aircraft was forced down on to the sea but, although underwater, Flying Officer Willerton managed to crawl through a side window, swim to a floating dinghy and, in a dazed condition, pulled aboard two members of his crew with him, one severely wounded. Without first aid equipment, he dressed his companion's wounds as well as he could and then paddled the dinghy for six days before being rescued.

That wasn't his only lucky escape. On January 27th 1942, while on a patrol over northern France, his plane was hit by anti-aircraft fire and he was forced to fly back to England on one engine. When overland, he parachuted out of the stricken plane. He noted in his log book: 'Landed on Dartmoor. Landed heavily, resulting in black eye.' (*Grimsby Telegraph Bygones*, 1940s edition, 1985)

~ November 22nd ~

1939: On this day an execution was due – but it never happened. It was the classic crime of passion: a woman strangled by her fisherman husband after she taunted him about leaving for another man. Thoma Cossey would have paid the ultimate penalty were it not for the intervention of the people of Grimsby – and his victim's mother.

The police were called to a house in Burgess Street to attend the body of Maud Steward in an upstairs bedroom. Cossey, 42, was nearby. His wrists had been slashed and there was a strong smell of gas. He said, 'What did you come so soon for? Give me some more gas. She's dead. I wish I was also. I hadn't enough money for the gas.'

Within three weeks, Cossey was found guilty of murder and sentenced to death. The execution date was set for November 22nd, but in Grimsby there was uproar. Cossey, who had been co-habiting with Maud, was well-liked and respected. There was a real feeling Cossey had been driven to commit his awful crime: Maud had been seeing another man while Cossey was at sea. The court case heard she was addicted to 'sexual excess' and his defence had argued and his was a crime of jealousy. A petition was raised by two of his neighbours and within days, 6,000 people had signed it. One signature was Mrs Bratley – the mother of Maud, whom Cossey had strangled with his leather bootlaces as she slept.

Just days before Cossey was due to hang, the Home Secretary granted a respite, replacing the death sentence with twenty years in prison. (Stephen Wade, *Foul Deeds and Suspicious Deaths in Grimsby and Cleethorpes*, 2007)

— November 23rd —

1947: On this day, well-known personalities of the sporting world were put through their paces at the Palace Theatre, in Grimsby. Alf Knight, Britain's Olympic hope and the country's strongest man at the time, set up an unofficial weightlifting record, while famous footballers Horatio 'Raich' Carter, Leon Leuty, Jimmy Frew and Tim Ward indulged in a heading competition. Eric Dolby and Des Wright boxed an exhibition round and demonstrated some of the finer points of the pugilistic art, and Johnny Leach, the table tennis ace, was also there.

The occasion was the presentation by the Central Council for Physical Recreation of Spotlight On Sport – a programme which, with its glittering sports stars, filled the theatre and would go on filling it for the rest of the week. Its aim was to get us all interested in and participating in sport of all sorts.

Television experts were there to watch a display of Indian club swinging by a team of seventeen girls from a Grimsby health club, with a view to televising their performance at Alexandra Palace, in London. (*Grimsby Evening Telegraph*, 1947)

~ November 24th ~

1951: On this day, the Grimsby Film Society launched its midnight showings at the Chantry Cinema, in Cartergate, with a screening of *Bicycle Thieves*. It stood empty for two years when it was sold to a West Bromwich firm of manufacturing electrical engineers in 1959. (*Grimsby Telegraph Bygones*, 1997)

1981: On this day, an oil rig with twenty men aboard was adrift in the North Sea in mountainous seas and gale-force winds after strong winds and 40ft waves dragged some of the rig's twelve anchors. But the owners said the men were in no danger and the rig was being shadowed by three tugs which would later try to take it in tow.

The incident came as most of the country was battered by wild weather. In Grimsby and the surrounding area, a mini whirlwind had lashed the landscape, ripping the roofs off several buildings, blocking roads and making several families homeless. Miraculously, no one was hurt in the gales, which approached hurricane force at times and caused even the 'unsinkable' Humber lifeboat to seek refuge in Grimsby's sheltered port. (*Grimsby Evening Telegraph*, 1981)

1997: On this day, history was made at the Great Grimsby Conservative Club, for male members voted unanimously to accept ladies as full members of the club for the first time. The move was described as the biggest change in the entire history of the association.

The club was founded in 1958, and ever since, women had been allowed to join as associate members only. They could not: hold official posts, speak or vote at general meetings, propose others for membership or sign guests into club premises.

At the time of the decision, club chairman Mick Smart said:

> This is probably the most significant change in the constitution of the club for almost 40 years. When we consider that the country was led by a lady Prime Minister of the Conservative Party as long ago as 1979, it is appalling that ladies have, for so long, been denied the same status as men.

The issue had been raised at the club before, but special meetings had failed to produce a quorum, meaning the proposal failed at the first hurdle. (*Grimsby Telegraph*, 1997)

— November 26th —

1906: On this day, the first school opened in Immingham. When the nineteenth century dawned, just 144 people lived in the town on the outskirts of Grimsby; 100 years later, only 241 had made it their home, and there was not much going on. The area was mainly marsh, and there was no school. But there was an upsurge in 1906 – when the Great Central Railway Company decided to build a dock on the River Humber. The massive construction process saw an influx of 2,500 navvies.

The first school was built as a mission for these navvies, their wives and children. The head was Robert Dukes and there were seventy-seven children on the roll on opening day. A log book entry for January 11th 1910 states that the girls would be unable to use two of their closets during the week. They were being partly demolished because the land on which they stood was sold for building purposes.

During the First World War, there are several references in history books to Zeppelin attacks on Immingham, with a typical entry in March 1916 stating several children were absent from school owing to 'Zeppelinitis'. (Grimsby Central Library)

~ November 27th ~

1901: On this day, Alice Ann Harper appeared in court to deny a murder charge. The 40-year-old, who had been a widow for four years, lived with her 13-year-old daughter in Lime Street, Grimsby. Mrs Harper was courting and fell pregnant. At an advanced stage, she called a doctor to examine a pain in her side. The doctor mentioned her pregnancy and Mrs Harper was shocked. 'I don't know what I shall do,' she told him.

In June 1901, the birth was imminent. She told her daughter to fetch the doctor. Almost immediately after the girl left the house, Mrs Harper gave birth to a girl, directly over a chamber pot.

When the doctor arrived he found the pot, with the infant inside, in a cupboard. It had been put in an empty bucket and a piece of old carpet placed over the top. Mrs Harper, who was in bed, said, 'I never touched the baby at any time. I hope I won't get into trouble over this.'

The doctor later told the inquest the child had been born alive, but only for about a minute, as she was asphyxiated. The inquest jury brought back a verdict of willful murder and on this day, Mrs Harper appeared in court. No evidence was offered against her, and the jury was instructed to return a not guilty verdict. (Adrian Gray, *Crime and Criminals in Victorian Lincolnshire*, 1993)

1924: On this day, the body of a baby was found in the garden of a councillor's home. The newborn boy was found in a yard behind Eleanor Street – the home of Councillor W.S. Beales, of Grimsby Council. Dr Duncan McLellan said the baby had lived for about two hours and had died because of a fracture to the skull.

The boy had been dead a day before he was discovered by the councillor's daughter, Eva, and the dustman, Robert West. The sad parcel had been placed near the bin, the baby wrapped in two pieces of cloth and paper. Clearly he had been thrown, already dead, over the 5ft tall passage wall which ran along the back of the garden.

The police came up with no evidence as to who the perpetrator was and on December 29th, the coroner's jury returned a verdict of murder against some person or persons unknown. (*Grimsby Evening Telegraph*, 1924)

1946: On this day, the *Barnett*, skippered by Alan Whitelam, smashed the landing record at Grimsby. Her 2,000 kits of White Sea plaice sold for a new record of £13,000. (*Grimsby Evening Telegraph*, 1946)

1979: On this day, Welholme Galleries officially opened. The large site was, in fact, two buildings in its original form. The 1907 Welholme Congregational Church, designed in a free Gothic Revival style by Bell, Withers and Meredith, and built by Hewins and Goodhand, incorporated the 1894 Congregational Mission Church and Sunday school, designed by H.C. Scaping, of Grimsby, and built by H. Thompson. This rich architectural history alone has made it a prominent site in North East Lincolnshire.

Once, it was a showcase museum, and many a local has whiled away an afternoon among its exhibitions. Among several collections lay an Aladdin's cave of diverse curiosities, including a self-propelled wheelchair, an old school bell and a pair of hand-knitted fisherman's long-johns. There were treasures from the fishing industry and wartime, a massive costumes collection, and photographs and artwork.

In 1998, it was taken over by a group of volunteers, who opened the venue up to the public. One of them said, 'We have some mannequins in a particular part of the gallery, where if you tread on the floor boards, they move. I remember someone walking past one, stepped on a board and the head fell off! They thought the place was haunted.'

In recent years, the venue has been used as a council store for office items and furniture. (*Grimsby Evening Telegraph*, 1979)

⁓ November 30th ⁓

1947: On this day, people had grown used to a new sight on the roads of Grimsby. The town's first lollipop ladies stepped off the pavement for the first time in that month. Earlier, the borough council had recruited eighteen mothers on a voluntary basis to train as crossing patrol wardens. Policemen acted as tutors and the women were equipped with a white coat and a blackboard, on which was chalked 'Stop: Children Crossing'. By the time the first mum had walked out to hold up the traffic in Carr Lane, the blackboard had been replaced by a proper board: the predecessor of the famous 'lollipop'.

1949: On this day, Roger, a 6-year-old mongrel dog, was mourning the passing of his master, George Cox. Whenever Mr Cox, a trawler hand, was at sea, Roger waited quietly for his return, greeting him with a friendly bark as Mr Cox threw his sea-bag off his shoulder.

At 2 a.m. on this day, Roger began to bark and pawed at the kitchen window's curtains, ripping down the blind. He then tried to escape the yard. Six hours later, a representative of Grimsby's Port Missioner called at the house to inform Mrs Cox her husband had died on board the trawler *Remexo*. The couple had ten children, aged between 8 and 30 at the time of his death.

(*Grimsby Telegraph Bygones* 1940s edition, 1985)

— DECEMBER 1ST —

1951: On this day, two Grimsby seamen refused to trawl because 'lives would have been in peril'. Two days later, two of them were jailed and three fined when magistrates took stern action against them.

In court, the men admitted they had combined together to disobey the commands of the master of the trawler *Salvini* at sea on December 1st about 100 miles north-east of Spurn Point. It was alleged that they had refused to shoot the gear, and that their ringleader had told the skipper to take the ship back home, and the court heard that their disobedience might have made the ship become unseaworthy. A solicitor for the prosecution said discipline at sea was getting 'steadily worse'.

In their defence the men said their lives would have been put in danger had they obeyed the skipper because the weather was too bad. It was about 8 a.m. when the gear was hauled and the skipper decided to wait as the weather was squally. By 11.15 a.m., it had improved and other small trawlers were fishing nearby, so the skipper decided to start fishing again – but the five men refused to shoot the gear and went below.

The orders of a ship's captain were law at sea and had to be obeyed. The magistrates said they viewed such cases with 'deep concern'. (*Grimsby Evening Telegraph*, 1951)

～ December 2nd ～

1997: On this day, something strange happened in the skies above Grimsby: there were dozens of reports of mysterious lights and objects above north-east Lincolnshire. But according to the Government's own X Files, they have posed no threat to national defence.

People can only speculate about the cause of strange happenings above our heads, but it has been officially recognised that there is public interest in unidentified flying objects. Documents published by the government revealed that over a ten-year period, fourteen mystery sightings were officially reported in the area including Grimsby, Scunthorpe, Immingham and Skegness. The published lists were not comprehensive, however, for there were many incidents which weren't on them.

One such incident was in Grimsby on this day, which came to light through a Freedom of Information Act request to the Ministry of Defence. The request asked if there had been 'any UFOs or extra-terrestrial designed craft controlled by homo sapiens over Grimsby on December 2, 1997, between 01.00 and 05.00'. According to the Ministry, the answer was a straight 'no'. (Ministry of Defence, 1997)

‒ December 3rd ‒

1969: On this day, Lincolnshire's old soldiers were ready to get the guns out again over a suggestion that they should sell their medals. British Legion members were disgusted that an offer to buy them should have been made in their journal, and registered a strong protest. The *Grimsby Evening Telegraph* reported:

> There is many a be-ribboned veteran who would starve rather than sell his decorations, and the collectors' offers will neither tempt nor harm him. Nor should he feel affronted – only tolerantly amused – when others try to put a price on what he knows is priceless. It is natural that they should be sensitive if commercialism tries to taint the honours which, in their winning, are beyond the power of the pound. A second-hand medal is, after all, as empty a symbol as you could pin on an unworthy chest. The first reaction is, understandably, one of anger at such impudence – but on closer scrutiny, is it not all rather flattering? If people wish to buy them, it can only be for their value as pieces of history, and there is no slight in that.

(*Grimsby Evening Telegraph*, 1969)

– December 4th –

1937: On this day in 1937, the Regal cinema, in Freeman Street, opened. It was built for the Associated British Picture Corporation Ltd on the site of the Prince of Wales Theatre, and had 686 seats in the circle and 1,280 in the stalls. The first film to be shown was *Shall We Dance*, starring Fred Astaire and Ginger Rogers.

The Regal was Grimsby's first 'super' cinema. The acoustics and seating were considered revolutionary. A Compton organ, played by Wilfred Southwark, was a popular feature of each evening's entertainment for many years.

It later went through changes of ownership, including ABC, when EMI converted it into a three-screen cinema, and Cannon in March 1987. For example, it closed during 1966 and reopened in March the following year. Rebuilding had cost £150,000 and seats were reduced to 1,280 only.

Television kept families at home and, despite showing 3D films, the novelty was not enough to keep the crowds returning. It closed some years ago as an Odeon and now stands empty. (Stuart Russell, *Memory Lane Grimsby*, 1999)

~ December 5th ~

1945: On this day, an elderly widow was knocked down and injured by an escaped bullock. Florence Lacy was in Albion Street, on which she lived, when a bullock ran into her and tossed her 'as far as it could throw her'.

As a result of her injuries, she was unable to walk for three or four months and received regular medical treatment. She was forced to employ household help because of the accident.

Two years later, Mrs Lacy, then aged 79, made an unsuccessful claim at Grimsby County Court for £200 damages from Messrs Wilkinson Bros, haulage contractors from Market Rasen. The court heard how cattle were being transported by Wilkinson Bros to the yard of the slaughterhouse in Albion Street when one escaped. The lorry driver said the cattle left the lorry in the normal way and went into a pen, but one bullock spun round and knocked him down. It then ran out into the street. The defence explained that responsibility for the cattle ended once they had left the lorry, and that the bullock had escaped from the yard, not the transportation. The court found in the firm's favour and Mrs Lacy was no doubt left disappointed. (*Grimsby Evening Telegraph*, 1945)

— DECEMBER 6TH —

2005: On this day, 50-year-old George McPhee began living his life as a free man – after spending eighteen years behind bars for a murder he did not commit.

The father of six, from Immingham, was handed a twenty-five-year sentence in 1985 in Scotland – the second highest in Scottish history at the time – for the murder of Elizabeth Sutherland at her home in the Highlands. He was condemned to time in some of Britain's most notorious prisons, including serving alongside serial killer Dennis Nielsen and murderer Michael Sams.

He told the media how he had always protested his innocence, and when his conviction was quashed on this day, called for the case into Ms Sutherland's death to be re-opened. He said:

> They are eighteen lost years I will never be able to get back. When I was sent to prison there were no such things as mobile phones or DVDs. I'm elated that I can now get on with my life, but I want to know why I spent so long in prison. I just made it clear to the officers and other prisoners that I did not commit any crime, but after a while, you just don't want to talk about it.

(*Grimsby Telegraph*, 2005)

‑ DECEMBER 7TH ‑

1982: On this day, an unusual pile-up in the centre of Grimsby caused a bit of a stink. Traffic was diverted after 4 tons of herring fell of the back of a lorry – straight on to the road at Victoria Street. The fish filled a lane at the traffic lights by Corporation Bridge for more than an hour.

The fish fell from a lorry when the tailgate came open as it pulled away from the traffic lights. 'It just came out of the back,' said the lorry's driver, Robert Stephenson, who lived on the Wybers Wood estate in Grimsby, 'and the first I knew of it was when someone started shouting.' He was carrying about 15 tons of herring to Grimsby Fish Meal Factory, on the Pyewipe.

Police diverted motorists to a different route while the council came to clear up the mess and later, the fire brigade washed the road down for good measure.

A spokesman from the fish meal factory said the fish eventually arrived safely on the premises. 'It's certainly been condemned now, even if it wasn't before,' he commented. (*Grimsby Evening Telegraph*, 1982)

— DECEMBER 8TH —

1962: On this day, Grimsby's very own Mae West took the next step in her stage career. After a spell in the West End hit *Gentlemen Prefer Blondes* with Dora Bryan, Grimsby-born actress Diana Noble returned to the scene of her previous successes in London – the Pigalle Theatre Restaurant. But Diana, who three years before played the lead in a £12,000 revue at the Pigalle, went back as a star in her own right, with an act of her own. The 21-year-old was better known to people in Grimsby as Dolly Crampin.

Before fame beckoned, Dora Bryan had lived with her family in Rutland Street. Her mother went to live with Diana in London, but her three brothers remained in Grimsby.

Auburn-haired, statuesque Diana had her first taste of show business as a singer at the Pier Pavilion, in Cleethorpes, with the Syd Kane Band. Her first break was in Manchester on the ABC TV series, *Top Numbers*. In 1959, she was picked from thirty other women to play the lead in the Pigalle show. The producer, Robert Nesbitt, said at the time: 'I wanted a statuesque girl who typified Edwardian beauty with a big boisterous voice. In fact, I wanted a young Mae West. Diana fitted the bill admirably.'

She also appeared on television and on the same bills as Shirley Bassey and Tommy Trinder. (*Grimsby Evening Telegraph*, 1962; Grimsby Central Library)

— DECEMBER 9TH —

1947: On this day, it was reported that two calves with TB had been found and condemned in Grimsby slaughterhouses. The incident had been reported to the government and officials were trying to find the mothers of the calves. (Grimsby Central Library)

1982: On this day, it was announced that an extra hour of drinking in pubs on Christmas Eve was going to be allowed. But the public was warned that no sympathy would be shown by the courts to anyone arrested for unruly behaviour over the festive season. (*Grimsby Evening Telegraph*, 1982)

2006: On this day, the famous statutes of two large lions – which stand guard at the entrance of Weelsby Woods – were put back on their plinths after being restored. The statues are more than 100 years old and were temporarily removed for cleaning and renovation work. For Grimsby children, it is a rite of passage to sit on their backs and pretend to ride them.

In 2011, the beauty spot gained Country Park Accreditation from Natural England, the public body responsible for the protection and improvement of the natural environment – at the time, one of only thirty-six in the country. (*Grimsby Telegraph*, 2006)

‑ DECEMBER 10TH ‑

1947: On this day, the seeds of modern-day Grimsby were planted at a meeting of the borough council's Reconstruction Committee. Members heard of a bold and ambitious plan to change the face of a predominantly Victorian town, packed with run-down and unhealthy homes around the docks and fish curing houses.

The plan included the wholesale clearing of the houses in Victoria Street, King Edward Street and Burgess Street, where some of the worst slums were located. They would be replaced by light industry and some shops. There would be a new railway station built in the Pasture Street area, replacing both the existing Town and Docks stations. The London North Eastern Railway Company had plans for this earlier in the year and was considering spending £1 million on the project.

With it would go a new bus station and a new road network around the town centre, including railway flyovers and the demolition of the Old Market and the Bull Ring. More redevelopment was planned in Freeman Street and a civic centre suggested for the area between George Street and Pasture Street. (*Grimsby Telegraph Bygones*, 1997)

– December 11th –

1987: On this day in 1987, it was reported that 'well-known down-and-out' 'Podgy' Hunt had died after collapsing in the street. Podgy – real name George – was discovered slumped outside The Mariner's Rest, in Albert Street, by a policeman. He was a popular character around the Freeman Street area of Grimsby.

Podgy was distinctive, with his white sideburns, weather-beaten complexion and an array of hats. Although he was barred from practically every pub in Freeman Street, and was regularly arrested, he was never regarded as anything other than 'a rather loveable nuisance'.

The 48-year-old used to be a deckhand. His father, Charles, was lost in the famous Leicester City trawler tragedy of 1953. His brother, Chuck, died in 1985 after falling down a flight of stairs. At the time of his death, Podgy still had two brothers living in Grimsby, Lol and Enoch.

Enoch said:

> I was fishing myself when things started to go wrong. He went burgling and went to jail and then, after returning to fishing, went off the road. He was one of the best and never caused anyone any serious trouble. He was a genuine bloke and if he had 50p, he'd give you 25p of it.

One landlord said, 'The town has lost a great character.' (*Grimsby Evening Telegraph*, 1987)

~ December 12th ~

1952: On this day, a War Damages Claim was paid out – eleven years after Grimsby's library was destroyed in an air raid. The raid killed five people, smashing to bits the library and adjoining buildings, breaking shop windows in Pasture Street and Victoria Street. Arlington Street and Lord Street were also hit.

Built in 1900, the library composed of a large reading room (where the newspapers were fastened down!) and an area of shelved books, most of which were half-leather bound with gilt lettering. There were brass rails and fittings everywhere, and it was overseen by a stern librarian who would order people out if they overstayed their welcome.

That splendour vanished when a German airman dropped his stick of bombs on February 4th 1941. Books, fittings, typewriters and desks remained strewn across Victoria Street until some attempt at salvage could be made.

In due course, a War Damages Claim was drawn up and submitted. The total came to £1,068 14*s*. It was paid out on this day in 1952. (*Grimsby Telegraph Bygones*, 2005)

⎯ DECEMBER 13TH ⎯

1962: On this day, the strength of modern synthetic fibres now being used in the manufacture of trawl cod-ends was proved by the *Ross Mallard*'s find of a two-and-a-half ton boulder. The boulder had the characteristic rounding of debris brought down by glaciers. It may well have been lying on the bottom of the North Sea for thousands of years. (*Grimsby Evening Telegraph*, 1962)

⎯⎯

1999: On this day, two Grimsby firefighters braved a hazardous boat blaze to search for a missing person – and were rewarded for their courage. Robert Kneller and Guy Smith rescued a man trapped on the burning *Zuider Kruis* in Grimsby Docks. Tragically, the trapped man on the vessel did not survive the fire.

The fire was out of the ordinary; shipping fires are particularly dangerous. As part of the rescue crew, they had to make their way through extreme heat and a narrow opening into the sleeping compartment of the vessel.

The pair were later presented with commendation awards by the Chief Fire Officer of Humberside. (*Grimsby Telegraph*, 1999)

~ December 14th ~

1967: On this day, many residents were on a waiting list to be connected to a phone line. But they were warned it was going to be some months before the GPO could install one. There was also a backlog in Humberston, Healing, Waltham and other areas of the borough, which was unlikely to be cleared before March or April 1968. But the reason for the delay in Grimsby was not the same as in the outlying districts, said the Lincoln area superintendent, Mr T.J. Gardner. He said at Healing, Humberston and Waltham, all the exchange equipment – in other words, numbers – were in use.

During the previous three months, more than 100 people in Waltham alone had been connected. During the past year, he said, about 350 new lines in all had been assigned to the area. At Humberston and Healing, the GPO had been able to do only a few numbers at a time as they became available. In each case, he said, more 'number equipment' was needed.

Mr Gardner said Grimsby residents had experienced problems obtaining numbers, many hearing an engaged tone before finishing dialing:

> It must be realised that we have a certain quality of service. We cannot allow more subscribers and lines to be connected until we have a different kind of specialised equipment which will permit this. We have had the new piece of equipment on order for some time.

(*Grimsby Evening Telegraph*, 1967)

~ DECEMBER 15TH ~

1905: On this day, a new venture called The Tivoli theatre opened in Duncombe Street, Grimsby. It was the dream of Henry James Curry, intending to provide a venue for light entertainment, in contrast to the drama staged by the already existing Prince of Wales Theatre.

The Tivoli did exactly this until March 1st 1908, when it was closed down for six years, re-opening during January 1914 as a cinema. In the spring of 1936, Mr Curry disposed of his firm to the Associated British Cinemas. The following year, the Tivoli reverted to live entertainment until July 1943, when it was destroyed in an air raid. (Edward Drury, *The Greater Grimsby Story*, 1990)

1962: On this day, it was warned that of the more than 450 children who would leave Grimsby schools that Christmas, fewer than half were likely to find work immediately.

The declaration was made by Alderman J.H. Franklin, the chairman of Grimsby Education Committee, who expressed concern over the level of unemployment among young people. It was a disturbing feature, he said, that 211 youngsters were unemployed – some of whom were still seeking their first jobs. (*Grimsby Evening Telegraph*, 1962)

– DECEMBER 16TH –

1947: On this day, poultry was scarce for Christmas. Leading meat trader Councillor C.W. Hewson described the poultry position as 'very difficult', but said there was about the same amount available as in 1946. There would be no pork or imported rabbits, but a small quantity of imported turkeys would be on sale in the town in time for the celebrations. Cases of frozen turkeys from the Argentine were in the Standard Ice Company's store in Victor Street – but few were to grace the tables of residents' homes. They belonged to the Navy, Army and Air Force Institutes, and were intended for units in the district.

Hanging in cold store were a few home-produced turkeys, but they were not for sale. Fearing they might be stolen, the owners had the animals killed earlier in the day and put in storage for safety.

Toy shops were experiencing better trade but the gifts in most demand – tricycles, dolls' prams and train sets – were still almost unobtainable. And a limited number of Christmas trees were heading for the town. Trees 2ft high cost 5s, with 5ft trees 12s 6d. Evergreen and mistletoe were in fair supply, but holly was scarce, at about 2s a pound. (*Grimsby Telegraph Bygones*, 1940s edition, 1985)

2007: On this day, a foul-mouthed Father Christmas was accused of being a grump after swearing at children and pretending to shoot them. Parents alleged their youngsters were queuing up at a grotto in central Grimsby when he emerged, swore and called the children 'brats'.

The incident began when the organisers started to turn people away before closing time. A shopper said, 'All the children were shouting "we want Santa". He came out of the grotto and turned around and said, "I am 73 years old". And when a small child shouted out he pointed his hand out and pretended he was shooting with his fingers.'

Another stunned onlooker, who had taken his younger sister to visit the grotto, said, 'Everyone was just looking around saying "what's going on?". Every time Santa comes on the television she points at it and says "bad man".' (*Grimsby Telegraph*, 2007; Gordon Jackson, *Grimsby and The Haven Company*, 1971)

~ DECEMBER 18TH ~

1964: On this day, one of Grimsby Town Football Club's most consistent goal scorers in its history passed away.

It was the summer of 1959 that the Mariners signed Ralph Hunt and although his stay was to last only two seasons, Hunt went on to claim thirty-nine goals in just fifty-three league games, helping the club to near-promotion in both campaigns.

The nephew of Sheffield Wednesday's pre-war forward Douglas Hunt, Ralph joined his hometown club, Portsmouth, as a 15-year-old in 1948, progressing quickly to become a regular player in their reserve side. Five goalless first team games and an equally unimpressive performance at his next club, Bournemouth, gave nothing to suggest he would become an accomplished scorer. However, three years at Norwich from 1955 saw him bag sixty-seven goals.

The chance to join Grimsby came after an unhappy season at Derby, where Hunt had been replaced once the goals had temporarily dried up. Apparently he had a fiery nature, which could explain why he played for nine clubs in all. Newly relegated to Division Three, Grimsby Town FC opened the 1959-60 season with a home game versus Chesterfield, Hunt took just ninety seconds to score. Chesterfield lost 5-1. In his first ten games for the club, he scored in every one.

In July 1961, he was exchanged for a Swindon player. Hunt died in hospital, a week after he was seriously hurt in a car crash. (Dave Wherry, *We Only Sing When We're Fishing: Grimsby Town FC The Official History 1878–2000*, 2000; *Grimsby Telegraph*)

~ December 19th ~

1893: On this day, Henry Rumbell, the captain of a Grimsby fishing smack, was executed for murdering his lover, Harriet Rushby. They lived in Stanley Street but while Rumbell was on a lengthy fishing trip in October, he arranged for Harriet to stay with relatives in Ayscoughe Street.

On November 7th Rumbell returned to shore and went straight to Ayscoughe Street, only to discover that Harriet had not stayed there once. Furious, Rumbell bought a revolver and fifty rounds from a gunsmith. At 8.40 p.m., Rumbell called on Ann Widall, who said Harriet had gone to the Empire Music Hall with a Mr and Mrs Bowdidge. Rumbell met Harriet and Mrs Bowdidge in Cleethorpe Road, so they went to the Exchange pub and then on to the music hall together.

He discovered that Harriet had been living with Mrs Bowdidge in Tunnard Street, and persuaded her to go back there with him. They were in a room downstairs, arguing about whether she had 'been' with other men, when Mrs Bowdidge returned with Burns, the lodger. Rumbell shouted: 'You have deceived me and no other man shall have you. You shall not leave this place alive.'

He then forced Harriet upstairs. Burns and Mrs Bowdidge heard Harriet yell: 'Don't murder me in my sins' and two shots were fired. Rumbell came downstairs covered in blood, asked for his hat and left.

Rumbell told his landlord about the murder and was persuaded to give himself up. He was sentenced to death, and his last request was for cigars to smoke. In the condemned cell, Rumbell was visited frequently by the Bishop of Lincoln. He never atoned for his crime, convinced that he would meet Harriet in the next world and all would be fine. (Adrian Gray, *Crime and Criminals in Victorian Lincolnshire*, 1993)

~ December 20th ~

1987: On this day, detectives unearthed the £57,000 snatched in Grimsby's biggest ever armed robbery. After hours of frantic digging all over the area, the stolen cash was found buried in a nearby wood.

The two robbers had struck a few days before at the Christian Salvesen premises in Grimsby before calmly cycling away with their swag, a sawn-off shot gun in a black bin-liner and a large khaki army-style kitbag, to a getaway vehicle parked a mile away. They pedalled off, leaving two Christian Salvesen workers gagged and bound in the wages office. Dressed in blue Salvesen-type overalls and dark blue Parka anoraks used by cold store workers, they cycled along various paths before reaching Grant Thorold Park and the getaway van.

Detectives, who had already made some arrests in Grimsby and Hull, were led to the buried cash after a number of telephone calls from the public describing spotting the white getaway van. Other items used in the raid were also found there.

Detective Superintendent Geoff Smith issued an appeal for more information, adding: 'I have to say this has all the hallmarks of being an exceptionally well-planned operation committed by professionals. This was certainly no opportunist job.' (*Grimsby Evening Telegraph*, 1987)

— December 21st —

1942: On this day, Grimsby soldier Tom Willis survived the dramatic sinking of the troopship *Strathallan*, torpedoed by a submarine. He was just 19 when, after a rough sea crossing from the Clyde, the ship entered the Mediterranean.

Tom couldn't sleep so went outside and saw the moon's rays lilting on the calm sea. He said:

> I went indoors and within a moment of lying down, there was a loud explosion. The lights went out. Amid all the shouting and pushing, we never heard that the captain had called 'abandon ship'. We met our unit; only then they told us of the order. There were nurses in the water screaming; overcrowded lifeboats were sinking. There was debris, troops in lifeboats and hundreds of others in the sea. It was an awesome sight. Another destroyer arrived and started to rescue people. The ship was leaning so much that any chance of getting off other than using ropes was out of the question. Daylight dawned to a still sea and a sunny day. The liner lay silent at the mercy of any enemy submarine.

A decision was made to evacuate to another ship – by jumping to it. Tom made it safely – only one man failed. Later, the liner caught fire and sank. 'It was to be five more years before I got back to dear old Grimsby,' Tom recalled. (*Grimsby Telegraph Bygones*, 2006)

~ DECEMBER 22ND ~

1883: On this day, the Mayor of Grimsby, Alderman T.B. Keeteley, handed to Superintendent Waldram £8 16*s*, to be distributed among members of the Borough Police Force as Christmas presents. Superintendents received 10*s*, sergeants 7 and constables 5. The previous day, Alderman James Veal had sent a hare to each member of the force. (*Grimsby Telegraph Bygones*, 1994)

1987: On this day, the story was told of Wally the wallaby, who went walkabout for Christmas … causing stares of disbelief! Railway worker Peter George thought he'd had too much Christmas spirit when he spotted the wayward wallaby hopping it across a farm field.

'A farmer called me across and said "Look in that field and tell me what you see",' said Pete. 'I said I thought it was a kangaroo and he replied, "Thank God, I thought I was seeing things!"'

Pete chased Wally into a nearby wood but even a police dog couldn't flush him out. The next morning, Pete arrived at work to find Wally cowering in a corner of his station. He was promptly cornered and caught by his owners, Alan Brett and Jean Chappell. Jean said, 'We kept him in a shed but he got out.' (*Grimsby Evening Telegraph*, 1987)

1966: On this day, the number of unemployed people in the Grimsby Employment Exchange area had topped the 2,000 mark. The actual total of those aged 18 and over who were registered as jobless in the latest round of published statistics was 2,001 – a rise of 178 since the last recording.

The new figures comprised of 1,792 men and 209 women. This did not include the twenty-six men who were severely disabled and were unlikely to obtain employment other than in special circumstances. Unemployed people now made up about 3.3 per cent of the working-age population in the area. (*Grimsby Evening Telegraph*, 1966)

1976: On this day, Grimsby dockers, who had the day before walked off a Norwegian frozen-fish ship, returned to work after dockside arbitration had settled the dispute.

The forty dockers working on the *Jostang* left the vessel after there was a dispute over handling rates of the cargo of 293 tons of frozen cod. But after a meeting with representatives of the port employers, the matter was resolved and the men went back to the ship.

Meanwhile, other dockers working on a neighbouring vessel, the *Shintoku Maru*, were uploading a cargo of frozen chips. A spokesperson for the Docks Board said, 'Not so long ago, we had one ship unloading fish, one with chips and another with peas!' (*Grimsby Evening Telegraph*, 1976)

～ DECEMBER 24TH ～

1997: On this day, gale-force winds caused widespread damage to buildings in the area – and even cancelled Grimsby's pantomime. Performances of *Aladdin*, which was midway through a three-week run at Grimsby Auditorium, were suspended for days after parts of the venue's roof were ripped off. Metal strips and insulation material were blown down Cromwell Road and police closed the carriageway until council staff, working on Christmas Eve, made the structure safe.

The high winds, with gusts recorded at more than 60mph, had wreaked havoc throughout northern Lincolnshire for two days. During an 'extremely busy' Christmas Eve, the emergency services also dealt with structural damage at a bathroom centre and two cars which had been blown over. Roads were closed as material was blown off buildings, and there were several accidents caused by trees falling down.

Unlike other parts of the country, no one was hurt, but many people awoke on Christmas Day to find fallen fences, destroyed garage roofs and damaged television aerials. (*Grimsby Telegraph*, 1997)

– DECEMBER 25TH –

1911: On this day, swimmers braved the icy waters of Grimsby Dock and plunged in, to take part in what would become an annual tradition in the town. The first ever Christmas Day swim was in the morning, before participants towelled off and went their separate ways for a hearty dinner. Some years, they would even have to break the ice on the surface of the water before being able to take the chilly dip.

Previous swimmers have included the famous Channel swimmer Hayden Taylor and Pete Winchester, who in 2013, completed his seventieth swim of the River Humber. The race has been taking place for more than 100 years and although it has been cancelled in the past, Pete has always made sure he at least had a dip into the water.

In 1968, the coldest year Pete can remember, the docks were frozen solid for thirteen weeks, but Pete punched a hole in the ice with a pick axe and jumped into the -2°C water. Known as the Humber King, he was also the only man to have ever swum from Hessle Foreshore to the Grimsby Dock basin – the equivalent of a marathon. (*Grimsby Telegraph* archives; verbal accounts by Pete Winchester and Brenda Fisher)

~ December 26th ~

1934: On this day, Miss Constance McDonald was preparing for her big day. She was one of four daughters of Mr and Mrs George McDonald, of Convamore Road, Grimsby, and her sisters – bridesmaids in their pretty velvet dresses – were almost as excited as she about being the bride of greengrocer George Todd.

Old Clee Church was packed with friends and family for the 3 p.m. service. George stood alone at the altar. He was the only child of Mr and Mrs John Edward Todd, of Freeman Street. His best man, Dick Pidgeon, shifted nervously waiting for the bride – but there was no sign of her.

There was a schedule of weddings that day and the guests for the next marriage had already begun to arrive. The vicar decided to move on to the next ceremony, and the congregation trooped miserably out into the cold afternoon.

The 3.30 p.m. bridegroom, Frederick Cumming, took his place by the altar. The veiled bride took her place by his side – but it wasn't his intended. It was Constance. The vicar, who did not know the brides, began the ceremony but there was a flutter of concern among the guests and someone stepped forward to halt proceedings.

Fred's true bride, Genetta Winkworth, turned up on cue and they married. And later on, so did George and Constance. (*Grimsby Telegraph Bygones*, 1994; verbal account by Peter Chapman)

~ December 27th ~

1955: On this day, the search was on for survivors after Grimsby trawler the *Prince Charles* succumbed to the icy waters of the Barents Sea. Nine men were killed when the vessel hit the rocks in a snowstorm and sank 60 miles off the Norwegian coast on December 23rd, but about a dozen managed to swim to a small island.

Skipper Thomas H. Baskcomb rescued two of the crew before he lost his own life searching for others in the icy sea. His last cry was: 'God save you all!' Exhausted and freezing, the survivors stood in darkness, moving about in the snow to keep their circulation going. The cook, Jim Smith, later told how some of the men were rescued in under three hours – but just in the nick of time. 'Myself and the galley boy saw one man lie down and freeze, but we could do nothing for him,' he recalled.

At first, relatives were unsure who was alive and the week following the sinking was enormously traumatic with the search for surviving crewmembers continuing for several days. Fifteen-year-old galley boy Edward Howard survived. Weeks later, at home, he told how he couldn't swim but that someone had grabbed his hair to stop him drowning. His clothes had been frozen so solidly that they had to be cut from his body with a knife. (Grimsby Central Library archives)

~ December 28th ~

1980: On this day, the Grimsby to Louth railway line closed for good, despite a public campaign to keep it open.

The pressure group was formed in 1978, lobbying under the name of the Grimsby-Louth Group. Now known as the Lincolnshire Wolds Railway Society, the group restored the section of track between North Thoresby and Ludborough, offering residents the chance to experience traditional travel by steam train.

The line actually closed to passengers in October 1970, but commercial wagons continued transporting grain to the malthouses in Louth for another decade. (*Grimsby Evening Telegraph*, 1980)

1987: On this day, mystery surrounded one of Britain's 'most startling mid-air near misses' which was alleged to have happened over RAF Binbrook. A national newspaper reported how an RAF Phantom jet came within seconds of crashing into an Air UK SD360 plane bound for Humberside Airport.

The report, published in the *Daily Mail*, claimed that 'it was the most startling incident in Britain's worst year of near-misses.' But the Ministry of Defence and Air UK both said, 'We've never heard of it.' (*Daily Mail*, 1987)

– December 29th –

1932: On this day, a shocking discovery was made on the LNER railway line near the Welholme Road crossing. The decapitated body of a man was found by the guard of a goods train. He was later identified as a retired builder.

It was customary for such trains to stop at the crossing, and it was during this halt that the guard, Mr Flint, came upon the man's severed head in a nearby '6ft' (alley). Other parts of his body were found elsewhere. It was discovered that the deceased had been struck by the onward bound mail train, which arrived in Grimsby at about 5.22 a.m. each day.

On the same morning, there was a drama unfolding in central Grimsby. Three terrified horses attached to a farm wagon galloped uncontrolled almost the whole length of Victoria Street. The horses and wagon was in the charge of Arthur Dowse, of Swallow, who was accompanied by his 7-year-old son. The animals, in two shafts, had not been in town before. They were bound for Messers Ogles sawmill, when they were spooked by the tramcars.

Luckily they did not do any damage and were brought to a standstill at Lock Hill, through the pluck of unemployed Frederick Henney. Jumping on the back of the wagon, he managed to get hold of the reins and succeeded in pulling up the tiring horses near the Oberon Hotel. (*Grimsby Evening Telegraph*, 1932)

— December 30th —

1959: On this day, two men had a miraculous escape when a New Holland to Immingham diesel train and a 10-ton petrol tanker crashed at an unguarded crossing at Killingholme. The tanker, which was empty, was overturned and almost completely wrecked. The front of the train – the driver's cab – was shattered. Neither driver was injured. (*Grimsby Evening Telegraph*, 1959)

1970: On this day, BP divers were still waiting for the weather to improve before investigating 'funny noises' which had been coming from beneath their unmanned static platform B, 12 miles off the Lincolnshire coast. High seas had prevented them from reaching the platform, in the middle of the West Sole gasfield. The noise was described as a tapping, 'similar to that you hear in water pipes in old hotels'. (*Grimsby Evening Telegraph*, 1970)

– December 31st –

1971: On this day, a third hoax SOS call of its kind in a month was made off the Grimsby coast. The latest prank call involved fifteen ships, an aircraft and the Scarborough lifeboat, which was out for more than four hours. The call was picked up by Flamborough Coastguard and said a vessel, the *Argosy*, was taking on water 18 miles east of Scarborough. The ship did not exist.

Bernard Ingham, managing director of the Grimsby tug firm J.H. Pigott & Son Ltd, told how one of their tugs was sent out about 25 miles up towards Flamborough Head before it became clear the SOS was a hoax. He said:

> The men are flaming mad but there's not much we can do about it except draw attention to the types of despicable swines who do this sort of thing. The men risk their lives when they go out to ships in distress. There will come a time when someone shouts wolf once too often and the men refuse to go.

(*Grimsby Evening Telegraph*, 1971)